Planned Giving Essentials

A Step-by-Step Guide to Success

Second Edition

Aspen's Fundraising Series for the 21st Century

Planned Giving Essentials: A Step-by-Step Guide to Success
Richard D. Barrett and Molly E. Ware, CFRE

Fundraising Basics: A Complete Guide, Second Edition
Barbara Kushner Ciconte, CFRE, and Jeanne G. Jacob, CFRE

Developing Major Gifts: Turning Small Donors into Big Contributors
Laura Fredricks, JD

Strategic Fund Development: Building Profitable Relationships That Last, Second Edition
Simone P. Joyaux, ACFRE

Capital Campaigns: Strategies That Work
Andrea Kihlstedt and Catherine P. Schwartz

Direct Marketing for Nonprofits: Essential Techniques for the New Era
Kay Partney Lautman, CFRE

Successful Special Events: Planning, Hosting, and Evaluating
Barbara R. Levy, ACFRE, and Barbara Marion, CFRE

Corporate and Foundation Fund Raising: A Complete Guide from the Inside
Eugene A. Scanlan, PhD, CFRE

Donor Focused Strategies for Annual Giving
Karla A. Williams, ACFRE

Aspen's Fundraising Series for the 21st Century

Planned Giving Essentials

A *Step-by-Step* Guide to Success

Second Edition

Richard D. Barrett
President
Barrett Planned Giving, Inc.
Washington, DC

Molly E. Ware, CFRE
Principal
Ware Development Consulting
Alexandria, Virginia

AN ASPEN PUBLICATION®
Aspen Publishers, Inc.
Gaithersburg, Maryland
2002

Library of Congress Cataloging-in-Publication Data

Barrett, Richard D., 1931–
Planned giving essentials : a step-by-step guide to success/
Richard D. Barrett, Molly E. Ware.—2nd ed.
p.   cm.—(Aspen's fundraising series for the 21st century)
Includes biographical references and index.
ISBN 0-8342-1905-0
1. Deferred giving—Handbooks, manuals, etc. 2. Fundraising—Handbooks, manuals, etc.
I. Ware, Molly E. II. Title. III. Aspen's fundraising series for the 21st century
HV41.2.B37 2001
658.15′224—dc21
2001045095
CIP

Orders: (800) 638-8437
Customer Service: (800) 234-1660

Editorial Services: Christie Matlock
Library of Congress Catalog Card Number: 2001045095
ISBN: 0-8342-1905-0

Printed in the United States of America

1 2 3 4 5

Table of Contents

Foreword

PLANNED GIVING—WHERE TO BEGIN?

In its simplest form, planned giving begins with a donor wanting to make a charitable gift. The contemplated gift is usually large enough to behoove the donor to consider the gift asset, the gift plan, and the timing. The gift asset, the gift plan, and the timing are three of the main components of every planned gift. The fourth, and sometimes overlooked component is always donative intent, a donor wanting to make a charitable gift.

In this scenario, the phrase "large enough" is a relative term. For some, this may mean a gift of $5,000 or $10,000. For others, this may mean a gift of millions of dollars. In any case, the gift is large enough from the donor's perspective to consider charitable gift planning. This process usually includes a charitable gift planning professional.

The ranks of "charitable gift planning professionals" has virtually exploded in the last decade or so. The Tax Reform Act of 1986 eliminated most tax deduction vehicles and plans, leaving charitable gift plans as one of the few remaining alternatives open to financial planners looking for tax deductions for their clients. Simultaneously, more and more charitable institutions have come to recognize and appreciate the tremendous potential planned giving offers to both donors and charities in providing cost-efficient, significant philanthropic support.

For each new member entering the ranks of charitable gift planning professionals, a logical question is, "Where to begin?" and a reasonable response is, "Talk to others in the field." So many people talk about planned giving but its meaning seems to differ in every conversation. To some it means a highly technical field involving discount rates, growth factors, and a seemingly endless vocabulary of legalese jargon: a field restricted, or perhaps they think it should be, to lawyers and financial planning professionals. To others, planned giving conjures up visions of an elderly donor making a life-statement by quietly including a bequest to a favorite charity, representing a gift from an estate, the fruits of a lifetime of work passed on to help others: the ultimate gift. Some say planned giving is mainly a marketing venture: build it and they will come. Others seem to see planned giving as a matter of product sales: match the proper gift plan with the donor and close the gift. To an increasing number of chief development officers of charitable institutions of all sizes and types, planned giving increasingly has come to embody a tremendous potential for growth in philanthropic revenue: a field of opportunity.

In a sense, all of these perspectives are true and accurate. A planned gift can involve highly technical legal and financial expertise for a donor structuring a complex, ultimate gift after responding to a marketing piece on a particularly attractive gift plan providing a tremendous impact on the bottom line philanthropic revenue for a charitable organization. All of these perspectives can be intertwined in the process involving a single planned gift.

Planned giving is a jewel with many facets and aspects. In successful practice, it often combines the sciences of finance and tax law with the arts of interpersonal relationships and human emotions.

The question remains, "Where to begin?" *Planned Giving Essentials* provides an excellent introduction to this many faceted field of charitable gift planning. Drawing from their extensive experience in the development and day-to-day practice of charitable gift planning programs, Dick Barrett and Molly Ware offer a comprehensive overview of the full spectrum of planned giving. From the nuts and bolts to the technical jargon, from the basic gift plans to the donors' emotional considerations intertwined in the planning process, this book explores in detail the many facets of the jewel of planned giving.

Planned Giving Essentials provides the knowledge needed to begin that first conversation with a donor wanting to make a charitable gift that is large enough in the donor's eyes to look to planned giving. After all, that is where to begin.

Jeffery W. Comfort
Director of Planned Giving
Georgetown University
Washington, DC
Past President (2000)
National Committee on Planned Giving

Preface

Why another guide to planned giving? The answer is simple: because there is no primer, no beginner's manual, no basic text on this subject despite all the lengthy how-to books sitting on bookstore shelves.

Why a second edition of *Planned Giving Essentials: A Step-by-Step Guide to Success?* It is, after all, a primer, a basic text concentrating on first principles that are on balance unchanging. All right then, why a second edition? The answer is still simple: there are new concepts and new interpretations of original concepts that have evolved, tax laws have changed, and the society that is the potential constituency of planned giving is changing in significant ways.

Fifteen years ago the only organizations that had "planned giving programs" and staff to promote these programs were major universities and large charitable organizations. Today, many people are entering the profession of fundraising, and numerous organizations are starting or interested in starting planned giving programs. Many are still not as familiar with all the terminology of planned giving, nor understand the role it can play in an organization's overall development program. This book is an attempt to supply the necessary background.

In this Second Edition, the authors identify and discuss the impact of the emerging trends that are affecting planned giving:

- a surge in interest among nonprofit organizations, many of which had been dependent upon corporate and foundation grants or support from state and local taxes
- an increasing volume of planned gifts from individuals as they learn of their benefits from the increasingly effective promotional efforts of nonprofit organizations
- the emergence of new wealth from young technology entrepreneurs, along with their requirement to track the effectiveness of their gifts

- the increasing use of commercial brokerage "charitable gift funds" as conduits between donors and charities
- the realization that the trillions of dollars in tax-advantaged retirement funds can be effectively used as charitable gifts at death, rather than as tax-depleted bequests to heirs
- the increasing use of the Web and e-mail by seniors, making it a viable promotional vehicle for planned gifts

The book is divided into two parts: (1) an introduction to basic planned giving principles and practices and (2) a guide to implementing a planned giving program. The first part sets forth the basic elements of planned giving and planned gifts, defines key terms, describes types of gifts, presents a history of planned giving, and discusses the importance of planned giving for maintaining an organization's viability. The second part provides detailed advice on starting a planned giving program from scratch.

This book is written for

- beginning fundraisers
- individuals thinking about development as a profession
- students at universities and colleges that offer certificate programs for not-for-profit careers
- planned giving departments that educate other departments about planned giving
- development departments
- community foundations
- advanced planned giving officers in need of a refresher course on getting back to the basics of planned giving
- board members and professional staff of organizations considering starting a planned giving program
- representatives of charities located outside the United States interested in learning U.S. fundraising techniques

It will tell you

- the history, purpose, and characteristics of not-for-profit organizations
- how planned giving fits into a total fundraising plan
- the differences between planned giving and cash fundraising
- how a planned giving program can be started easily and for minimal cost
- practical suggestions for implementing the numerous activities required to start a planned giving program
- tips on what to do and what to avoid
- how to progress realistically
- when to ask for help and how to get it
- the advantages of teamwork
- why it is important to listen to donors

Acknowledgments

We have been fortunate in our different careers, and we each have encountered some wonderful people along the way. Among the very best have been the generous, knowledgeable fundraisers and gift planning professionals who have shown a refreshing willingness to share information and their gift planning experiences. We would like to thank especially the following individuals for their guidance: Debra Ashton; Ronald A. Brown; Charles W. Collier; Andre Donikian; Nancy G. Fax, Esq; James P. Gelatt, PhD; Fisher Howe; Arthur Keefe; Frank Logan; Jerry J. McCoy, Esq; Phillip E. Melberg; James B. Potter; Ronald E. Sapp; Robert F. Sharpe, Jr.; and Adele L. Wells. We would also like to express our gratitude for the extraordinary helpfulness of Mary Smith at the AFP Resource Center.

There are others without whom this book would not have been possible and whom we wish to thank. We are much obliged to Barbara A. Chandler, Molly's sister, who encouraged Molly to start by dictating answers to questions. Barbara would then transcribe the results. She gave generously and encouragingly her time and talent by transcribing dictations with incredible accuracy. Ruth Fidelman, a virtuoso on the word processor, worked long hours producing the many drafts of this book. Finally, we owe to our spouses, Thomas E. Ware and Pamela Soldwedel Barrett, a special thanks for helping us with the endless editing and giving us patient encouragement. We couldn't have done it without you.

Part I

Planned Giving: Its Characteristics and Its Importance

Part I sets the scene for planned giving. Use it as a guide for learning the basics: the history, philosophy, and concepts; the types of gifts and the ways of giving; the importance of planned giving and the role of gift planning professionals. This first part has the basic information you need in order to use the second part effectively.

Read it and be challenged. The professional practice of planned giving presents you with a wonderful opportunity to help build your organization's future, to help your donors, and to help you have a rewarding career.

Chapter 1
Planned Giving Defined

WORDS TO WATCH FOR

- fundraiser
- donor
- planned giving
- charitable organization
- capital improvement
- endowment
- feasibility study
- gift acceptance policy
- accountable
- outcomes

Entitling this chapter "Planned Giving Defined" risks raising expectations that a clear understanding of **planned giving** (or **gift planning**) can be acquired from reading a few brief phrases. If only that were really possible. Ask several fundraisers what planned giving is, or for that matter ask a number of donors, and the responses are likely to be varied and incomplete. Furthermore, most definitions provide at best a partial understanding of planned giving. That's because many planned giving professionals have their own specialized definitions, and donors also see planned giving from the perspective of their own particular circumstances. That is why this primer begins by focusing on first principles.

There are two complementary ways of characterizing planned giving. The first emphasizes the attributes of planned gifts, and the second describes planned giving as a process, a series of related activities carried out over time, designed to achieve the goal of producing a gift (Paulus 1966). These two ways of characterizing planned giving can be used to develop more specific definitions related to your particular circumstances. Indeed, the variety of charitable opportunities, the diversity of planning processes, and the differences in donors' desires and circumstances have produced a multitude of specialized definitions.

> *There are two complementary ways of characterizing planned giving.*

A number of professional organizations and writers on fundraising have tried to define both the major characteristics of planned gifts and the process of gift planning from the donor's point of view and the recipient organization's point of view. The definitions can be used to identify some of the essential qualities of planned giving and show how it relates to fundraising as a whole.

PLANNED GIFTS

First, let's examine planned gifts. Note that any kind of gift can be a planned gift, the gift can be of any size, and it can be used for any purpose. The gift can be used when it is given, or its use can be deferred to some time in the future. If it is given to a charitable organization, the donor benefits by receiving a charitable tax deduction.

There are four general categories of use for a gift:

1. operations—the day-to-day expenses, such as expenditures for salaries, rent or mortgage, utilities, marketing materials, office supplies, etc.
2. capital improvements—buildings, building renovations or improvements, building equipment of all kinds, furnishings, landscaping, etc.
3. endowments—invested funds whose interest and dividends are used for operations or capital improvements
4. mission-furthering projects—projects focused on particular aspects of an organizational mission, immediate pressing needs, and current problems

The above description of what constitutes a planned gift, the purposes for which it can be used, when it can be used, and its benefit to the donor is equally applicable to any type of gift. How then, you may ask, does a planned gift differ from other gifts?

First, the purpose for which a planned gift is used and when the gift is used can be controlled by the donor through the placement of restrictions on the gift.

Second, a planned gift donated to a charitable organization can benefit the donor in any one or a combination of the following ways: it can allow the donor a charitable income tax deduction, minimize capital gains taxes, reduce estate taxes, or provide the donor or others with an annual income for life.

Third, a planned gift has been carefully considered by the donor (typically the gift is decided upon as part of a thorough financial and estate planning review).

Also, planned gifts often are

- used in the future even though the recipient organizations have received present commitments
- in some form other than cash
- not considered by the recipient organizations to be an annual gift (that is, to be repeated in subsequent years)
- used to fund capital improvements and endowments rather than operations
- relatively large (that is, of significant size for both the donor and recipient organizations)

Note that many characteristics of planned gifts, or other kinds of gifts for that matter, are typical but not universal.

> *Note that many characteristics of planned gifts, or other kinds of gifts for that matter, are typical but not universal.*

One of the best ways to understand the nature of planned gifts is to compare them to gifts from other types of fundraising programs. Table 1–1 compares planned gifts and two other categories of gifts: major gifts and all other gifts. Major gifts was selected as a separate category because the distinction between planned gifts and major gifts is often not well understood.

THE PLANNED GIVING PROCESS

The process of gift planning has two essential attributes that set it apart from preparing for the solicitation and receipt of any other kind of gift:

1. The donor and the donor's advisors carefully and thoroughly consider the donor's financial condition and estate plan before making the gift commitment.

2. The recipient organization's professional development or planned giving officers provide assistance and needed information to the donor to supplement the advice given by the donor's advisors.

Given these two attributes, it makes sense that planned gifts are usually not outright cash gifts, are typically to be used in the future, and are major gifts of significant size. Planned gifts can be from loyal, less wealthy donors but more often are from wealthy donors. They include gifts of real estate, trust funds, and investment portfolios; complicated gifts with restrictions or conditions on their use; and gifts that provide benefits to the donors until death, when the benefits are finally transferred to the recipient organizations.

> *Given these two attributes, it makes sense that planned gifts are usually not outright cash gifts, are typically to be used in the future, and are major gifts of significant size.*

The fundraising process an organization uses to solicit funds and to receive gifts consists of a series of activities arranged sequentially. Depending upon the size of the organization, some of these activities are carried out by the organization's personnel (both staff and volunteers), some by donors, and some by both donors and personnel. This is true of all fundraising processes no matter what the program is. But while most activities are common to every fundraising process, each program adds its own special activities.

Planned giving activities are organized in the following six broad phases or stages. Each phase consists of a number of steps, and these are detailed in Appendix 1–A.

1. **Phase 1—Feasibility.** Determine if there are resources and opportunities sufficient to produce a successful planned giving program.
2. **Phase 2—Preparation.** Develop your marketing plan, including marketing materials and strategies; train staff, board members, and volunteers; and identify potential donors.
3. **Phase 3—Marketing.** Contact prospective donors in accordance with your marketing plan.
4. **Phase 4—Cultivation.** Concentrate on contacting prospective donors who have expressed interest and on developing their interest further.
5. **Phase 5—Acquisition.** Work with the donors and their advisors until the planned gifts are defined, understood, and realized. This phase is unique to planned giving, and it consists of two principal

Table 1–1 A Comparison of Planned Gifts and Gifts from Other Fundraising Programs

	Planned Gifts	Major Gifts	All Other Gifts
Any kind of gift (asset)	Yes	Yes	Usually cash
Any size of gift	Yes	Yes	Yes
Used for any purpose	Yes	Yes	Yes
Used when given, or deferred to some future time	Usually deferred	Usually used when given	Usually used when given
Donor of gift to a charitable organization is allowed charitable tax deduction	Yes	Yes	Yes
Used to fund operations	Not encouraged	Not encouraged	Yes
Used to fund capital improvements	Yes	Yes	Sometimes
Used to fund endowments	Yes	Yes	Not usually
Used to fund mission-furthering projects	Yes	Yes	Yes
Purpose and/or time of use can be controlled by donor	Yes	Yes	Not usually
Gift to a charitable organization can provide an annual income, minimize capital gains taxes, and reduce estate taxes	Yes	Sometimes	Not usually
Carefully considered by the donor as part of a financial and estate planning review	Yes	Sometimes	Not usually
Usually used in the future even though commitment is in the present	Yes	Sometimes	Not usual]ly
Some form other than cash	Usually	Sometimes	Not usually
To be repeated in subsequent years (annual gift)	Not usually	Not usually	Yes
Major or significant size	Yes	Yes	Not usually

parts: donors and their advisors make financial analyses and estate plans, and the recipient organization's planned giving professionals provide assistance and additional information to donors and their advisors.

6. **Phase 6—Stewardship.** Honor donors for their gifts, maintain relationships with them, sustain their interest in the organization's cause, and present them with additional opportunities to help meet the organization's current and future needs while providing benefits for themselves.

The planned giving activities in each phase relate in important ways to activities in the other phases and also to activities in the fundraising processes of other programs. For example, in some cases, planned giving activities from different phases can occur simultaneously, and indeed some phases are continuous, as noted below.

Phase 2 (Preparation) need not be totally complete before Phase 3 (Marketing) is begun. Work activities can be completed as seems appropriate for you and your organization. In addition, Phase 2 activities (developing a marketing plan and training personnel) are repetitive. For example, as time goes on and the philanthropic environment changes, the marketing plan will need to be reviewed and periodically updated—and eventually completely redone.

Phase 3 (Marketing) is a continuous activity that lasts the entire life of any planned giving program.

Phase 4 (Cultivation) and Phase 6 (Stewardship) are also continuous. Cultivation begins once the first prospect who has expressed serious interest has been identified, and stewardship begins with receipt of the first planned gift.

Phase 5 (Acquisition) is (hopefully) repetitive. Each time a planned gift is in the process of being made, the activities of this phase are called into play. Multiple sequences of this phase could occur simultaneously if multiple donors offer gifts at nearly the same time. Ideally, once your planned giving program is successful, the acquisition phase would go from being repetitive to being virtually continuous.

Planned giving and other fundraising programs have many activities in common. Stewardship activities are the planned giving activities most often shared with other fundraising programs, especially major gift programs. These activities include sending letters of appreciation to donors, which is something all fundraising programs should do.

The preparation of a marketing plan, planned giving Phase 2, may include devising ways to coordinate planned giving activities with the activities of other fundraising programs. If it does, the next phase, marketing, will certainly involve sharing activities with these other programs.

Cultivation activities may in some instances be shared by a planned giving program and a major gift or capital campaign program. When a donor has expressed interest in making a major gift but appears to have assets that would make a larger planned gift seem like a reasonable possibility, it may be to the organization's advantage to have personnel from both programs shoulder the responsibility for cultivating this donor.

The acquisition phase of planned giving is unique. Its activities are not generally shared with other fundraising programs.

The integration of activities in many of the phases of all types of fundraising processes is possible and may be effective in reducing fundraising costs and increasing donations. Combining planned giving fundraising activities with activities of other fundraising programs requires coordination, teamwork, and a willingness to pursue the organization's goals and renounce competition between programs.

> *Combining planned giving fundraising activities with other fundraising programs requires coordination, teamwork, and a willingness to pursue the organization's goals.*

PLANNED GIFTS, DONORS, AND ORGANIZATIONAL SURVIVAL

The presentation of the planned giving process was intended to help you understand the concept of gift plan-

ning and compare gift planning programs with other fundraising programs you might be familiar with (see also Exhibit 1–1). Of course, you will need more than a brief introduction before you can list planned giving among your fundraising skills. In fact, there is a lot of technical information you will eventually need to learn. Donors, while not expecting planned giving professionals to be tax experts, do want to be informed about the mission of any organization to which they are considering donating a gift, how the gift will aid the organization, and what benefits they can obtain by making the donation. Remember, gift planning, if done correctly, can provide opportunities for donors to be involved with an organization over the course of a lifetime of giving.

There is a new aspect to the current fundraising environment. Donors are requiring nonprofit organizations to be more accountable. This is not anything dramatically different. We have always needed to provide 990s upon request. However, what we are seeing now is an emphasis on outcomes. Donors want to know there are some results from their "collective" charitable gifts.

Donors come in many forms. Some consistently give one large annual gift whereas others give smaller gifts—some at frequent intervals, some infrequently. Fortunately, there are also donors who give major gifts. For each donor, no matter which type, cultivation and stewardship will increase the chance that the donor will assist in providing for the organization's future.

Exhibit 1–1 Important Facts about Planned Giving

- Some of the **largest gifts** ever made have been bequests and other planned gifts.
- Planned gifts usually made out of donor's **assets** rather than from current income.
- Often these gifts come from individuals who have never viewed themselves as being in a position to part with cash. They represent **an additional group of donors.**
- Frequently, the discussion of a **planned gift** leads to an **outright** gift.
- A planned giving program **need not be expensive** to administer. Staff can handle the day-to-day paperwork and the specialist can be on call.
- With an effective education program, planned gift **prospects identify themselves** and ask for further information. Thus, each contact is with a receptive individual.
- Planned gifts **expand options for your donors** and allow them to focus on personal needs as well as philanthropic goals.
- The sooner an institution embarks on a successful planned giving program, the sooner the **pipeline of future money** will start to deliver usable funds.

Loyal donors want the organizations they support to present them with interesting giving opportunities. Donors want to leave their mark! They want to participate in the achievement of their favorite organization's goals.

> *Loyal donors want the organizations they support to present them with interesting giving opportunities.*

The long-term survival of charitable organizations is in part dependent on contributions. A strong planned giving program, in conjunction with the vigorous cultivation of loyal long-term contributors, should be an integral part of a charitable organization's overall survival strategy. Although excellent annual fundraising programs are absolutely necessary for any charitable organization's day-to-day operations, without a vision of the future, well thought out plans, and a planned giving program to support the development of new programs, an organization's viability will remain in question.

POINTS TO PONDER

- Planned giving has many definitions, is a multifaceted type of fundraising, and has many similarities to other types of fundraising.
- Donors come in many forms.
- Gift planning can play a role in raising needed funds for almost every organization.
- Donors want not only to give and to leave their mark, they also want to participate in their favorite organization's future.
- Donors expect us to be accountable.

REFERENCE

Paulus, W.K. 1966. Methodological aspects of problem formulation. *IEEE Transactions on Systems Science and Cybernetics* 2, no. 1: 1–4.

Appendix 1–A
The Planned Giving Process

Each of the phases of the planned giving process is made up of a number of steps. These are described below. Included in each description are the activities needed and the participants or parts of the organization responsible for performing the activities.

Phase 1: Feasibility

- **Step 1.1.** The board and/or top management, often at the urging of the development department or office, want to find out if a planned giving program will benefit the organization and direct development personnel to do a feasibility study.
- **Step 1.2.** Development personnel conduct a feasibility study. They examine, analyze, estimate, and project the possible costs for personnel and consultants, facilities, supplies, travel, entertainment, etc., and the possible benefits from gifts for a variety of gift types and time horizons. As a part of this study, they should find a reasonable number of potential donors who are committed to the organization's cause and able to make planned gifts, and they should also determine what types of gifts—bequests, pooled income funds, annuities, etc.—the organization wants to solicit and can properly administer (gift acceptance policy).
- **Step 1.3.** Using the roster of previous donors, development personnel choose potential prospects to survey in order to establish their commitment to the organization's cause and to identify their ability to donate a significant gift. They may have to arrange and pay for an age overlay (a breakdown of donors by various characteristics, such as age, sex, and location).
- **Step 1.4.** Upon completion of the feasibility study, development personnel provide copies for top management and the board to study. They also arrange to present, in a meeting, the findings and conclusions of the study to top management and the board,

offer a proposal for a planned giving program, and seek approval for it.
- **Step 1.5.** The board and/or top management should be kept informed of the study throughout its course. They perform a final review, suggest needed revisions, and, if appropriate, declare that a planned giving program is feasible.

Phase 2: Preparation

- **Step 2.1.** Development personnel research and create a detailed time- and cost-based business plan for the program that includes all staffing; marketing, cultivation, and stewardship strategies and materials; training programs; and the means and methods to identify candidate donor populations and, if possible, specific potential donors. Outside consultants may be needed to assist in this work. Development personnel should check with other departments or offices of the organization for potential prospects for planned gifts. They also need to review the charitable solicitation laws in the states in which the organization expects to solicit, and, as necessary, they need to register with state insurance agencies for certain types of gifts. Finally, they must do research and analysis to determine which types of gifts are to be solicited. The research will be based on the list (established during the feasibility study) of the gift types the organization wants to solicit and the assessment of what it would take to administer them. It includes verifying local, state, and federal requirements, if any, that apply to the selected gift options. Note that the amount of work in this step depends on the size of the organization and its fundraising ambitions.
- **Step 2.2.** Development personnel research, design, and produce required marketing materials, such as brochures, flyers, solicitation letters, thank-you letters, and telephone questionnaires. Preparation also

needs to be done for the cultivation and steward-ship phases. For the cultivation phase, development personnel plan seminars on the benefits of estate planning and on the tax advantages of giving. They need to provide information on the organization's mission, and the organization's effectiveness. For the stewardship phase, personnel research and create a program to honor planned gift donors and keep them substantively involved with the organization, including the giving of future gifts. Program elements might include certificates, medals, plaques, trophies, or other tokens of gratitude, membership in a legacy society or club, or involvement in a special activity. Literature on the benefits of additional generosity could be helpful.

- **Step 2.3.** Development personnel research, develop, and produce sample prototype documents required for Phase 5, the acquisition of planned gifts. Sample documents such as will clauses, simple trust agreements, and stock powers should be provided, complete with the organization's name in the appropriate places. Donors are not expected to use these prototype documents except as instruments of education. Their advisors will provide the proper documents when the donors need them.
- **Step 2.4.** Using the organization's donor database and if appropriate, a donor overlay, development personnel do a breakdown of donors by type, age, sex, profession, marital status, location, financial condition, special interests, and history of giving to the organization (including amounts given, frequency, recognition, etc.). From the available data, they develop a donor pool and segregate donors into classes by an assessment of the probability of contributing. Assessment criteria need to be developed in order to establish this segregated donor list. (The activities in this step should only be done if time allows and they are warranted by the size of the planned giving program.)
- **Step 2.5.** Development department and/or office staff and top managers, board members, and other volunteers who will participate in the marketing, cultivation, acquisition, and stewardship work receive training. Special consultants can be used for this training if development staff are limited by time, not expert in the subjects, or are inexperienced as trainers. Emphasis needs to be placed on the training of selected top managers and board members. Without their full participation in the marketing, cultivation, acquisition, and stewardship phases, the planned giving program could fail completely or at best produce an insignificant increase in the endowment fund. If a relatively high acquisition quota

has been set, maximum participation by top managers and board members is essential. The purpose of training staff, managers, board members, and volunteers is not to create a cadre of planned giving professionals but simply to provide them with an understanding of the subjects that will allow them to talk easily and convincingly with prospects.
- **Step 2.6.** Top managers and board members will have reviewed and participated in the previous steps in this phase, as well as received relevant training. At this point, approval to move to the next phase should occur. In practice, not all of the work of this phase needs to be completed before the work of the next phase can begin.

Phase 3: Marketing

- **Step 3.1.** The identification of potential donors, which was begun in Phase 2, Step 2.4, continues. As the marketing effort goes on, new names will be added to the donor pool and, of course, some names will be dropped. Keeping the list of potential donors current is a continuous activity.
- **Step 3.2.** Marketing begins in accordance with the marketing plan. Over time, new marketing opportunities will become apparent and the marketing plan should be revised accordingly. Marketing is the lifeblood of the planned giving process and its importance to the success of the program cannot be overemphasized. As personnel change, additional training will be needed.
- **Step 3.3.** Periodically top managers and board members should be thoroughly informed of current marketing activities. In addition, from time to time they will be called upon to assist fundraising professionals in marketing efforts, and new top managers and board personnel will need training to bring them up to speed.

Phase 4: Cultivation

- **Step 4.1.** When marketing identifies potential donors who have a real interest in donating planned gifts, cultivation of these prospects begins. The purpose of cultivation is to show prospects that donating planned gifts will be beneficial to them and the organization both. Newsletters, flyers, telephone calls, personal visits, seminars, and invitations to special events, annual conferences, or a ground-breaking ceremony for a new building are some of the means that can be employed to inform them of the organization's mission and effectiveness and to intensify their interest in making a planned gift.

- **Step 4.2.** Top managers and board members need to participate in cultivation activities. They may make phone calls, write letters, make personal visits, or provide introductions for potential donors at special events. In addition they must receive periodic reports on cultivation activities and successes.

Phase 5: Acquisition

- **Step 5.1.** Development personnel talk with prospects who indicate a desire to make a planned gift. In the discussions, which can occur using any form of communication (letters, phone calls, meetings), the development personnel provide detailed information about the types of possible gifts, the uses the gifts can be put to, the means by which the gifts can be made, and the possible benefits to donors. The purpose is to give the prospects information that they and their advisors can use to make an informed, fiscally sound decision whether to make a planned gift.
- **Step 5.2.** Outside consultants can be contracted to assist staff. (They are often most helpful in the start-up phase of a planned giving program.)

- **Step 5.3.** Potential donors consult with their advisors on financial, legal, and estate issues and the terms and conditions of possible planned gifts. The consultation and decision-making process does not directly involve the organization's development personnel, but close contact with these representatives of the organization must occur. The conclusion of this step is the donation of a planned gift.

Phase 6: Stewardship

- **Step 6.1.** Donors are honored for their gifts. Stewardship activities are designed to maintain relationships with donors. A legacy society to recognize donors, special projects or programs in which they are encouraged to participate, and the mention of their contributions in the organization's newsletter are possible means of keeping donors interested in continuing to give.
- **Step 6.2.** Top managers and board members also participate in these activities and, where appropriate, act as liaisons with planned gift donors.

Chapter 2

Philanthropy and the Philanthropist

Knowing the history behind philanthropy can help you understand why philanthropists give of their time and treasure. Knowing what motivates philanthropists can help prepare you for fundraising, especially for planned giving.

A HISTORICAL PERSPECTIVE

Philanthropy is not a new practice (AAFRC Trust 1989; Sills 1965). In ancient Babylonia, Hammurabi decreed that "justice be done to widows, orphans, and the poor." The Egyptian Book of the Dead includes praise for those who gave bread to the hungry and water to the thirsty. The Old Testament of the Bible contains the pledge of Jacob to offer up one-tenth of all that God gave him. The giving of a gift of ten percent—tithing—is fully compatible with the Hebrew concepts of love of mankind and sharing with the poor. Ancient Greek and Roman societies concentrated on supporting the general good rather than assisting the individual poor (Murray 1982).

The rise of Christianity brought with it an ethic according to which giving was more important than the gift and there was virtue in poverty—especially if it was the result of a pious vocation. Although in the Middle Ages the Catholic Church appropriated to itself a significant portion of charitable giving, it took responsibility for a substantial program of charity.

The rise of the secular state and the decline of feudalism brought major social changes. For example, Protestantism, early in its history, took a harsher view of poverty, and it favored the idea that many poor people were to blame for their own poverty.

At the beginning of the seventeenth century, an age of growing urbanization and fragmentation of religious authority, the English Parliament enacted the Statute of Charitable Uses. That statute underlies American charity laws. It was intended to create, control, and protect charitable funds and thus it provided for the collection of public funds by taxation to assist the poor. The statute initiated the intervention of government into charitable activities.

American philanthropy certainly owes a debt to English charitable philosophy and law, but, owing to the spirit in which this country was founded, American philanthropy is very different from the English version. American philanthropy from the beginning was characterized by volunteerism. In the communities that existed before government was established, social services were provided by collaborating volunteers. Community members organized to meet community needs. Most governments fund, control, and even operate the main national social institutions, but not the U.S. government. In the United States, such institutions are established, organized, governed, and supported by private citizens who have volunteered their services.

> *American philanthropy from the beginning was characterized by volunteerism.*

Some two decades after the Pilgrims landed on Plymouth Rock, three clergymen were sent to England by the Massachusetts Bay Company to raise money to start a new college in Cambridge. Many years later, an individual offered what could be the first instance of a planned gift in the Colonies. The gift was in return for granting a special request. What do you imagine the request was? To retitle the college. Who was the donor? Reverend John Harvard, after whom Harvard College, now Harvard University, was named.

Throughout the eighteenth century, churches and higher education were aided by philanthropy. Eventually, social and civic causes began seeking contributions, as did the arts. In the nineteenth century, the tradition of philanthropic giving was carried on by a growing population of successful citizens. This was an era in which personal humanitarianism flourished. People felt a need and perhaps an obligation to contribute not only money but also time and energy to help the needy and support organizations such as hospitals and "old folks' homes."

The tendency to become personally involved with humanitarian causes, to show selfless concern for others' well-being, lasted until after the Civil War, when philanthropy began to become institutionalized. Personal involvement was replaced by charitable fundraising and the creation of charitable organizations. By the end of the first third of the twentieth century, a large number of charitable foundations had come into existence, and the separation of givers from recipients steadily increased. The epitome of this trend was the gala or ball used by more urbane societies and organizations to raise money for charity.

Remarkably, in the last decade of the twentieth century, there continues to be some evidence of a trend back toward personal humanitarianism—but it is too early to assess its significance, if any.

A LESSON FROM HISTORY

There is a lesson for planned giving in the history of philanthropy: concepts of giving, charity, altruism, and philanthropy evolve over time as society's attitudes and behaviors change. The means and methods of fundraising, the way of presenting a case for support, must also change. This makes it even more important for planned giving professionals to understand the attitudes and behaviors of potential donors. Donors of major gifts are likely to have behaviors and attitudes different from those of society as a whole. Understanding how these donors think and act and how they differ from other people requires insightful research by planned giving professionals.

> *Concepts of giving, charity, altruism, and philanthropy evolve over time as society's attitudes and behaviors change.*

PHILANTHROPY AND CHARITY

From before the American Revolution, when philanthropy was the sole means of creating and supporting community charity, until today, the true meaning of philanthropy has not really changed. Its purpose has been, and undoubtedly will continue to be, the improvement of human welfare.

In casual discussion, *philanthropy* and *charity* are used interchangeably. Philanthropy, however, encompasses attempts to deal with the problems of society as a whole, whereas the focus of charity is on helping needy individuals and groups. In addition, philanthropy is generally thought of as more impersonal than charity and not as closely associated with religion and altruism. Philanthropy is characterized by independence and voluntarism, whereas charity, because it deals more with immediate needs and problems, does not rely nearly as much on voluntary organizations. In fact, government has gradually taken over to a significant degree the provision of charitable services.

Philanthropic institutions, with their mission of social change and bettering the human condition, are neither business nor government organizations, although they share aspects with both types. The business sector of society is controlled by market economics and the profit motive. The government sector in a democracy, at least in theory, acts in accordance with the will of the majority. The third sector, the not-for-profit sector, is oriented toward meeting social needs that are neglected by the other sectors. Philanthropy can be thought of as a counterbalance to the business and government sectors—a way of responding *compassionately* to social needs (Douglas 1983).

> *Philanthropy can be thought of as a counterbalance to the business and government sectors, a way of responding compassionately to social needs.*

HOW GIFTS ARE MADE

The United States, it appears, is first in the world when it comes to private wealth committed to the public good. More benefits are dispensed, it is thought, by this country's many philanthropic organizations than by the philanthropic organizations of any other democratic country. These funds overwhelmingly come from individuals. Although today's individual donors do not have, on average, the great resources of the major donors at the end of the nineteenth century and the beginning of the twentieth, there are still many potential donors with significant resources (Rudney and Rudney 1992).

In fact, today, we are seeing that three-quarters of the very wealthiest Americans have their own private foundations. These foundations are set up by people in the top third of the Forbes 400—those whose net worth exceeds $2 billion. We do not know if these wealthy individuals are what is referred to as the New Philanthropists; however, we do know there is a significant increase of wealthy individuals in our country today.

Indeed, the number of potential donors is much greater than before. But that is only half the story. While the number of potential donors with significant resources (a million dollars or more) has increased, the amount of giving by these contributors, as a percentage of their total available resources, seems to have significantly decreased. In the 1980s, for example, the number of potential donors with significant resources was calculated to have increased by a factor of 14, but by the end of the decade the average amount of yearly gifts was about two-fifths of the amount given in the decade's first year.

However, new statistics on charitable donations have come out. In 1999, $197 billion was donated to charitable organizations; approximately 75 percent or $147 billion came from individuals, and 9 percent and 11 percent came from corporations and private foundations, respectively. These gifts are equivalent to about one-third of the domestic federal budget or 2 percent of our national income. These statistics are based on the reporting of monetary gifts (cash, stocks, etc.) and goods (equipment, real estate, etc.) to the Internal Revenue Service. The amount of time people volunteer is not included. Trends in volunteering time have gone largely unquantified. Even though there are indications that volunteering is on the increase, it is not known whether that presumed increase is ahead or behind increases in population and income.

Something else to think about is the information in *The Millionaire Next Door*. This book came out in the late 1990s and certainly has given many of us in the profession food for thought in how we evaluate donor or prospect potential. Of course, no one knows in detail who the richest Americans are, where the source of their money lies, how it is invested, or where it will go when they die. There are numerous large family trusts, but information about them is scarce and often inaccurate. Consequently, it is impossible to make anything but gross order-of-magnitude estimates of how much Americans give.

For the United States, information from many sources suggests that more than three-quarters of the funds donated to not-for-profits comes from individuals. This figure is plausible given the American Judeo-Christian ethic of charity and good works, a continuing influx of immigrants in search of a better life, an economy that has a sterling record of expansion over 200 years, and a tax code that has helped create great wealth, especially in the past, for a relatively large segment of society and provided significant financial incentives for giving.

Considerable time and effort have been spent trying to understand the recent history of the philanthropic sector and its pattern of giving. Research has provided important insights into recent changes in the giving of significant gifts. Perhaps the two most important conclusions are these:

1. Surviving spouses are especially likely to give to charity.
2. At death, gifts to family members are as common as gifts to charity in spite of the tax advantages of giving to charity.

The census shows that women outlive men on average. Given that the future is always unknown, it makes sense that a surviving wife would wait until her death before giving to charity. It is also understandable that people want to provide for family members before helping others. Historically, gifts from men far exceeded in value gifts from women, no doubt because men gained and controlled virtually all of the wealth. It is generally believed that gifts at death are made by something less than one-quarter of the wealthy but that the more wealth people have, the more likely they are to give through an estate plan. Recently, gifts derived from the income of wealthy individuals may have roughly equaled gifts at death.

It is thought that the tax laws affect giving in a number of ways. For example, they

- encourage wealth accumulation
- place a maximum on charitable deductions
- make it advantageous to give during a lifetime rather than at death

Strangely, it appears that planned giving does not decrease in difficult economic times, such as the years of the Great Depression. The reasons for this are not obvious, but perhaps part of the explanation is that people not so adversely affected can see the need for charitable institutions more clearly in tough times and respond accordingly.

Or the main reason may have something to do with how charitable institutions present their case and state the need. Organizations that continue to present a clear, concise, consistent case for support, during good and bad economic times, continue to receive contributions from philanthropic donors. Donors who believe in your organization but may not currently have ready cash might well bequeath a substantial gift from their capital assets through a will or trust. This means you should never stop conveying your case for support.

> *Organizations that continue to present a clear, concise, consistent case for support, during good and bad economic times, continue to receive contributions from philanthropic donors.*

Although the wealthy appear to be somewhat less than generous when it comes to charitable gifts, the opposite appears to be true of poor minorities. The evidence shows that they contribute a greater percentage of their income than more affluent minorities. Minority giving patterns and attitudes presently seem to emphasize the group rather than the individual, and minorities have created their own organizations and institutions. As the minority populations grow and their income increases, they may contribute to yet another evolution in society's modes of giving.

Considerable research has been directed toward understanding how potential donors view giving opportunities over time, and it has uncovered a correlation between available resources, desire or motivation, and age. It is not surprising that the motivation to give seems to decrease sharply at or near retirement (roughly 62 years of age and up) even though resources are typically close to their maximum at that time. On the other hand, young potential donors, although often desirous of helping to better society, usually have a low level of resources. It is reasonable to conclude that somewhere between youth and retirement an individual's motivation and resources will coincide, and for as long as they do there could be an opportunity to turn the potential donor into an actual donor of regular and special gifts. The period after retirement, because resources are generally diminishing then, is a time of potential deferred giving (Mann 1994). This picture of the changing motivations and resources of a typical potential donor can aid in understanding the opportunities and constraints that pertain to planned giving.

Understanding the financial, social, cultural, and family attributes of your constituents will help you create effective development strategies. These strategies should include efforts to educate potential contributors and turn them into actual contributors. Conversely, for current programs and development strategies, demographic information can be used to identify donors likely to be receptive to your message. Finally, like social attitudes

and behaviors, the demographics of a society or region can undergo changes, and you need to keep abreast of any such changes.

> *Understanding the financial, social, cultural, and family attributes of your constituents will help you create effective development strategies.*

WHY GIFTS ARE MADE

It is important for you, as a planned giving professional, to understand not only how people donate gifts but also why they do it. Besides the gaining of a tax advantage, many reasons exist that cause people to give, including these:

- Donors are often motivated by social, religious, or philosophical convictions; gratitude; a commitment to public service; or a desire to better society.
- Some donors wish to share their good fortune, win love or appreciation, receive public recognition, or achieve redemption.
- A donor may want to create a memorial in remembrance of a person, a family, or an event.
- A donor may desire to keep his or her life's work in the family's control.
- On the negative side, donors occasionally are driven by guilt or competitiveness.

Whatever reason motivates a potential donor, you must listen carefully for clues and identify the source of the potential donor's desire to give. Frequently, the motivation behind a gift is very personal and private, and only by achieving a degree of intimacy with the potential donor can you get a glimpse of it. Creative cultivation and stewardship is the means that planned giving professionals employ to reach out to donors and achieve the necessary degree of closeness.

PHILANTHROPIC ORGANIZATIONS: POWER AND CONTROL

One of the most important developments in American society has been the creation by the very wealthy of many large and well-funded philanthropic institutions over the last 125 years. Not only has no other nation encouraged the growth of private philanthropic organizations like America has, but no other nation has given them the same freedom to act. And nowhere else have private philanthropic organizations played such a significant role in a nation's growth (Douglas 1983).

The largest and wealthiest philanthropic organizations have a degree of political and social influence commensurate with their size. They can, if they choose, affect the course business or government will take on issues concerning them. That kind of power creates public fear of potential wrongdoing. Large philanthropic organizations have also become more institutionalized and more bureaucratized. As a result, government participation in the philanthropic sector has increased.

Government participation has taken two forms: regulation and involvement in charity (welfare). In some ways, regulation and welfare are interrelated. The government, in order to ensure welfare expenditures constitute a proper use of taxpayer money, sets standards to control the distribution and use of funds. It also may intervene to meet social needs that philanthropic organizations do not have sufficient interest in or adequate funds for. Nonetheless, government intervention has deprived private American philanthropic organizations of a major portion of the autonomy that they have traditionally enjoyed.

Government controls may offer a form of protection, but they can also constrain planning and restrict the purposes and operations of programs. Of course, philanthropic organizations are also quite capable of setting restrictions for the institutions and individuals they fund. Private grants to universities, for example, may limit academic freedom, freedom of expression in the arts may be constrained by conditions set by donors, and the range of social programs designed to solve social problems may be likewise confined by conditions set.

The shift in government philosophy that is occurring has led to a reduction in the government's role in philanthropy. The extent of the effects of this shift is not yet clear, but the very fact that the government's role is being seriously questioned is itself significant.

Clearly, for the planned giving professional it is essential to understand government restrictions affecting fundraising and planned giving. It is equally important to understand the policies of the not-for-profit organization that employs you. In addition, you must also be aware of the ethical principles that apply to planned giving and know which types of actions can threaten ethical standards. One useful tool is the Model Standards of Practice for Charitable Gift Planners, which has been adopted and promulgated by the National Committee on Planned Giving.

POINTS TO PONDER

- The history of philanthropy can help in understanding the characteristics of donors and current trends in giving.
- You need to be aware of your prospects' attitudes and behaviors regarding planned giving.
- You should have some understanding of why philanthropists give of their wealth and time.
- Not every nonprofit organization can afford to pursue the New Philanthropist.
- The financial, social, and cultural attributes of your prospects are determinants of their ability and willingness to give and need to be researched.
- Planning is one key to better fundraising.
- The standards of professional ethics are of extreme importance to the profession.

REFERENCES

AAFRC Trust for Philanthropy. 1989. Understanding philanthropy: Fund raising in perspective. *Giving USA Update* (May–August):3–10.

Douglas, J. 1983. *Why charity? The case for a third sector*. Thousand Oaks, CA: Sage Publications.

Mann, B.T. 1994. Philanthropy and the aging process. *Give and Take* 26, no. 9:1, 7.

Murray, M. 1982. *Philanthropy: Its roots and history*. Washington, DC: Adventist World Headquarters.

Rudney, G., and S. Rudney. 1992. *Generosity of the wealthy: Facts and speculations*. New York: AAFRC Trust for Philanthropy.

Sills, D.L., ed. 1965. *International encyclopedia of the social sciences*. Vol. 12. New York: Macmillan and The Free Press.

Chapter 3

Planned Giving and Fundraising

WORDS TO WATCH FOR

- donor focused
- integrated fund development
- segmentation
- grants
- endowment
- mindset
- serendipitous contributions

There is an old adage, "the more things change, the more they stay the same." Well, the news is that more nonprofit organizations are starting planned giving programs, and others are expanding their planned giving offices. And the *other* good news is we are seeing the basics—wills and trusts—as the "bread and butter," so to speak, in these programs.

In this chapter, the various fundraising activities of a development office are examined and the opportunities for planned giving explained. Planned giving provides a means for you to create opportunities for long-term donors to stay involved with the organization. The chapter concludes with an enumeration of perceived obstacles that may prevent the establishment of a planned giving program.

> *Planned giving provides a means for you to create opportunities for long-term donors to stay involved with the organization.*

Numerous studies have been conducted for the purpose of exploring both the desire for planned giving and the obstacles preventing the seeking of planned gifts. The results indicate that the potential for fundraising through planned giving still is largely unrealized. They also indicate that the obstacles to planning and implementing a planned giving program are becoming fewer and fewer. Therefore, the best strategy is to assess the potential for planned gifts within your organization and, if the potential is at a high level, to find a way to overcome any obstacles to implementing a planned giving program. Sometimes the major obstacle is simply a lack of education. Of course, the necessary additional education will take time, time you may think you do not have, but keep in mind that patience and perseverance are worthwhile attributes, useful in other efforts, as well as in a planned giving program.

A solid foundation in fundraising principles is essential for a successful planned giving program and for the integration of planned giving into the other components and activities of a development office. Once you have established a planned giving program, it provides you with one more opportunity for raising money—an additional building block in your development program structure.

> *A solid foundation in fundraising principles is essential for a successful planned giving program.*

The term *development program* brings up recent trends regarding fundraising in general. There is an evolution going on in both the use of terms and in the approach to fundraising by focusing energy on the integration of all the campaigns in an organization. This new approach is called integrated fund development, and it is donor focused. *Fund development* is the new term for enhanced fundraising. Integrated fund development with a donor-focused approach has as its purpose securing the long-term commitment of donors to your nonprofit organization and its cause. It is an effective means to successfully encourage donors to give. This approach is intended to inspire casual donors to become more than just annual givers, if possible by increasing their gifts; and then if they can, by making a major gift; and finally for those who are able, to become planned gift donors and give from their estate. The hope for this is to take donors at the base of the fundraising pyramid of giving to the pyramid's apex (see Figure 3–1). As many of you may know, more than 80 percent of our organizations' donations are provided by fewer than 20 percent of donors, and these gifts are either given as a major or planned gift.

The fundraising activities needed to implement a donor-focused integrated fund development program are the same as those used in upgrading donors. The most important component requires full cooperation and co-ordination by all the players from your organization's team: the development staff, program staff, executive leadership, and, in some cases, board members. The cultivation activities have a focus on donor interest and needs. The full concept of donor-focused integration applies to engaging donors more and more with the organization and to higher and higher levels of giving. It is also the integration of fundraising activities between each level and type of giving and the involvement of all the various players in the process. This book presents planned gift fundraising activities in detail, and many of these activities are applicable to integrated fund development. How planned giving fundraising activities in particular are integrated into fundraising activities for different levels of giving will vary by cause, organization, and the donors themselves . . . you make those decisions.

Successful nonprofit groups have embraced integrated fundraising, and, more importantly, a donor-focused philosophy in their fundraising planning and activities. It can be a seamless process, one that seeks to discover how best to involve interested donors within the organization and to keep their interest in giving over a lifetime. However, this approach also requires planning and teamwork from within, and hence the integration of efforts from all concerned, from the top down to make it happen. "Friend-raising" requires coordination and consistency in cultivation and plans to build these relationships. If your goal is to seek investment from your donors in time, talent, and the ultimate gift, prepare yourselves to do it well.

Your development program requires thoughtful fundraising plans if it is to accomplish all its programs and projects. This includes marketing materials the organization finds necessary to garner financial support for current and future needs. Development officers must look for assistance not just outside the organization but also inside. Ultimate success will depend upon staff teamwork and fundraising support from board members.

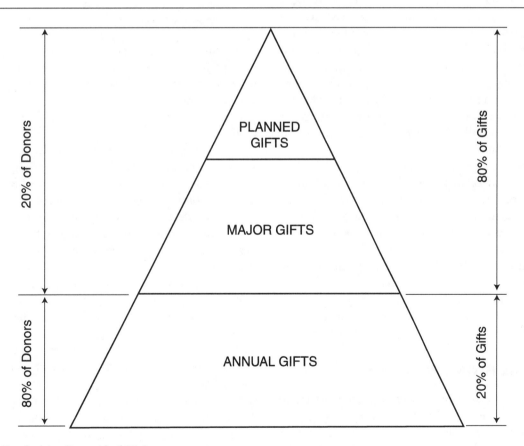

Figure 3–1 Fundraising Pyramid of Giving

Many people have the misguided view that fundraising is only one activity and that the results of this activity are always in the form of cash. This is far from the truth. In the real world of fundraising there are many methods and techniques used in the solicitation of gifts. Each element of an organization's development program needs to be carefully thought through and coordinated with every other element, and though these elements must be intertwined, they need also to function independently of each other—not an easy feat to achieve, but doable. Some elements are meant to support today's needs, while others are intended to support the organization's perceived future needs. For all contributions the competition is stiff. Creativity teamwork and persistence are absolutely necessary for success.

Fundraising is much more competitive than it used to be. Every opportunity needs to be explored. The more we do, the more, it seems, there is to do. Planned giving is one more way of offering loyal donors an opportunity to make a major financial contribution and to significantly help the organization in the enormous task of fundraising.

THE DEVELOPMENT OFFICE

An organization's development office tends to be a very complex department. It also plays an essential organizational role because it is the place where money is raised and where relationships with donors are built. Its importance, however, is not always recognized, and therefore you, as a fundraiser, will have to inform management and colleagues what the department and team have accomplished on behalf of the organization. In other words, you will have to provide education and training within the organization.

Whether your development office is large with several professionally staffed and individually managed units or it consists of only one or two people, it must attract donors and raise money in its own particular way. Therefore, it needs to provide a creative environment in which innovative solutions to fundraising obstacles can be hammered out and implemented. To see how planned giving opportunities can be coordinated with a development office's fundraising, consider the descriptions of annual giving and special purposes programs provided below along with the sample planned giving applications.

THE ANNUAL GIVING PROGRAM

Organizations need to generate enough income to take care of all their general operating expenses. The annual giving program, sometimes called the annual campaign, should do just that. It is usually designed to provide an organization with the bulk of its annual operating funds.

Annual fundraising has two major objectives in addition to raising funds:

1. to recruit new donors
2. to renew and upgrade gifts from prior donors

An increase in dollars and donors over the previous year's levels are two important indicators of success.

Most fundraising that organizations undertake requires both professional staff and volunteers, including board members. Volunteers are usually needed to help deal with the myriad details and tasks that are part of fundraising.

The frequency of annual fundraising solicitations is different in different organizations. Most charities have several solicitations in the course of the year: churches have the weekly collection plate, and the United Way and federated campaigns use a payroll deduction as a mechanism for regular payment.

Whatever your method for annual fundraising, its main purpose is to satisfy the organization's need for general operating funds for the year. There are a number of effective methods. The following four are typical and will be used to demonstrate how planned giving can fit into an annual fundraising program.

Direct Mail Solicitation

As stated before, after raising funds, the main objectives of your annual fund campaign will include renewing and upgrading current donors, reviving past donors, and acquiring new donors.

Renewing and upgrading current donors is easier said than done. Indeed, it takes a lot of effort. You should survey your current donors periodically to uncover new ways to keep and upgrade them. The surveying can be done by various means: by phone, in writing, or through a focus group. You will have to determine which is the most cost-effective method for you. Often the best way to obtain worthwhile information is to go outside the organization and hire a consultant. (For more information, see *Donor Focused Strategies for Annual Giving* by Karla A. Williams, also in this series.)

When attempting to acquire new contributors, you should begin by selecting an audience that is likely to favor your organization's particular cause or purpose. To do this, you can either update your existing mailing lists or buy or rent lists from other organizations or a list broker.

Before any direct mail is sent, you need to plan the project in detail. (For more information on direct mail fundraising, see *Fundraising Basics: A Complete Guide* by Barbara Kushner Ciconte and Jeanne G. Jacob, also in this series.) Once the plan is complete, you need to write the solicitation letter (the text should reflect the content established in the plan). Next, you should have the letter signed by your executive director, president, or board chair (hopefully someone whose name is easily recognized and who is identified with the organization in the public mind). Lastly, but certainly very important, you need to develop a response form containing a suggested gift amount, a form donors can use to request specific organizational information (this is where you invite requests for information on planned giving), and a reply envelope.

The direct mail plan must include a time schedule in addition to the details of the direct mail project, such as how contributions will be processed and how donor files and records will be organized. Prototype thank-you letters that can be modified to personalize acknowledgment of any large gifts should also be created.

The direct mail portion of the annual giving program usually is the most expensive component of any fundraising program. This is because of the high cost of printing, postage, package materials, list brokers, and labor. However, direct mail campaigns provide the quickest means for gaining a list of people who might be planned giving prospects. By looking at donor records, you can determine who has been loyal to the organization—who has made frequent gifts and whose gifts have increased in size over time. The records, therefore, need to be kept in a form that allows for analysis. In particular, you should be able to determine the frequency of giving over time, the size of gifts, donor names, and related donor characteristics, such as age, marital status, sex, and location. From this information establish specific criteria for your planned giving prospects. For example, you could establish a gift level you consider appropriate for your search. Similarly, search for loyal donors, those who give every year, or every so many years. Whatever criteria you establish, the most important thing to keep in mind is: your segmented donor records are a *very* valuable asset for planned giving, and up to a point, the longer an individual has been consistently on your records, the better. An age overlay is valuable information to include in your database for planned giving prospects.

> *Direct mail campaigns provide the quickest means for gaining a list of people who might be planned giving prospects.*

Telephone Solicitation

A number of not-for-profit organizations, both large and small, use phonathons to solicit gifts. An organization's phonathons are tied to its direct mail program and are usually part of its annual giving program. Both prospects and prior donors appear to respond favorably to personal phone calls, and the financial return rate is traditionally higher than for direct mail alone.

Phonathons are especially appropriate for organizations that have a sizable number of volunteers. For one thing, they allow the volunteers to actively participate in the development office's fundraising. One strategy is to set aside a week for phone calling by staff and volunteers. You contact current or previous donors to solicit their annual commitment and at the same time ask a few questions. After phonathon callers have identified themselves and the organization and mentioned the purpose of the phonathon, they could say, "I'm also calling to get your response to a few questions. We are trying to improve our fundraising performance as well as our understanding of your needs and wishes. Why did you decide to give this Worthy Organization your support? Worthy Organization has introduced a planned giving program. May we send you some information on our membership society?" The callers could provide information about any major activity, new program, change in administration, or event that the organization is currently promoting and also note any comments or questions asked in the donors' files. Of course, any questions asked by a donor would be followed up by the appropriate staff person. Phone solicitation is also a good way to verify names, addresses, and phone numbers, and to find out the best time for a staff person to call.

Because the response rate traditionally has been very good for phonathons, larger organizations sometimes hire people from outside to make the solicitation calls. Targeted or selective telephone solicitations, as opposed to phonathons, are often made by development office staff. However, consultants are also used to make these kinds of telephone solicitations.

Telephone "thank you" campaigns provide a wonderful opportunity to gain direct information about and feedback from donors. If your organization uses phonathons or other types of phone solicitation, the volunteers or staff who make the calls are another group you need to train. It is important to educate as many staff and volunteers as possible about planned giving, because if you do, you will be able to collect all the information about donors you need. Callers should ask if they would like any information mailed to them, if they would prefer having a personal contact, or whatever the primary purpose for which the phonathon is being conducted. At the same time, also consider updating donor records. Always be creative in looking for additional sources for planned giving prospects. The annual giving program traditionally has been fertile ground. Prospects usually want to be apprized of the various opportunities available to them as participants in your organization's future.

Special Event Sponsorship

Special events (benefits) can be very helpful to an organization, especially from a public relations point of view. They are very popular with volunteers and often with the general public. The most important thing to keep in mind when you take on a special event: first cover your costs, then make some profit.

Special events come in a variety of forms. They include something as simple as a bake sale or a car wash. The best type of event to sponsor will depend on your organization and your constituents. You can choose from sporting events, such as golf or tennis tournaments, walkathons, and running or bike races; cultural events; zoo parades; and of course formal balls and other black-tie events.

Many organizations have held clever, fun, moneymaking benefits. The good news is that most of these events are well managed and they sometimes make a 50-percent net contribution. The bad news is that they can be quite expensive to put on and may not be as profitable as they have been in the past due to rising costs or changes in social attitude.

Special events involve lots of details, and are labor intensive and time consuming. Your organization may not have the expertise in available staff or difficulty gathering the number of volunteers necessary to work on a special event. In spite of the obstacles, special events have a public relations potential that should not be dismissed lightly. Therefore, it may make sense to hire consultants who specialize in special event planning. They could be called upon to supplement staff. The publicity alone could be of such great value to your organization that it just may be worth the effort and cost. (For further information on special events, see *Successful Special Events: Planning, Hosting, and Evaluating* by Barbara R. Levy and Barbara Marion, also in this series.)

> *Special events have a public relations potential that should not be dismissed lightly.*

Educational organizations offer a unique type of special event—the alumni weekend. This special type of gathering is known as a means for generating large amounts of revenue and is a perfect example of how an organization can devise its own particular method of generating funds.

Special events could be an excellent way for your organization to gather new names and increase its donor base. Some of the participants at special events are likely to be totally new prospects—possibly even individuals who would not otherwise be known to your organiza-

tion. Once you get their names, you can explore their interest in the organization and, at an appropriate time in the future, their potential for a planned gift. Remember, you're always on the lookout for new sources of prospects to educate about planned giving.

> *Remember, always be on the lookout for new sources of prospects to educate about planned giving.*

Always try to get information about any prospects you personally meet, but also develop a means to help the person in charge of the special event to acquire the following information:

- names, addresses, and phone numbers of all attendees
- reason for attending the event (volunteer or guest)
- personal information about attendees (such as prior contributions to the organization, family connections, etc.)

The purpose, of course, is to separate out good prospects quickly. You have to be as efficient as possible in the use of your time.

Commemorative Gifts Solicitation

Many organizations receive commemorative or memorial gifts and actively solicit for these funds. This type of fundraising offers an opportunity to honor individuals and provide financial assistance to the favorite charities of the honoree.

Friends and family often contribute money to an organization instead of sending flowers at the time of someone's death. By remaining in touch with the person in your organization who is responsible for keeping track of these gifts, you may be able to work with a family and develop a larger gift. For example, the family might be persuaded to match contributed gifts with enough money to establish a scholarship in memory of the deceased family member. There are times when opportunities present themselves if only we think creatively. When you work as a team with other colleagues, it is amazing what can happen.

SPECIAL PURPOSES PROGRAM

Organizations need to generate funds for unique or special purposes as well as income for their general operating expenses. Special purpose gifts differ from annual gifts: they are of a significant size and are given in order to support a particular project or program.

They are usually "one-time" gifts and the funds may be disbursed over a period of time.

There are a limited number of special purposes fundraising methods. The following three are the most common: major donor fundraising, grants seeking, and conducting a capital campaign.

The special purposes program seeks major gifts from individuals, foundations, corporations, and government agencies. Often these gifts are a result of written proposals asking for funds to support or to underwrite a specific project or program. A long period of cultivation is usually required to qualify for and to receive the funds, and often some special preparation is necessary, such as research or proposal writing.

Major Donor Fundraising

The major donor solicitation process for special purpose gifts is quite different from the solicitation process for annual gifts. Just think of how much preparation you might need if you were asking someone for a large sum of money, such as a million dollars or more.

Soliciting major donor gifts usually involves the participation of a team consisting of professional staff and volunteer leadership, especially willing board members. After solid preparation, a personal solicitation in the form of a person-to-person visit following a preliminary phone conversation is the best way to begin. Your prospect will know the reason for the visit and, assuming you are properly prepared and have done your homework, will likely be receptive to your plans. If that is not entirely the case, you will have gained additional information through listening and will have established at least the beginning of a relationship, which, with creative cultivation, could result in a major gift at a later time.

Working closely with everyone in your organization is never more important than when a major gift or the potential for a major gift is at hand. Your training or coaching of the organization's fundraising team should include tips on how to listen for planned giving clues (Exhibit 3–1) and how to cultivate prospects. In short, help your development team help you. Consistent training and coaching of colleagues will pay off for everyone.

> *Consistent training and coaching of colleagues will pay off for everyone.*

Seeking Grants from Government Agencies, Foundations, and Corporations

Whether to write proposals for grants is a decision each organization must make for itself. This decision

Exhibit 3–1 Clues That Can Help in Matching Potential Donors and Giving Opportunities

"I'm planning to sell the house."
- **Outright or life income gift** (allows charitable deduction and avoids capital gains tax).

"My funds are all tied up in my company."
- **Outright or life income gift of company stock** with possible company buy-back.

"I can't give now because I'm saving for retirement."
- **Charitable deferred gift annuity or charitable remainder trust** paying life income.

"The kids are up and out, but how can I help my grandchildren with those college bills?"
- **Charitable remainder trust or gift annuity** with deferred payout for a fixed time period.

"I'd like to help, but I want to leave my estate intact for my family."
- A gift only of income, with eventual return of the assets—**a charitable lead trust.**
- A gift with **wealth replacement insurance trust.**

"This place is really getting to be a burden, but if we sell it, the capital gains tax bite will be huge."
- Gift of house to fund a **charitable remainder trust or retained life estate.**

"I'm locked into stock I've had for years. It doesn't pay as much as I'd like, but I'd be hit with capital gains tax if I sold it."
- **Charitable gift annuity or charitable remainder trust** (saves capital gains tax and increases income).

"I can't give anything now because of my health problems, but I think that Worthy Charity is doing wonderful things."
- Provision in the donor's will for **a bequest, charitable gift annuity, remainder, or lead trust.**

needs to be made on an organizationwide basis and at the highest level. Many, many not-for-profit organizations write proposals and never qualify for grant funds. A significant amount of research must go into a successful proposal. (For more information on grant writing, see *Corporate and Foundation Fund Raising: A Complete Guide from the Inside* by Eugene A. Scanlan, also in this series.)

Should your organization decide to pursue grant funding, there is a specific process that should be followed. Whether you are applying to government agencies, corporations, or private foundations, the first step is to determine through research which grantor is most likely to fund your type of organization and the particular type of project you are thinking of proposing. After you have narrowed the field, write for the grantors' proposal guidelines. When preparing your budget for the program or project, make certain you add in all expenses, including overhead, administrative, and general expenses. All of this takes a considerable amount of time and energy and could be very tedious for anyone who does not have an accountant's mentality. This is the time to bring in the organization's financial manager. The proposal writing team could benefit greatly from the financial expertise and information as well as from direct experience with grant seeking.

Your next step is to prepare a proposal specifically designed to fit the guidelines of your selected grantors. These guidelines, which must be followed exactly, will include a schedule and deadline dates. Many applicants have had their proposals disqualified for failure to follow the guidelines—even for the omission of minor details. Grant proposals, unlike proposals made directly to individuals, should never be emotional appeals. Grantors usually avoid emotion when making decisions as to which proposals to fund. Hundreds, maybe thousands, of proposals are received by institutions, which must have some rational basis and rigorous process for making award decisions.

While it is possible that someone in your organization might have a good contact on a corporate or foundation board, this rarely happens. Furthermore, it is not essential to receiving a grant. Grantors have finite resources, and many organizations are vying for the same funds. Usually what you propose must match the grantor's goals perfectly in order for you to receive the grant.

In general, grants are awarded to specific organizations or individuals for specific projects or programs over a specific time period. Planned giving, on the other hand, is available to an indeterminate number of individual donors who frequently have no specific time frame in mind. How could there be a planned giving application in the case of grant seeking?

There have been occasions when a foundation has provided funds for board training. Take this one step further: if your organization needs funding to bring in an outside consultant to train the board in the planned giving basics to help "get the board on board" prior to starting a program, maybe you could apply for a grant for this purpose. Receiving a grant might be the only way for a small organization to get a planned giving program going.

Conducting a Capital Campaign

Another way an organization's special purposes program can raise money is through a capital campaign. A need may arise for a new building, a building addition or renovation, a major new program, or a large research project. Or the organization may decide it is time to establish an endowment. In such situations the organization will seriously consider raising funds through a capital campaign.

Prior to embarking upon a capital campaign, the organization conducts a feasibility study to determine whether there *is* a base of financial support, who the leaders are, where exactly the sources of money are, and whether there is sufficient internal support for this kind of campaign. Feasibility is tested by actually soliciting contributions selectively and without fanfare. If half or near half of the funding goal is pledged, the capital campaign is formally announced.

A capital campaign is a means to gather staff and volunteers together in a significant fundraising effort for a very large project. It is the most cost-effective way for an organization to raise a considerable amount of money in a relatively short period of time. A campaign will usually run for a few years; there is a definite beginning and end. This is the sort of effort that board members, alumni or former patients, and dedicated major donors are usually willing to become involved with, and many of them will have given their own gift prior to asking others for a contribution. The time frame announced for the campaign may appear to the public to be surprisingly short and the funding goal surprisingly big, but in actuality the majority of the work was done while the feasibility study was being conducted and what is referred to as the "quiet stage" of a campaign.

Planning and preparation could take one to three years prior to the campaign announcement, and it is common for everything to come together beautifully during the campaign. Most capital campaigns are successful, both from a fundraising standpoint and from the volunteers' point of view—all participants are happy to have been contributors to the victory.

Some capital campaigns are planned specifically to build an endowment. However, many capital campaigns are not, and still a significant number of planned gifts are donated. Some are major gifts from donors who never thought they were capable of giving a gift of this size. A planned gift usually comes from a donor's assets rather than current cash, and when the potential donor understands the difference, he or she views the gift as a more achievable stretch.

And then there are capital campaigns where a "once-in-a-lifetime" gift is received. Such gifts, which can run into the millions, are frequently donor instigated: the donor feels such a connection with the organization that he or she has already determined the assets to be donated and presents the gift proposal to the organization.

ENDOWMENT

An important part of long-range planning for any organization is to understand the purpose of an endowment and more specifically, what your endowment needs are. In general, the purpose for which endowments are created is for perpetual financial independence. There are many reasons why your nonprofit organization would establish endowments. Endowments can provide a safeguard against the changes in priorities of the organization and its environment and a hedge against the extremes of the marketplace, even while it is subject to the fluctuations of the marketplace. Without such a hedge, the changes in market conditions, especially in volatile and down markets, can have a tremendously negative impact on current operations for your organization.

Endowments can serve as a source for existing programs, and take pressure off other sources of revenue. They can be used for initiating or expanding new programs and ideas. Whatever the stated purpose for establishing an endowment, this stated purpose is the basis for the board's resolution in establishing an endowment.

There are two broad types of endowments: *donor designated* and *board designated*. In the first type, a donor has stipulated that the endowment's principal is preserved and only the earnings can be spent, whereas in the second, the board has set aside money with the intention of preserving the principal and spending only the interest. Board-designated endowments can be changed at any time by the full board's approval, but donor-designated endowments cannot be changed by the board.

PLANNED GIVING

Planned giving provides a way for donors to sustain an organization into the future—to be one of the organization's foundation builders. As mentioned, these special benefactors are found by researching the organization's donor base to identify loyal donors who have given regularly to the organization over a period of three years or more.

Educate your targeted special audience of donors continually. Write articles on various gift planning subjects, such as writing a will. By advising potential contributors of the fact that many people have not written a will, and by describing the difficulties this has caused their families and their favorite charities, you can provide an important service.

Another good approach is to selectively send letters with planned giving information directed at this target audience. The information you provide will serve your donors and the organization well. Donors want to know the organization is making plans and is bullish on its own future. They want to know that their help is necessary, that you are offering solutions to their estate tax problems, and that you are providing opportunities for them to be part of the organization's future.

THE FUNDRAISING MINDSET

Here we are into the second year of the new century, and one cannot help but think about the new and the old: new philanthropists, new century, new terminology, or new meaning for old words, such as "dot.coms," gigabytes, e-mail, logon, mouse, etc. However, fundraising basics do not change; we "fine-tune" them or analyze the results more, but in fact there are some old sayings that can afford to be restated: "You get what you put in," "Nothing comes from nothing," "Stick to the basics." Carrying this forward into professional fund development and planned giving, it can be said the results received from your planned giving program are in direct proportion to the investment of time, talent, and budget dollars that are put into it. This brings up the case for a defined budget for your planned giving program. In order to go forward, you will need the "go ahead" from leadership and a reasonable budget. It is not necessary at first to have a full-time staff person. You will need backing by the head of the organization and the board, a budget, and time to have your planned giving program pay off. Management, staff, and volunteers are all part of the organization's fundraising or development team. Each person has a responsibility to contribute ideas that assist the organization in achieving its mission. Whether your organization has a small or large staff, members of the development team must exchange ideas. They must not isolate themselves. Often, members of the team have a mistaken belief that they are not knowledgeable enough in the basics or the nuances of fundraising to make worthwhile suggestions. Almost anyone can think of a good suggestion if properly engaged mentally with the issues. Some people appear to be too shy to participate in team efforts, but shyness is usually overcome with encouragement and a sharing environment.

Keeping up to date is a necessity in fundraising. You need to stay abreast of the successful activities of other organizations and share relevant information with your team. Knowledge is the lifeblood of the development efforts. Understanding the economic environment in your community and in your particular sector of the "not-for-profit world" is just as essential as understanding the needs of potential benefactors. You may have donors who are encountering financial difficulties because of the ups and downs of the economy. You may have donors who have recently retired from work, received a promotion, or gotten divorced or remarried. You need to be attuned to such changes as best you can.

Planned giving prospects can be identified in many ways. Many do not realize they can afford to give a gift of significance in the future or that their gift could strongly affect the future of the organization. It is of extreme importance that you continually nurture friends of the organization and continually search for and identify others who might become friends. You must also develop the ability to explain to prospects and donors alike how their gifts can make a difference to the organization and assist them in analyzing their asset base to determine the feasibility of donating a planned gift.

SERENDIPITOUS CONTRIBUTIONS

There are times when money just comes in! You may not have made any effort to inform, cultivate, or encourage participation in your organization, but someone might decide nonetheless to leave his or her assets to you in a will or in trust. You may never know exactly why the person gave so generously. Trying to track down a connection could be difficult and time consuming, but if the gift is significant, it is usually a worthwhile thing to do. Who knows, you might uncover new donors—perhaps relatives of the deceased who want an opportunity to honor their loved one.

Unsought gifts are called windfalls. It is very difficult to plan for them. However, some organization do budget a certain dollar amount to cover any difference between the planned budget and the eventual result. Regardless of how your organization handles this anomaly, windfalls certainly are nice to receive.

OBSTACLES TO ESTABLISHING A PLANNED GIVING PROGRAM

Some circumstances within an organization may seem to prevent it from establishing a planned giving program, even though there are donors who believe in the organization's mission and are willing to help support it with contributions. The three principal obstacles that are thought to hinder an organization from starting a planned giving program are

1. insufficient staff (paid or volunteer) to develop or follow up on leads
2. insufficient expertise in managing the financial aspects of planned gifts
3. an overriding need for immediate funds that directs fundraising toward activities that produce immediate results but fewer funds in the long run

The six favorite excuses for not pursuing planned giving are these (see also Exhibit 3–2).

1. Planned giving hurts annual giving.
2. Planned giving is too technical and complicated—we wouldn't know what to say.
3. We don't have time to start a planned giving program.
4. It requires hiring staff who do nothing but planned giving.
5. Planned giving is so mysterious.
6. We don't think we have the right kind of donors.

As the person responsible for planned giving, you may experience one other obstacle that might adversely affect the program or even end it prematurely: a lack of understanding on the part of top management or the board of how long donor cultivation will take before planned gifts are finally received. Unrealistic expectations could seriously jeopardize or at least call into question the effectiveness of the gift planning program and your abilities. Educating top management and the board about the time needed to develop a viable program and involving them in the creative cultivation and the stewardship of donors who have said the organization has been named in their estate plans is essential to the survival of the program.

Any expression by top managers or the board of the attitude that you, the person responsible for planned giving, "should just get out there and collect those planned gifts" or "should just be able to set a goal and go out there and meet it" endangers your program and shows that more education about planned giving is needed. Planned giving is a joint endeavor. It requires a team approach—and the team must include top managers and the board. No planned giving professional can do it alone.

POINTS TO PONDER

- How can you fit planned giving into your existing fundraising program?
- How can you educate your colleagues about or coach them on planned giving? (See Appendix 8–A).

Exhibit 3–2 Top Ten Planned Giving Myths

Myth 1:   Planned giving is not appropriate for a new organization.

          Reality: Planned giving can be a powerful source of larger gifts to assure an organization's future. Assure donors their executor or trustee can be empowered to assign an "alternate charitable organization" designation in the event the first donee organization is no longer a viable choice when the gift becomes effective in the future.

Myth 2:   Planned giving applies only to older people.

          Reality: Gifts of life insurance policies and deferred charitable gift annuities and bequest designations are particularly appropriate for younger donors.

Myth 3:   We need money *now*. Can't possibly think about planned giving.

          Reality: Many planned gift donors feel an increased commitment to the organization and, as a result, give larger outright gifts.

Myth 4:   I need more technical training before I can even *begin* to raise the topic of a major planned gift.

          Reality: Listen to how the donor would like to be benefited (e.g., a steady income to support an elderly parent), then select the gift that produces the benefit (e.g., a life income gift). Stick with the understandable benefits rather than using the technical words.

Myth 5:   People who make outright gifts are not planned giving donors.

          Reality: When the donors learn about planned gift options, many find that they can give a larger gift to the organization than they ever thought possible.

Myth 6:   Planned giving hurts annual giving.

          Reality: Frequently donors increase their annual gifts after making a planned gift due to the closer connection they feel they've made by investing in the future and mission of the organization.

Myth 7:   Only wealthy people are planned giving prospects.

          Reality: Many people may not appear to lead an opulent lifestyle, yet have assets such as stock or real estate, the value of which has risen over the years.

Myth 8:   We can't launch a successful program without an experienced planned giving officer on our staff.

          Reality: A beginning planned giving program can be outsourced to a consultant, who can provide the technical expertise. Later, as the program matures, the organization can match the investment of the planned giving professional's salary with the money as it comes in.

Myth 9:   Our organization could *never* manage to pay a lifetime of checks.

          Reality: Outsource this function to organizations expert in the management of planned gifts (see Appendix B).

Myth 10:   I will suffer *eternal mortification* if a prospect or donor asks me a tax question I can't answer.

          Reality: Even seasoned professionals are faced with this. Many will say: "Well, I don't have that answer to that right now, but I'd like to research that and I'll get back to you."

Chapter 4

First Steps

WORDS TO WATCH FOR

- assets
- bequest
- cultivation
- stewardship
- will

This chapter introduces you to the first steps in starting a gift planning or planned giving program. It describes a type of beginning program and discusses ways to sustain and make it grow through cultivation and creative stewardship.

Within the development community, predictions have been put forward that by the year 2000-something more than half of all charitable gifts will be made through planned giving arrangements. If that proves to be the case, then a gift planning program, as well as the creative cultivation and stewardship that support it, will be a necessity.

We live in a very competitive environment and many charitable organizations are vying for the same limited resources. Do not jeopardize your organization's survival by delaying the planning or implementation of a planned giving program. The most important question confronting you should be: How do we get started?

FEASIBILITY TEST

You can begin to develop a planned gift program when you know these two criteria are satisfied:

1. You and a significant number of your donors believe the organization should continue into the future.
2. A relatively large number of those donors are willing and able to back their belief in the organization with gifts of significant size.

The size of the organization and the size of its donor base are the most important variables in testing the feasibility of starting a planned gift program. That is because what will be considered a significant number of donors (or a significant gift size) is relative and will be determined by the size of an organization. No organization is too small, or for that matter too large, to have a planned giving program. When you are testing the feasibility of starting a planned gift program, it is the balance between program size and cost and the amount of donor support and resources that requires careful consideration.

According to the common wisdom of the profession, almost 80 percent of the money that organizations raise through fundraising comes directly from individual donors. In 1999, $197 billion was donated; of this approximately 75 percent or $147 billion came from individuals, and 9 percent and 11 percent came from corporations and foundations, respectively. This represents one-third of the domestic federal budget, or 2 percent of the national income (AAFRC Trust 2000). Offering various contribution options and providing donors with every available opportunity to give is critically important for your organization. A planned giving program will add to the set of options donors can pick from.

There is no single kind of gift planning program. Programs are designed and adapted to address specific needs. Start to plan a gift planning program as you would any practical enterprise: define your needs, ask yourself common-sense questions, and pursue the answers through research.

> *Define your needs, ask yourself common-sense questions, and pursue the answers through research.*

HOW TO THINK ABOUT STARTING

Consider questions like the following; these should help you jump-start the planning process.

Whom does your organization serve (or who benefits from it)? Try to analyze your constituents using as many defining characteristics as you can (such as age, sex, and location). Try to quantify each characteristic. Think of this task as akin to a market survey.

Are those you serve also your fundraising audience? If they are not your fundraising audience, wholly or even in part, who is your fundraising audience? Again, imagine you are doing a market survey of your potential donor market.

What types of gifts does your organization receive? How have those gifts been solicited? Who are the donors of major gifts? Have any of the gifts your organization has received been a bequest? Try to break down the gifts by type, program, and size and use a reasonable period of time as your time frame.

Seek the support of your chief executive officer and the board president. Describe to them the market potential and convince them to help you define the time and resources the organization needs in order to implement a planned giving program.

What kind of help will you need? Will you need the assistance of staff or volunteers? What skills will you need? How much time is available? What are the costs you will incur?

How much time can you personally devote to planned giving? How does the necessary time commitment fit with your other responsibilities? Establish time and cost budgets for yourself.

What other programs does your organization have that could benefit from and/or contribute to a planned giving program? Define the benefits and contributions and involve other program managers in your planning process by showing them how, with some support from them, a planned giving program can benefit their programs.

Conclude the planning process by securing the approval of your chief executive officer and board president to initiate gift planning.

BEQUESTS AND WILLS

By far the simplest and easiest first step you and your organization can take to start a planned giving program is to seek bequests from potential donors. A bequest is a way for an individual to transfer ownership of specific assets to other persons or charitable organizations upon death. A will is the document through which the transfer is accomplished.

The implementation of any fundraising program will take some startup money. However, a bequest program can be undertaken with a minimum cash outlay.

FIRST STEPS

Keep in mind that you will need to devote time to your planned giving program in order to reap any benefits. Start by setting a specific goal for the program, a goal that is reasonable but requires some "stretching" from you. Then set aside the amount of time per week you will need to achieve this goal. Initially, try to set aside four continuous hours a week and avoid interrupting this work period except for the occasional emergency (Ashton 1991). The work sessions should focus on accomplishing the following:

Prepare a specific, detailed one-year plan for your program and yourself, but be realistic about what can be completed.

Educate yourself, board members, donors, and other staff about the bequest phase of the planned giving program and lay out your vision of the future of the program.

Start involving your constituents immediately. For example, reply envelopes included in the organization's publications should have a request (with check-off box) like the following: "Please send me information on how to include Worthy Charity in my will." Draft a reply letter and have it ready to mail when you receive inquiries. Include in the letter the wording potential donors should use when naming your organization in their wills.

Write articles about the planned giving program for your organization's publications (see Appendix B).

Search your organization's files, find loyal constituents, and send them educational materials that describe the benefits of planned giving and how they can participate in your program by naming your organization in their wills.

In all writings, ask donors if they want information about your planned giving program. Your marketing piece will be a brochure on writing a will. When you get a response, contact the prospect immediately.

Get out of the office and visit prospects who have expressed interest in your planned giving program. Also make appointments to see local advisors—lawyers, trust officers, accountants, investment managers, and others—who might suggest your organization to their clients as a worthy gift recipient. All of these activities could take considerable time, so you must weigh them against other uses of your time and your staff's time to determine which are the most cost-effective.

Have patience and faith that your efforts will result in a successful program.

COMPLEX GIFTS

A small organization that is just beginning a planned giving program is likely to be on a limited budget. More importantly, it probably does not have extra staff nor expertise to help with the details and the administration of the program. On the other hand, a large organization might have the necessary time and expertise to pursue more complex gifts such as a variety of trusts and to appropriately administer them. If it does not, it is still more likely to have sufficient funds to secure outside assistance.

UNREALISTIC MANAGEMENT EXPECTATIONS

There is one not-so-obvious reason why it is important to set aside a specific amount of time per week so that you can devote your undivided attention to the planned giving program. Top managers and board members often develop expectations that a planned giving program will quickly result in the securing of large gifts. When that does not happen, the credibility of the development or planned giving professional and the viability of the program are called into question. Working consistently on the program is one way of ensuring that the payoff will be sooner rather than later. You can also use the work sessions to keep managers and board members informed of the program's progress and to hammer in the point that cultivation of donors is a drawn-out process.

> *Working consistently on the program is one way of ensuring that the payoff will be sooner rather than later.*

PLANNED GIFT BENEFITS

There are many benefits for donors who make a planned gift (see Exhibit 4–1). It is extremely important for you to emphasize these benefits when talking to potential donors. Not only is this helpful for the donors, but it is a good marketing tactic. You might throw in a remark like this: "Did you know that charitable bequests may be deducted from your total estate and could lower the amount of estate taxes that you owe?"

Also point out that planned giving provides a means for a loyal donor to participate in the organization's future. A well thought out bequest can help ensure that the organization will survive and fulfill its mission after the donor has died.

Exhibit 4–1 Planned Gifts and Corresponding Benefits

Outright gift of appreciated stocks or bonds. This type of gift allows the donor the potential to **save taxes three ways:** through the charitable deduction, the avoidance of capital gains tax, and the reduction of estate tax.

Life income gifts. Funded by appreciated stock, bonds, or real estate, this type of gift allows the donor to **save taxes three ways** (as above), while providing **dependable income** for the lifetime of the donor and/or others through pooled income funds, charitable gift annuities, or charitable remainder trusts.

Life insurance policy. The charitable organization can be either the beneficiary or owner of the policy. This **gift has a modest out-of-pocket cost** and is particularly attractive to younger donors and those of any age who have a paid-up policy that is no longer needed for its original purpose.

The gift you can live in for the rest of your life. In giving a home or farm, a donor can retain the **right to live in the property** for the donor's lifetime through retained life estate.

The gift you get back. A gift of income, with the income-producing assets placed in a charitable lead trust for a fixed time period, can be returned later to the donor or heirs.

The gift with wealth replacement. A gift plan can be devised in which the donor and/or others are paid a life income and insurance is used to replace the asset value that would have passed to the heirs. The cost of premiums may be defrayed by tax savings and/or increased income from the gift plan.

WILLS

Everyone should have a will. It is a privilege, a way of exercising one's freedom. It can also be a tool for helping one's family or supporting one's beliefs. Anything a person owns while living is still owned by the person after death. A will provides the means to transfer ownership post-mortem.

All planned gifts, from the simplest bequest to the most technical trust, are fully detailed in a will. Unfortunately, six out of ten people do not have a will. By introducing your donors to planned giving, you can provide a tremendous service for them and for your organization. Through simple straightforward explanations to donors, you can help them make wills or update them.

> *Six out of ten people do not have a will.*

RESPONSE CARDS

When educating donors, whether through articles in your organization's publications or targeted direct mail, make certain that you keep your educational information and your response devices (tear-offs, coupons, forms, surveys, etc.) clear, concise, and easy to understand and use. One way to do this is to provide check-off boxes (see Exhibit 4–2). By making relevant information as accessible as possible, you will help make giving to your organization as easy as possible.

DONOR RECOGNITION SOCIETIES

Donor recognition groups have been around for many years. However, in recent years many new recognition societies, especially legacy societies, have been established. This has generally occurred because of the increased interest in gift planning.

Gift planning principally concerns estate planning and all the emotional issues that surround that important subject. If it makes sense to ask donors to give major gifts through their estates, then obviously you should take the time to honor the contributors and show your organization's appreciation as part of your creative cultivation and stewardship efforts.

There are many different reasons to establish a legacy society, but most are established for two principal reasons:

1. to publicly recognize individuals for their charitable gifts
2. to gather donors together in an exclusive group

Another reason to establish a bequest or legacy society is so you can use it as a platform to educate the community about gift planning. For example, the society and the organization might jointly sponsor estate planning seminars to pique people's interest and supply them with needed information.

Bequests are referred to as a *revocable intention:* an individual can change his or her will or "revoke" a bequest up to the point of death. Membership in a legacy or bequest society, while not ensuring that a bequest will not be revoked, can provide an additional way to maintain the trust and confidence of donors and discourage them from changing their wills.

Once you have been informed that an individual has named you in his or her will or estate plan, maintaining

---

Exhibit 4–2 Sample Response Card

Worthy Charity

CONFIDENTIAL

_____
Name (PLEASE PRINT)

_____
Address

_____
City   State   ZIP

_____
Signature

_____
Telephone

❏ I accept membership in the Legacy Society and qualify on the following basis:

❏ I have included Worthy Charity in my insurance/will/estate plans.

❏ I have established an irrevocable life-income plan with Worthy Charity.

❏ I have an insurance policy naming Worthy Charity as ❏ the beneficiary.   ❏ the owner.

❏ I have made other estate provisions for Worthy Charity (please describe):

_____
_____
_____

(Over)

[Reverse Side]

❏ Please send me more information on
  ❏ providing for myself and others through a life-income gift to Worthy Charity.
  ❏ providing for Worthy Charity through my will.
  ❏ becoming a member of the Legacy Society.
❏ Please send me a copy of *Planned Giving Opportunities.*

❏ I am enclosing a donation of $ _____.

Please return this card in the enclosed reply envelope and mail it to:
Mary Jones
Director of Development
Worthy Charity
1800 Main Street
Goodtown, USA

the relationship with this donor should become a priority. Your success at building and sustaining relationships with donors will depend on the plans you developed for creative cultivation and active stewardship. A bequest society could be one vehicle for accomplishing your main goal. Remember, care, cultivation, and inclusion go a long way toward sustaining donor interest and loyalty.

> *Care, cultivation, and inclusion go a long way toward sustaining donor interest and loyalty.*

Planning is one of the most important components of your planned giving program. Prior to establishing your society, you need to proceed through these five steps.

1. **Get approval.** Gain senior management and board approval and any other approval you deem necessary. Securing the support of your organization's leaders is your first step. Without their endorsement, the other steps will not be necessary. The goal is to have the board take a principal role in establishing the donor recognition society.
2. **Develop membership criteria.** What type of planned gifts are you willing to accept? Will you want documentation or will the donor's word be enough? Do you want to have a dollar amount? What about a form for the donors to fill out? Remember, there is a fine line between involving donors and scaring them away by requesting too much documentation and asking too many questions. However, you will want some information, so plan what you need.
3. **Choose a name.** Many organizations use "legacy society" or "heritage society," whereas others use a name that alludes to their particular purpose. Your main objective should be to choose one that is appropriate for your organization.
4. **Decide on a symbol.** What will you use as an outward sign of membership? A certificate or scroll suitable for framing, a pin, or another tasteful personal memento?
5. **Develop a marketing plan.** How are you going to promote the society? Will you have a spokesperson? Who will that person be? Check your network and research how other organizations have established their societies. Buy or develop brochures and other necessary marketing materials. Count on a minimum of three years of promotion before benefits accrue.

Admission to membership in your legacy society is an opportunity to thank donors today for their future gifts. Establish an annual event to recognize these wonderful individuals and allow them to meet each other. Following are some ideas to help get you started:

- Establish different gift levels and hand out extra "perks" at the annual event depending on the size of the donor's commitment. One suggestion is to hold a reception prior to the event for donors of large gifts. Another is to provide special seating for those donors at the event.
- Invite all individuals who you know to have named your organization in their estate plans.
- Take lots of pictures of donors with various staff and board members. These pictures can be used in future promotional materials.
- The annual event could be where the members receive their membership symbol.
- Plan a special newsletter that promotes the legacy society. Include stories about your members as well as information on wills and bequests. You could maximize the use of pictures you have taken by publishing them not only in the legacy society newsletter but also in other newsletters or organizationwide periodicals that are regularly sent to constituents or potential donors.

Devoting a reasonable amount of financial resources and staff time to nurturing the legacy society could mean an enormous future return for the stewardship effort the society represents.

STEWARDSHIP

Webster defines a steward as someone who manages another's property, finances, or other affairs. Stewardship in the context of planned giving is more than just minimal oversight. It can be thought of as the art of building confidence and trust for the purpose of developing a donor–organization relationship in which additional gifts are possible.

Relationship building is what fundraising is all about. You could call this relationship building *friend raising*. Fundraisers have a saying: "People give to people." This is never more true than in planned giving. People do not usually include "strangers" in their wills. They give to family, loved ones, friends—whomever or whatever they believe in.

> *Relationship building is what fundraising is all about.*

How do you help a bequest gift to be made? The answer is this: know your mission; develop an ability to convey your story with logic, passion, and conviction; and build relationships inside and outside your organization. If you succeed in each task, eventually you will see the results in all your fundraising, but particularly in your planned giving efforts.

Because planned gifts are usually of a significant size, they are rarely given spontaneously. They often require advance planning and a legal instrument such as a will or trust agreement. Stewardship should be an integral part of your organization's comprehensive development program, especially in the case of planned giving. Raising funds for an organization's future needs and survival is different from all other fundraising. It is based on creative cultivation and stewardship.

Fundraising is a social art, not a science. However, underlying any successful planned giving or stewardship program is the "law of return": if you do a good job, you will reap a reward. In various settings, services are provided in the hopes of gaining financial support. For example, universities often provide information about planned giving in adult education courses. A social service or health service organization might promote its planned giving program by publishing needed estate planning information in its newsletter. Churches frequently present planned giving as an extension of the principles of biblical stewardship: return a portion of the good fortune God has bestowed.

Although cultivation and stewardship have a role in other fundraising programs, in planned giving they are essential. In general, planned giving requires roughly three years from the first sowing of seeds to the bearing of fruit. The initial period is a time of heavy effort and little to show for it. However, the eventual rewards are often so significant that your planned giving fundraising might turn out to be the most cost-effective of all your fundraising activities.

Your initial marketing will probably have a low response rate. Consequently, the amount of staff time needed to follow up on requests will be low, making your first steps very doable.

Some organizations need all the funds they can raise in order to maintain day-to-day operations. An organization in this situation might conclude that it cannot afford a planned giving program. In fact, nowadays it seems that any solicitation program that fails to produce immediate income is in danger of being considered too expensive. Unfortunately, creative cultivation and stewardship, as noted, take a long time to attract gifts, and so they are reduced or eliminated, their potential for return notwithstanding. One common result is that a planned giving program simply never is undertaken.

At present, fully developed stewardship plans are typically found only in the development programs of organizations with financial strength; organizations with a long history of fundraising; and large, well-established universities, hospitals, and national or international charities with broad public appeal.

Your organization's stewardship program is a means to provide your donors with the information, encouragement, care, assistance, and nurturing that is necessary to get them to make major gifts. Many donors need encouragement, reassurance, and emotional support during what is often a long period of education and decision making, and handholding of donors can prove to be a major component of the stewardship role.

> *Your organization's stewardship program is a means to provide your donors with the information, encouragement, care, assistance, and nurturing that is necessary to get them to make major gifts.*

The emotional support provided is intertwined with the technical information provided on tax benefits and the finances of estate-related gifts. The technical information can lead the way by helping the prospective donor feel comfortable with the idea of donating a large gift. The donor then might be inclined to ask his or her own advisors to explain how to make a planned gift. However, you will often be regarded as someone who is merely supplementing the information given by the advisors.

Many fundraising professionals find cultivation and stewardship to be difficult because of the complexities of planned giving itself and the degree of emotional closeness sometimes necessary. Not everyone has a temperament or personality suited to the patient care of donors. And not everyone has the social skills required to engage and hold the interest of donors and the accompanying ability to explain gift opportunities clearly. Lack of confidence and the fear of embarrassment or failure have discouraged many fundraising professionals from participating fully in this important function.

However, anyone who has a sincere desire to develop the necessary social skills—skills that are truly essential for a planned gift officer—should seek out other professionals with these skills for advice or mentoring. Most of us in the profession of fundraising have a certain measure of sociability, so success in achieving good social skills is likely.

Planned giving, cultivation, and stewardship are fundamentally interrelated. The professionals who practice stewardship, the long-term supporting element of planned giving, need not only tenacity and knowledge of the subject but also, and perhaps even more importantly, the personal skills to communicate courtesy, appreciation, and respect to donors as well as the common sense to build confidence and to create emotional partnerships.

Do not get discouraged; many different-sized organizations are introducing gift planning into their fundraising programs. Of course, you have lots to do in order to get your program started, but be encouraged. Others are now beginning to see positive results. You can soon be among the high achievers.

POINTS TO PONDER

- A gift planning program can be started on a shoestring, but time and money must be allocated.
- You are performing a wonderful service to your constituents and your organization by providing information about wills and bequests.
- Creative cultivation and stewardship are vital to any fundraising program, but especially to a planned giving program.

REFERENCES

AAFRC Trust for Philanthropy. 2000. *Giving USA 2000: The annual report on philanthropy for the year 1999.* New York: AAFRC Trust for Philanthropy.

Ashton, D. 1991. *The complete guide to planned giving.* Cambridge, MA: JLA Publications.

Chapter 5
Not-for-Profit Organizations

This chapter provides a basic understanding, from a fundraising perspective, of the major differences among various types of not-for-profit organizations.

Nonprofit organizations make up the "third sector." Just as the business and government sectors provide services that satisfy our needs, so too do nonprofit organizations enhance our lives in various ways. Nonprofit organizations are not in business to make a profit, nor are they part of the government. The organizations represented in the third sector cater to our spiritual, cultural, and educational interests and respond to our mental, physical, and social needs in a manner that distinguishes them from other types of organizations.

The nonprofit sector is special because many of its services and functions are intended to improve people's well-being. Furthermore, organizations in this sector are structured to allow participants a level of self-determination that is often impossible elsewhere. Each is governed by a board comprising representative members of a community who are entrusted to set a responsible course in pursuit of a public mission. The structure, management, and governance of a not-for-profit can allow for much more flexibility than is possible in the more tightly organized world of business or in bureaucratically controlled government agencies.

> *The not-for-profit sector is special because many of its services and functions are intended to improve people's well-being.*

Not-for-profit organizations are uniquely situated. They can address social needs as those who direct and manage the organizations see fit. They are free to define their own performance criteria. They must decide for themselves what it is they are in business to do and how to judge success and failure.

Not-for-profit organizations are like business organizations in at least one regard: they must at least break even. That is, they must generate as much revenue as they spend, or otherwise they fail and must dissolve. Contrary to popular belief, a not-for-profit actually can make a profit—in the sense that it can generate more revenue than it spends. However, surpluses cannot be annually distributed to those who control the organization, as is done in business. Rather, any surplus is used to pursue the general purposes for which the organization was established.

Not-for-profit organizations also resemble government in one important way: they address the needs and goals of a collective public nature, although on a voluntary basis and without the power of taxation to support themselves.

Because not-for-profits are not primarily driven by the marketplace, nor by politics and government directives, they are in the unique position to define the public good and the public's needs as they see them and to pursue their mission undeterred so long as they operate lawfully and at least break even.

Exact classification of not-for-profit organizations is difficult because their variety is almost endless. A good place to start is the federal tax code, which divides not-for-profits into different groups for tax purposes. With few exceptions, not-for-profit organizations are exempt from corporate income tax (tax on the difference between operating revenues and expenditures) and are classified under Section 501 of the Internal Revenue Code. The broadest distinction is between **mutual benefit organizations**, which produce services for their own members, and **charitable or philanthropic organizations**, which produce services for a segment of the general public.

MUTUAL BENEFIT ORGANIZATIONS

Many mutual benefit organizations provide commercial services to benefit their own members economically and professionally or to support the industries or professions that they represent or are a part of. While there are several different groupings in the tax code, the general category includes trade associations, associations of manufacturers, social and fraternal clubs, mutual insurance companies, professional organizations such as the American Medical Association, and labor unions such as the United Auto Workers and the AFL/CIO.

PHILANTHROPIC ORGANIZATIONS

The largest and most prominent third-sector group consists of charitable or philanthropic not-for-profit organizations. Classified under Section 501(c)(3) of the Internal Revenue Code, these not-for-profits serve external constituencies—segments of the general public. For example, hospitals are intended to serve the sick, universities to serve students, orchestras to serve music lovers, and environmental organizations to preserve the environment for present and future generations. Of central importance for us who work as fundraisers in the not-for-profit world is the fact that organizations in this 501(c)(3) category are permitted to receive charitable contributions from individuals, corporations, and foundations and that these donors may take a charitable deduction from their taxes.

Section 501(c)(3) not-for-profit organizations can be divided into three categories: (1) public charities, (2) private foundations, and (3) community foundations (Blevins et al. 1985).

The largest of these is the category of public charities. This group includes hospitals, colleges and universities, social agencies, museums, orchestras, religious institutions, and large charities such as the American Cancer Society and the Red Cross. All of them raise funds through charitable solicitation, and some, like the United Way, allocate the solicited funds to other charitable organizations. In general, their work is intended to benefit the public at large or some segment of it, and they are supported by public resources, including grants, special gifts, and other charitable contributions from a variety of individual, government, and corporate contributors.

A private foundation, unlike a public charity, is established using an individual's or corporation's fortune as the exclusive source of funds (Nielsen 1985). Although the purpose of private foundations is to serve the public, tax laws treat them less favorably than public charities.

This is partially due to the nature of private foundations. There are two categories of private foundations: (1) operating foundations and (2) grant-making foundations. Rather than giving money away, operating foundations use their funds primarily to carry out a direct service or research agenda. For example, the Salk Institute was established to perform medical research. Grant-making foundations, such as the Ford Foundation or the Robert Wood Johnson Foundation, generally restrict their activities to the disbursement of grants to other organizations and to individuals undertaking projects or programs consistent with the grant-making foundations' stated purposes and guidelines.

Unlike private foundations, community foundations, such as the Foundation for the National Capital Region and the New York Community Trust, are funded with gifts from people in their localities. These foundations administer portfolios of gifts, bequests, and endowments, and the donations may be designated for particular purposes. Community foundations direct their funds toward projects and programs intended to benefit their communities. In a sense, community foundations are conduits for the local distribution of charitable contributions. Because community foundations are deemed to be supported by a broad-based public, they are classified as public charities under Section 501(c)(3) rather than as private foundations.

There is a final important not-for-profit category. The organizations in this category have a public purpose, but it is political advocacy rather than philanthropy or providing public services. They are classified under Section 501(c)(4) of the tax code and are not eligible to receive tax deductible contributions.

NOT-FOR-PROFITS AND PLANNED GIVING

This discussion has covered only the most basic types of organizations, and additional distinctions could be made. However, by now it should be clear that the third sector plays a significant role in delivering an enormous array of needed and desired services.

Although there is chance for error, like in any human endeavor, the incentive to profit by cheating or compromising on quality is less prevalent and less strong in the third sector than in the profit-making sector. Moreover, in comparison with government agencies, not-for-profit organizations are generally responsive to public needs and market demands within their particular service areas. Having the largest portion of the not-for-profit world made up of charitable and philanthropic organizations should give us all some hope for the future.

> *The incentive to profit by cheating or compromising on quality is less prevalent and less strong in the third sector.*

Charitable and philanthropic organizations clearly need to survive, and planned giving is an excellent way these organizations can help to ensure their future. First they need to understand that they can include planned giving in their fundraising without the expenditure of substantial resources. A focused program can be introduced even if the development program is staffed by a single person. With insight, careful marketing, and a bit of luck, the smallest program can identify interested major donors, garner gifts, and ultimately achieve significant results. Not-for-profits no longer have the luxury of ignoring the potential of planned giving.

> *Not-for-profits no longer have the luxury of ignoring the potential of planned giving.*

Knowledge of federal and state tax codes and related regulations is of course essential. Tax relief is, after all, one of the principal benefits donors are receiving for contributing a charitable gift, and a fundraiser's knowledge of the technical aspects of gift planning and taxes can help donors feel comfortable with the idea of transferring ownership of a substantial portion of their assets.

POINTS TO PONDER

- A not-for-profit organization's profits must be used to provide services to its constituents.
- Not all not-for-profit organizations can receive tax deductible charitable contributions, only those with an Internal Revenue Code 501(c)(3) designation.

REFERENCES

Blevins, R. et al. 1985. *The trust business.* Chicago: The American Medical Association.

Nielsen, W.A. 1985. *The golden donors.* New York: Truman Talley Books.

Chapter 6

The Business of Philanthropy and the Practice of Planned Giving

No other type of fundraising provides as many challenges as planned giving. Nor does any other type offer such creative opportunities to advise prospects and donors in ways that could bring major benefits to them, to your organization, and perhaps to society. This chapter briefly describes how not-for-profit organizations do business, how the professional practice of fundraising is carried out, and what attributes a fundraising professional needs.

FUNDRAISING AS A PROFESSION

Few people begin careers in fundraising with the expectation of making a lot of money. Instead, idealism, the belief in a cause, is the primary motivation for the majority of those attracted to the fundraising profession. Consequently, it is rare for fundraisers early on to plan every career move or decide on ultimate goals. They are people who care about other people and want to do something that will make a difference in the lives of other people. Getting ahead in life is not their primary concern.

Something incredible has happened over the past few years; there has been an explosion of younger people choosing fundraising as a career. One reason why some are moving into this sector is due to their work experience in college. But others are choosing fundraising as a profession because of their ideals; they want to make a difference. From their perspective, "it begins with me." And many others are finding out that larger organizations are expanding their planned giving departments and they need planned giving associates, and it is a career opportunity for them.

> *Something incredible has happened over the past few years; there has been an explosion of younger people choosing fundraising as a career.*

However, it is not just younger people who are entering the profession; older workers on their "second career" are entering the fund development field. And why would they be doing this? Because they have a need, a need to be productive members of society and to augment a less than desirable retirement income. The reduction of government services has resulted in an increase of nonprofit organizations that are filling the gap. You may ask, are there enough positions? You bet there are. In fact, there is a great demand for development experience. And for major gift and planned gift officers, in some instances, these higher level positions are receiving significant increases in compensation.

The term *fundraising professional* by necessity is a broad one. Consider who does the fund development for an organization. The development staff? Senior leaders of the organization? Members of the board of trustees? The answer is: all of the above. Anyone else? Oh yes, other staff members, program or project leaders, and, of course, volunteers all can do fundraising (Cohen and Young 1989).

Yet there is an important difference between individuals who happen to do fundraising and the professionals who staff the development office. Neither top managers, nor board members, nor volunteers can completely replace development professionals when it comes to running a fundraising program.

The term *professional* signifies specialized knowledge, extensive preparation, and payment for services. For members of the fundraising profession, that specialized knowledge and preparation needs to be in the field of fundraising. Although volunteers and senior management staff at certain times should be actively involved in various aspects of fundraising, the major share of the workload is on the shoulders of the professional development staff.

To meet their fundraising responsibilities, development staff professionals who do charitable gift planning require not only general fundraising knowledge but also a diverse set of skills, specialized training, and a certain mindset.

Several changes have influenced the world of planned giving over the last few years. First, donors have become more knowledgeable and savvy. Second, competition for financial support has increased. As a result, planned giving professionals not only must be very creative in their approaches to planned giving but must gain a thorough understanding of tax law, estate and financial planning, marketing, banking, and donor management. In addition, they need to develop excellent social skills.

There has been talk of making the study of philanthropy, volunteerism, and not-for-profit organizations and management an educational requirement for those pursuing careers in this not yet well-defined field (Hodgkinson et al. 1989). The first and second sectors, government and business, have had education programs for years. With full-time employment in philanthropy approximating the combined employment in federal and state government, some kind of curriculum seems overdue. Education has always been an important focus of professional organizations such as the Association of Fundraising Professionals (AFP) formerly (NSFRE) and the National Committee on Planned Giving (NCPG), and therefore some of the groundwork for an education program has already been laid.

Philanthropic studies will not be developed so rapidly that careers in philanthropy in the near future will be restricted to people with specific educational credentials. However, as the curriculum expands and new opportunities emerge in the field, those who began their careers before formal education was available will feel pressure to become better prepared and keep up to date.

Philanthropy has always been complex, and, like other fields, it is becoming even more so. Philanthropic decisions depend on too many issues to be made solely by lawyers or accountants or administrators or fundraisers. For those who want to continue to work in the field, continuing education will be essential. No doubt there are more professional positions available for individuals with philanthropy-related education and experience than there are individuals with the desired background. Yet, more individuals with potential, enthusiasm, and commitment are being attracted to philanthropy, and there finally appears to be a growing awareness of the need for more professionalism and more continuing education.

If a curriculum is developed, it should reflect the fundraising profession's two aspects: the business side of philanthropy and the fundraising side. The first concerns the operation of not-for-profit organizations—their activities or functions and their structure. The second concerns the relationship between not-for-profit organizations and potential donors. By looking at these two aspects of the profession together, we can not only identify subjects for study but also learn something about the character of successful development professionals.

THE BUSINESS OF PHILANTHROPY

A not-for-profit organization or institution has essentially the same business functions as for-profit businesses. It must deal with financial matters, accounting, employment regulations, and personnel. Depending upon its size and mission, public relations, legal counsel, and facility management may also be important needs. And like any for-profit business, it must manage its resources and assets.

> *Like any for-profit business, it must manage its resources and assets.*

The not-for-profit organization will have officers: a president and vice-president(s) and possibly other senior officers. It will also have a board of directors or trustees. If the organization is large, it will have department heads and administrators as well as officers. Some of the larger organizations even have lower tier officers, such as assistant or associate vice-presidents and program managers.

Both large and small not-for-profits carry out the same basic business functions. Large organizations do it with more people, and staff roles are thus more limited and functions more compartmentalized. Small organizations do it with fewer people, who must therefore "wear many hats."

THE DEVELOPMENT DEPARTMENT

The mission of a not-for-profit organization is what really differentiates it from a for-profit organization. However, another distinguishing feature of not-for-profits is the development function—the fundraising activities, the work of securing gifts through contributions. The development department (or development office) is the place where a not-for-profit organization concentrates the responsibility for planning, implementing, and managing its fundraising activities. The department typically is operated by an administrator with a title such as "development director," "director of institutional advancement," or "vice-president for development." Many staffing arrangements are possible, ranging from a one-person office with an assistant to a fully staffed department comprising numerous subdepartments and their directors (e.g., director of annual giving, director of corporate giving, and director of planned giving).

THE PRACTICE OF FUNDRAISING

The development office, whatever its size, has the responsibility to

- Define and state clearly the case for supporting the organization's mission.
- Provide the staff with sufficient information to enable them to fully understand the organization's mission.
- Identify individuals and organizations that are likely sources of support and present them with donor-focused opportunities that support the organization's mission.
- Hire staff with a "can do" attitude who are willing to present donors with opportunities to enhance or expand programs or meet future needs.

> *Hire staff with a "can do" attitude who are willing to present donors with opportunities to enhance or expand programs or meet future needs.*

The word *support* as it's used here includes all types of gifts. The fundraising activities are performed in a series of carefully planned steps based on a schedule reflecting specific development needs and objectives (see Chapter 1). All successful fundraising by organizations requires varying amounts of planning, preparation, unearthing philanthropists' needs, problem solving, professionalism, and patience. If planning and carrying out fundraising sounds difficult for the planned giving officer and development personnel to do, you are right—it is difficult.

An organization's officers and top managers and the board of directors act as the principal leaders and planners of the organization's policies. For example, they set fundraising policies and establish the principles for development activities. The success of an organization's fundraising efforts depends in great part on how effectively officers, top managers, and board members work with development officers and communicate fundraising policies and principles to them. It depends even more on the ability of the development staff to plan and implement the fundraising activities efficiently and effectively.

Beyond their role in policy guidance, officers, top managers, and board members are expected to be active participants in some fundraising functions, usually in two ways: first as contributors and second as catalysts in identifying and securing gifts—particularly major gifts. Because of their positions in business, society, or govern-ment, they are well positioned to influence others to contribute to the organization.

Top managers and board members are not likely to have been fundraising professionals. Consequently, the fundraising staff have the added responsibility of coaching them, along with other volunteers, during the pursuit of major gifts. A large portion of this responsibility easily falls on the shoulders of the planned giving professional.

PLANNED GIVING PROFESSIONALS

Planned giving is a profession in which past experience can be advantageously brought to bear on current responsibilities. Many planned giving professionals have had previous careers. They often have experience in accounting, banking, law, teaching, social work, ministry, insurance, and financial planning. Quite a number have advanced degrees.

However, though their backgrounds may be wide and varied, they must exhibit a willingness to continue to learn. And besides this willingness, they must possess, if they are to be effective, the following abilities and attributes: integrity, communication and interpersonal skills, creativity and resourcefulness, common sense, superior listening skills, and patience.

For the aspiring planned giving professional, some of the necessary skills are technically complex, but simple enough that a motivated individual can learn them. However, understanding technical terms and applying the concepts they define does not make a complete or well-rounded planned giving professional; the role is not limited to quotas and charts. It also depends upon social consciousness and relationship building.

While each organization has its own culture and its own gift planning emphasis, the planned giving professional must believe in the mission and have empathy for others. You must also have strong leadership qualities: faith in what you are doing, patience to wait for results, and foresight to know that your work will ultimately benefit the organization. As a planned giving professional, you will need to practice the skills of technical consultation and emotional support.

POINTS TO PONDER

- Fundraising professionals can specialize or wear many hats.
- Each type of fundraising, including planned giving, requires a distinctive mindset, as well as a determination to work as a part of the whole.

- Planned giving professionals need to train or coach other members of the development staff, top managers, board members, and volunteers in their area of fundraising.

- The **five Ps** of fundraising are **p**lanning, **p**reparation, **p**hilanthropy, **p**roblem solving, and **p**rofessionalism.

REFERENCES

Cohen, L., and D.R. Young. 1989. *Careers for dreamers and doers: A guide to management careers in the non-profit sector.* New York: The Foundation Center.

Hodgkinson, V.A., and Richard W. Lyman & Associates. 1989. *The future of the nonprofit sector.* San Francisco: Independent Sector.

Chapter 7
Planned Gifts

- appreciated property
- adjusted gross income
- closely held stock
- deed of gift
- qualified appraiser
- gift acceptance policy
- annuitant
- disclosure statement
- gift value
- donor advised fund

What constitutes a gift? The simple answer is, anything of value—your time or a treasured possession. However, that is not a very helpful answer. A better approach might be to divide gifts into categories, such as **tangible property** (things that can be touched physically; sometimes called tangible personal property or real estate) and **intangible property** (cash, securities, and life insurance). A competing way to analyze gifts is to use the categories of money, goods, and services.

- **Money** includes cash or documents that eventually become cash, like checks and the whole range of securities (stocks, bonds, treasury bills, mutual funds, closely held stock, promissory notes, royalties, and life insurance policies).
- **Goods** include real estate (land and buildings), other personal property (automobiles, boats, jewelry, art, furniture, clothing, timber, and livestock), and gifts in kind from manufacturers or retailers.
- **Services** include help given by individual volunteers and work donated by service companies and professionals (such as free transportation provided by

a taxi company, free food service provided by a caterer, and pro bono advice given by lawyers, financial planners, and accountants).

Use whichever way of thinking about gifts that works for you in your gift planning efforts.

PLANNED GIFTS AND HOW THEY ARE MADE

Different kinds of donor assets can be used as the basis for a variety of different types of gifts. As a planned giving professional, you must understand the types of gifts and the assets that can be used to put them into effect. You do not need to be a lawyer, but you do need to understand how and when the law applies. In addition, you need to be able to speak to potential donors and members of your organization knowledgeably and in lay terms about specific assets and the types of planned gifts your organization offers as well as the tax and other donor benefits of each (see Table 7–1 and Appendix 7–A).

> *Different kinds of donor assets can be used as the basis for different types of gifts.*

The following is a list of the more frequently used types of planned gifts:

- outright gifts of appreciated property
  1. securities
  2. real estate
  3. tangible personal property

Table 7–1 Guide to Donor Benefits of Planned Gifts

Donor Benefit	Outright Gift of Appreciated Property	Charitable Gift Annuity (CGA)	Pooled Income Fund (PIF)	Retained Life Estate (RLE)	Charitable Lead Trust (CLT)	Charitable Remainder Annuity Trust (CRAT)	Charitable Remainder Unitrust (CRUT)
Income tax deduction for gift value	X	X	X	X		X	X
Partially tax-exempt income payments		X					
Capital gains tax paid over life expectancy of annuitant		X					
Avoids capital gains tax	X		X	X		X	X
Federal estate tax savings	X	X	X	X	X	X	X
Property retained by donor for lifetime				X			
Income tax deduction for income payments to charity					X		
Pays fixed income		X				X	
Pays variable income; potential for inflation protection			X				X
Assets returned to donor or heirs					X		

- life income gifts
  1. charitable remainder trusts
     - annuity trusts
     - unitrusts
     - net income unitrusts
  2. pooled income funds
  3. charitable gift annuities
     - immediate
     - deferred
- life insurance policies
  1. charity as beneficiary only
  2. charity as owner and beneficiary
  3. policy as "wealth replacement"
- retained life estate
- charitable lead trusts
- bequests

OUTRIGHT GIFTS OF APPRECIATED PROPERTY

Donor Benefits:

- Charitable deduction for market value
- Avoidance of capital gains tax
- Reduction of estate tax

Securities

When a donor makes an outright gift of readily marketable stocks or bonds that have grown in value, he or she can save taxes in three ways:

1. The donor can take a charitable deduction for the market value of the stock.

2. The gift is removed from the assets subject to estate tax.
3. The capital gains tax is avoided, as there is no sale.

The charitable deduction for a gift of appreciated securities for a donor who itemizes deductions on his or her income tax returns is presently limited to 30 percent of the donor's adjusted gross income (AGI) for the year in which the gift is made. If a donor cannot use all of the deduction in the first year, it may be carried forward and used over the next five years, within the 30 percent of AGI ceiling. The tax savings reduce the out-of-pocket cost of the gift to a donor.

Example
Outright Gift of Appreciated Securities

Current Market Value	$10,000
Original Cost	$2,000
Capital Gain	$8,000
Income Tax Charitable Deduction	$10,000
Income Tax Refund	
$10,000 x 39.6% Tax Bracket	$3,960
Capital Gains Tax Avoided	
$8,000 x 20% Capital Gains Tax	$1,600
Total Tax Savings	$5,560
"Cost" of Gift of $10,000	
$10,000 less $5,560	$4,440
Value of Gift to Recipient	$10,000

A gift of closely held stock can yield some special benefits to the donor if he or she has built a business and is considering either selling it or passing control to the children. For example, if the donor, instead of selling the closely held company directly to a purchaser, contributes the stock to a charity, he or she will be allowed a charitable deduction for the fair market value of the stock and will avoid the potential capital gains tax on any appreciation value. The purchaser could buy the stock from the charity, making the cash available to the charity for its current needs. It is important that there is no contract of sale prior to the gift being executed and that the charity is not obligated by the donor to sell the stock to the purchaser.

Passing control to the children may be accomplished by giving them a few shares in the company. The donor then gives the controlling shares of the closely held stock to charity. The business represented by the stock uses its retained earnings to purchase the stock from the charity and "retires" the stock. Result: the children's shares increase in value and the charity has the cash to further its mission. Again, it is important that there be no written agreement of sale prior to the gift.

What if your donor is considering a gift of stock that is worth less now than when it was bought? The best advice is to sell the stock, take advantage of the loss for tax purposes, and then make a charitable gift of the proceeds of the sale.

See Appendix 7–B for procedures for transferring gifts of appreciated securities, Appendix 7–C for a gift data sheet, and Exhibit 7–1 for a sample advertisement for the giving of such gifts.

Real Estate

A donor may wish to give the title of a home, farm, apartment building, shopping center, or industrial property to a charity, which can retain the gifted property for its own use or sell it and use the proceeds to further its mission (see Appendix 7–D and Appendix 7–E). Much of America's wealth is tied up in real estate, so it is important for a charitable organization to be adept at handling these valuable gifts in a prudent manner.

For example, the charity assumes the expense of mortgage payments if it accepts a gift of mortgaged property. It is less expensive and simpler to avoid accepting gifts of mortgaged property. Also, when a charitable organization accepts a gift of real estate, it assumes the carrying costs and environmental liability involved. There are ways to manage the risks that attend the acceptance of such gifts, by adopting a sound gift acceptance policy, for example, and by utilizing the services of a firm that specializes in the handling of charitable real estate gifts (see Appendixes 7–D, 7–E, and 13–A).

Tangible Personal Property

Tangible personal property is property that can be physically touched, such as artwork, books, jewelry, automobiles, and equipment.

To transfer tangible property, the donor must sign a letter (deed of gift) describing the property and the donor's intent to give the property to a charity for its exempt purposes.

If the donated property is related to the exempt use of the organization (related use), such as books given to a school library, the donor is entitled to a charitable deduction in the amount of the property's cost basis if it has been owned by the donor for less than one year (short term) or for the appraised market value if it has been held for more than one year (long term). If the charity intends to sell the property immediately and use the cash, the gift would be deemed to fail the "related use" test and the donor would be entitled only to a charitable deduction for the cost basis of the property.

If the gift is more than $5,000 in value, in order to qualify for a charitable deduction the donor must obtain an appraisal by a "qualified appraiser" and file IRS Form 8283 (see Appendix D). The detailed instructions on the form are quite explicit and should be used as a guide. If the gifted property is sold by the charity within two years of the date of the gift, the organization must file Form

Exhibit 7–1 Sample Advertisement for Gifts of Appreciated Securities

---

Worthy Charity

Gifts of Appreciated Stocks, Bonds, or Mutual Funds

If you are considering a gift to Worthy Charity, it may be to your advantage to give stocks, bonds, or mutual funds instead of cash.

Any securities that you have owned for twelve (12) months or more and that have increased in value since you bought them are subject to the capital gains tax if you sell them. However, if you make a gift of these securities to Worthy Charity, you get a charitable deduction for the full fair market value as of the day of transfer and avoid the tax on the capital gain.

This allows you to make a gift using an asset which might have been considered frozen because of the capital gain that would be experienced if you sold it. Because you get a charitable deduction for the market value, avoid the capital gains tax, and reduce the potential estate tax, you are making a gift that can save taxes three ways!

Please give us a call if you would like to discuss this or any other gift.

Mary Jones
Director of Development
Worthy Charity
1800 Main Street
Goodtown, USA
(800) 123-4567

Example: *Mary S. owns $10,000 worth of XYZ Corporation stock, which she purchased for $2,000 two years ago. By donating this stock to Worthy Charity, she receives a charitable deduction of $10,000 and avoids tax on the $8,000 of capital gain.*

8282 (the "tattletale" form) and the donor's charitable deduction for the gift may be reviewed by the IRS.

In order to confidently answer donor questions about proposed gifts to your organization of tangible personal property, it is helpful to have an approved gift acceptance policy in effect (see Appendix 13–A).

LIFE INCOME GIFTS

Donor Benefits:

- Charitable deduction for gift value
- Income for life
- Reduction or avoidance of capital gains tax
- Reduction of estate tax

Life income gifts have become increasingly popular because of the financial and estate planning benefits they afford. The donor makes an irrevocable gift of cash or property and retains a life income for one or more persons (income beneficiaries). When the last income beneficiary dies, the assets that produced the income (the remainder) will pass to the charity (the remainderman) named in the document (instrument) that formalizes the gift.

The donor will enjoy a charitable deduction in the year in which the gift is made. If he or she cannot utilize the full amount of the deduction (50 percent of adjusted gross income if the gift is cash, 30 percent if appreciated securities or real estate is used), the deduction may be carried forward and used to offset income for five more tax years.

The charitable deduction is determined by the annual amount of income paid times the life expectancy of the income beneficiaries according to the actuarial tables. The IRS then "discounts" the total amount using a rate of interest linked to the current rate of government bonds at the time the gift is made. The result of this calculation is the "present value" of the stream of income, which is deducted from the market value of the securities to arrive at the "gift value." It is this gift value that is the amount deductible. The larger the income portion, the less the gift portion and hence the smaller the charitable deduction.

If the gift is made with appreciated property, the capital gains tax is reduced or avoided completely.

Example
A Gift of Stock with Retention of Income for Life

Donor's Age: 72

Value of Stock	
Current Market Value	$100,000
Original Cost	$20,000
Capital Gain	$80,000
Donor's Benefits:	
Annual Income of 7%	$7,000
Income Tax Deduction	$46,829
Capital Gains Tax	$0
Ultimate Value to Recipient	$100,000

Note: This example assumes a discount rate of 7.4 percent.

Charitable Remainder Trusts

Donor Benefits:

- Charitable deduction for gift value
- Income for life
- Avoidance of capital gains tax
- Reduction of estate tax

In this type of gift a donor irrevocably transfers assets into a trust created by the donor and governed by a trust agreement modeled after documents approved by the IRS (see Appendix C at the back of this book for examples). The trust pays income for life to the donor and/or others named in the trust instrument. The payments may not exceed 50 percent of the initial amount contributed, and the present value of the amount that will eventually pass to the charity (in most cases the charitable deduction amount) must be at least 10 percent of the market value of the assets transferred to the trust. The donor usually names a bank or trust company of his or her choice to serve as trustee to invest the funds, pay the income, prepare the annual tax reporting forms, and, when the last income beneficiary (recipient) dies, distribute the remainder (remaining assets in the trust) to the charity named. In some instances, a large and experienced charity will serve as trustee.

Trust income is fully taxable to the beneficiary (or beneficiaries) unless the trust is invested entirely in tax-exempt bonds.

Because of the legal expense required to draft a trust instrument (the cost of which can be defrayed by the donor's tax savings), the charitable remainder trust is more suitable for gifts of $100,000 and more. Life income gifts of less than that amount are most cost-effective for the donor when the pooled income fund or charitable gift annuity options are used as described below.

There are three variations on the charitable remainder trust theme: (1) annuity trusts, (2) unitrusts, and (3) net income trusts.

Charitable Remainder Annuity Trusts

Donor Benefits:

- Charitable deduction for gift value
- Fixed income
- Avoidance of capital gains tax
- Reduction of estate tax

A charitable remainder annuity trust pays a fixed income set by the donor at the time that the trust is created. It is stated as a percentage (at least 5 percent) of the initial trust assets. The resulting dollar income can be specified for the lifetime of one or more individuals or can be for a fixed period of years. Additions to the annuity trust are not permitted, as they are in the unitrusts or pooled income funds (see below).

The fixed payment feature makes the annuity trust particularly suitable to meet the steady income needs of many elderly beneficiaries. Sometimes the payment over a fixed term of years is selected to pay tuition for grandchildren.

> *The fixed payment feature makes the annuity trust particularly suitable to meet the steady income needs of many elderly beneficiaries.*

Example
Charitable Remainder Annuity Trust

John, age 70 had been a devoted volunteer for Worthy Charity. His great regret, however, was that he had never been able to give generously, as the support of a disabled family member had placed a heavy burden on his resources through the years. He was surprised and delighted to read in Worthy Charity's newsletter that it was possible to make a gift to the charity, save taxes three ways, and receive a dependable income for life.

After conferring with Worthy Charity's planned giving representative and his legal advisor, he placed $100,000 in low-dividend-paying stock that he had acquired many years ago for $25,000 into a charitable remainder annuity trust for the eventual use of Worthy Charity.

John benefits in a number of ways.

1. For the year in which he makes the gift, he qualifies for a federal income tax deduction of approximately $60,310, which, in his 36-percent tax bracket, will save him approximately $21,712. He can use the deduction to offset up to 30 percent of his adjusted gross income this year and may carry the unused portion of the tax benefit forward for up to five more years.
2. His designated income beneficiary, the disabled family member, will receive fixed payments in quarterly installments totaling $5,000 each year for life. This doubles the income John was receiving from the stock before the gift plan was put into effect.
3. John would have owed tax on $75,000 of capital gain had he sold the stock. With this plan, the entire market value of the stock was available for reinvestment.
4. The value of the stock was removed from John's estate, thereby reducing estate tax and probate costs.
5. John got the satisfaction of making a larger gift to Worthy Charity than he ever thought possible.

Note: This example assumes a discount rate of 7.4 percent.

Charitable Remainder Unitrusts

Donor Benefits:

- Charitable deduction for gift value

- Variable income
- Avoidance of capital gains tax
- Reduction of estate tax

The charitable remainder unitrust provides a payment to the income beneficiary in an amount that will vary. The donor selects the payout rate. The trust pays that percentage of the assets as revalued each year. The annual income will increase or decrease with the market value of the trust assets. Additions to a unitrust are permitted and will afford the donor additional charitable deductions for their gift value.

The unitrust gift option is attractive to donors who desire some income growth potential, and the permissibility of additions to the trust provides greater flexibility.

Example
Charitable Remainder Unitrust

When Worthy Charity's newsletter article about life income gift plans reached Jane, she was fascinated to learn that she could provide major support for this favorite charity without lowering her spendable income. The "icing on the cake" was that she could save taxes three ways and have the potential for increased income from the gift through the years.

After getting from Worthy Charity's director of development an illustration of the specific gift she had in mind, she sent the information to her advisor, asking him to help her put the plan into effect. Her lawyer drafted the trust agreement based on the IRS-prepared sample documents provided by Worthy Charity. She named her bank to serve as trustee, and started the trust with $100,000 in highly appreciated stock that she had inherited from her parents 25 years ago. She selected quarterly payments totaling 5 percent of the market value of the trust, as revalued each year, and will thus be receiving a variable amount that has the potential of growing with the market value of the trust investments. The annual payments will be made out of trust income, or trust principal if the income is not adequate. When the term of the trust ends at her passing, the value of the investments in the trust will go to Worthy Charity.

As Jane, age 72, will receive the income for her lifetime, she will qualify for a federal income tax deduction of approximately $57,078. The deduction can be used to offset up to 30 percent of her adjusted gross income when she prepares her tax return. To the extent that she cannot utilize all of the deduction for the year in which she made the gift, she can carry over the deduction and reduce her taxes for an additional five years. She completely avoided the capital gains tax she would have had to pay if she had sold and reinvested the $100,000 worth of appreciated stock. Another tax saving derives from the fact that the value of the stock will not be taxed in her estate. The primary benefit for Jane, however, is the knowledge that she has made a far greater contribu-

tion to the mission of Worthy Charity than she had ever contemplated.

Note: This example assumes a discount rate of 7.4 percent.

Net Income Charitable Remainder Unitrusts

Donor Benefits:

- Charitable deduction for gift value
- Variable income according to assets used
- Avoidance of capital gains tax
- Reduction of estate tax
- Helpful with gifts of real estate

This variation of the unitrust provides for the distribution to the beneficiary (or beneficiaries) of either the net income of the trust or the fixed percentage specified in the agreement, whichever is less. The donor may wish to add a "makeup provision" that allows the trust, in any subsequent year in which the income exceeds the selected percentage, to distribute such excess of income to make up for any deficiencies that might have occurred in previous years.

The net income unitrust is particularly useful in instances where the donor wishes to fund the trust with an appreciated asset that may not be immediately marketable, such as real estate. As there is no requirement to pay out an annual income based on a fixed dollar amount (annuity trust) or a fixed percentage of the assets (unitrust), the net income provision allows the trustee to sell the property on an orderly (not fire-sale) basis and replace it with income-producing securities. As with any unitrust, tax deductible additions are allowed. The donor may wish to use these additions to help the trust pay the carrying charges for the real estate until it is sold by the trustee.

Flip Unitrusts

The flip unitrust is a gift option that allows the payment of income to "flip" one that pays the net income with makeup (as the one immediately above) to a straight unitrust paying out a fixed percentage of the market value of the trust assets as revalued each year. The event that triggers the change must be one that is outside the control of the trustee or any other person, and includes the sale of a marketable asset, marriage, divorce, birth, or death. The flip occurs as of the first day of the taxable year following the year in which the triggering event occurs.

Example
Net Income Makeup Charitable Remainder
Unitrust with Flip Provision

Fred, age 70, is a psychologist who has built a successful practice over the years. He recently set up a gift plan to benefit the scholarship programs offered by the charitable foundation of his professional society to help deserving young people enter the field. In a meeting with the director of the foundation and her planned giving specialist, Fred considered the gift example and sample trust documents. He then discussed them with his advisor and decided upon the following plan.

Early in his career, he had purchased an apartment building for $35,000. Recently this building had been appraised for $500,000. He set up a net income charitable remainder unitrust into which he would place the apartment building. The trustee would sell the building and with the proceeds would purchase an investment portfolio of income-producing securities. As the trustee of the charitable trust (not Fred) liquidates the property, no capital gains tax would be paid, thus making it possible to reinvest the entire proceeds of the sale. (In other words, the proceeds are undiminished by the tax on $465,000 of capital gain that would have been due if Fred had sold the apartment himself.)

Fred qualifies for an income tax charitable deduction of approximately $270,965, which he can utilize to offset up to 30 percent of his adjusted gross income on his tax return for a total of six years or until used up, whichever comes first.

Fred will receive annual payments of 5 percent of the trust's value as revalued each year for his lifetime. In the first year, these payments will be the lesser of about $25,000 and the income earned by the unitrust. Payments in future years will vary with the value of the unitrust and will be limited to the trust's earned income. As the trust incorporated a makeup provision, payment shortfalls below the 5 percent may be made up in future years when the trust earns more than 5 percent. The net income provision will relieve the trustee of the requirement to make predetermined payments while the trust assets are still in real estate form, thus providing some leeway to sell the building in an orderly fashion to maximize the value of the trust.

On the first day of the year following the sale of the real estate, the trust "flips" its income payment to Fred to 5 percent of the market value of the trust, as revalued each year, regardless of the income produced by the trust's investments.

The plan upon which Fred embarked will save income tax, capital gains tax, and estate tax; will provide Fred an income for life; and will later make it possible for the charitable foundation to use his wealth to provide deserving students the opportunity to share the values of his profession.

Note: This example assumes a discount rate of 7.4 percent.

Other uses for flip unitrusts:

- Educational Trust—A grandfather funds a flip unitrust for his 12-year-old granddaughter. The trust flips when she is 18 years old. He structures it as a term trust to meet the 10 percent payout rule.

- Retirement Trust—A surgeon funds the unitrust during his peak earning years. The trust flips upon the donor reaching his retirement age. The triggering event should be a specific age or date to qualify.

Pooled Income Funds

Donor Benefits:

- Charitable deduction for gift value
- Variable income
- Avoidance of capital gains tax
- Reduction of estate tax
- No setup cost

In this type of gift, the donor joins a "pool" of donors and the gift assets are irrevocably commingled with those of other donors in a pool of investments similar to a mutual fund. The pooled income fund is governed by a trust instrument established by the charity. A disclosure statement must be given to and signed by the donor prior to making the gift. The donor may contribute cash and/or appreciated securities but not tax-exempt securities. After the last income beneficiary dies (there can only be one or two), the proportion of the fund represented by the donor's gift is withdrawn and becomes the property of the charity. Additions to the pooled income fund are permitted, and income distributions are fully taxable to the recipients.

Pooled income funds, because of their "off-the-shelf" quality, do not require legal fees of the donor and are especially advantageous for donors of gifts less than $100,000.

Example
Pooled Income Fund Gift

For years, John and Mary, 68 and 66, had made modest contributions to Worthy Charity's annual fund. Recently, however, they had learned that it was possible to give more major support through the new pooled income fund and get back an income for life, along with some attractive tax advantages. To fund the gift, they selected shares of XYZ Corporation stock that, although it paid only a small dividend, they were hesitant to sell because it had grown in market value from $10,000 to $50,000 over the years that they had owned it and they would have to pay a hefty tax on the $40,000 of capital gain.

Their gift is commingled with the gifts of others, like in a mutual fund, and they will receive over their lifetimes an annual income consisting of their proportional share of the varying income earned by the investments in the pool, which is managed by a bank trust department.

They will qualify for a federal income tax deduction of $17,680, which, if they cannot use fully for the year in which they make the gift, they can carry forward for as long as five more years. They will receive payments in quarterly installments for life. In the first year, these payments will be approximately $2,750, as the fund is currently yielding

5.5 percent. Payments in future years will vary with the income of the fund.

They avoid tax on the capital gain and reduce their estate tax bill in addition to gaining the satisfaction of making a handsome future gift to Worthy Charity, one that, far from diminishing their spendable income, actually increased it.

Note: This example assumes a discount rate of 7.4 percent.

Charitable Gift Annuities

Donor Benefits:

- Charitable deduction for gift value
- Fixed income, partly tax free
- Reduction of capital gains tax
- Reduction of estate tax
- No setup cost

One of the oldest, simplest, and most popular methods of making a life income gift is to use a gift annuity, which is a combination of a gift and an investment. With what is usually a simple one-page agreement (see Appendix C), the charity accepts the gift and agrees to pay a specified fixed dollar amount (annuity) to the donor (annuitant) and/or another recipient. It is an irrevocable gift and immediately becomes the property of the charity, which is then legally responsible for paying income for the lifetime of each annuitant. The charity would be well advised to set aside the entire amount of this asset and place it in a fund for the express purpose of paying gift annuity income. With this strategy, if the asset is invested wisely, the other assets of the charity are protected (see Chapter 14).

> *One of the oldest, simplest, and most popular methods of making a life-income gift is to use an annuity, which is a combination of a gift and an investment.*

Most charities pay annuity rates based on the recommendations of the American Council on Gift Annuities, which was established in 1927 to help prevent cutthroat rate competition between charities. This voluntary group now consists of the representatives of more than 1,400 charities. Its rates are developed using mortality (actuarial) tables and are revised periodically to reflect current rates of interest in the investment market. They are designed to result in a gift of at least 50 percent of the value of the initial gift when the last income beneficiary dies.

An increasing number of states are imposing their regulation of charitable gift annuities in varying ways. It is important to check the status of these regulations for the state in which the charity is located as well as the state of the donor's residence. The most current information with respect to this changing scene can be obtained by contacting Planned Giving Resources (www.pgresources.com) or Planned Giving Services (www.plannedgivingservices.com). Please refer to Resources in Appendix B.

For tax purposes, the income stream (annuity) will be divided into these portions during the actuarial life expectancy (see Glossary of Planned Giving Terms in Appendix A) of the income recipient(s):

- A tax-free portion. Because part of the income is regarded as a return of principal, it is not taxed.
- An ordinary income portion. The remaining portion is taxed at ordinary income rates if the original gift was made with cash.
- A capital gains portion. If the original gift was made with appreciated securities, the taxable income portion of the annuity is split between "ordinary" income and "capital gain" income and spread out over the annuitant's expected years of survival, after which it becomes taxed at the ordinary income rate.

One of the reasons for the great popularity of the charitable gift annuity is that the tax-free portion of the income stream in effect raises the return above the quoted rate, as the tax-free portion is not diminished by the requirement to pay income tax on it. The tax-free portion is greatest when the annuity is funded with cash.

Although cash and marketable securities are the most common assets used to fund a charitable gift annuity, real estate can also be used. Extreme caution must be exercised to avoid a cash drain on the charity incurred as a result of the carrying costs of a real estate gift prior to its sale by the charity.

Note that the administration of charitable gift annuities requires investment management and administrative skills that may not be present in a small organization (see Chapter 13).

There are two types of charitable gift annuities, immediate and deferred. These are discussed below.

Immediate Charitable Gift Annuities

Donor Benefits:

- Charitable deduction for gift value
- Immediately beginning fixed income for life
- Reduction of capital gains tax
- Reduction of estate tax

In this type of charitable gift annuity, income commences immediately after the agreement is signed.

Example
Immediate Charitable Gift Annuity

Mary, age 70, had been a loyal alumna of Welsford College, giving every year to the annual fund. She had always wished she could contribute more because of the excellent education she received there.

When she read in the Welsford newsletter that she could make a gift that could pay her back a life income, part of which was tax free, she returned the reply card to request more information. She was pleased when she immediately received a phone call from the college development office to thank her for her interest and to say that the information that she requested would be in the mail that afternoon.

Based on the material she received, she thought a charitable gift annuity would fit her need for a dependable income and a generous rate of return. She phoned to get answers to specific questions and spoke with Welsford's planned giving specialist, Nancy Truehart. Nancy explained in everyday terms the benefits and features of the plan Mary had in mind and sent her a written illustration based on the specific dollar amounts that Mary had discussed with her. Nancy included a gift annuity agreement and encouraged Mary to discuss it with her advisor before making her decision.

After consulting her advisor, Mary sent Welsford $50,000 worth of low-dividend-paying XYZ Company stock that she had purchased years before for $10,000 to establish a charitable gift annuity. She will qualify for a federal income tax deduction of approximately $20,233 (the amount is based on her age and the size of the annual payment). The deduction can be used to offset up to 30 percent of her adjusted gross income when she prepares her tax return. To the extent that she cannot utilize all of the deduction for the year in which she made the gift, she can carry over the remaining deduction for an additional five years or until it is used up.

She will receive payments of 7.5 percent in quarterly installments totaling $3,750 each year for life. In addition, $374 of each year's payments will be tax free for the first 15.9 years.

She will owe no capital gains tax at the time of her gift. Instead, $1,497 of her annual payments from the gift annuity will be taxed as capital gain in each of the first 15.9 years of payments, the actuarial life expectancy of an individual aged 70. If Mary were to have sold and reinvested this stock, she would owe tax on $25,000 of capital gain.

Mary has increased her income; saved income tax, capital gains tax, and estate tax; and received the great satisfaction of making a much larger gift to her alma mater than she had ever thought possible.

Note: This example assumes a discount rate of 7.4 percent.

Deferred Charitable Gift Annuities

Donor Benefits:

- Higher charitable deduction for gift value
- Deferred higher fixed income for life
- Reduction of capital gains tax
- Reduction of estate tax
- Increased retirement income

In a deferred charitable gift annuity, a variation on the charitable gift annuity theme, a gift of cash, marketable securities, or real estate is exchanged for the charitable organization's promise to pay the donor an income stream (annuity) starting at a future date. The donor's charitable deduction is larger than with an immediate charitable gift annuity. As the income does not begin until a future time and will be paid for fewer years, its present value is a smaller portion of the market value of the gift, and the deductible gift is a larger portion. Also, because the fund will have a period of time to grow without withdrawals for annuity payments, the income rate is higher than with an immediate annuity (see Table 7–2).

Deferred charitable gift annuities are beneficial in retirement planning for working professionals who may have reached the maximum on their contributions to such tax-qualified plans as IRAs, Keoghs, and 401(k)s. As there is no maximum on contributions to a deferred charitable gift annuity, the donor can continue to build retirement income while helping a favorite charity.

A deferred charitable gift annuity is particularly appropriate when the gift is real estate. The annuity agreement can be written in such a way as to delay the payment of the annuity until the charity has had ample time to sell the property and substitute income-producing securities. In this way, the charity ensures that it has an appropriate source of funds from which to make the annuity payments.

Example
Deferred Charitable Gift Annuity

Ralph, a 50-year-old surgeon, decides to increase his retirement income and to make a major future gift to Worthy Charity. He has reached the ceiling on contributions to his tax-qualified Keogh plan and has been advised that there is no ceiling on contributions to deferred charitable gift annuities.

After conferring with the development office of Worthy Charity, he instructs his broker to transfer $50,000 worth of shares of a mutual fund that he acquired for $10,000 to Worthy Charity in exchange for a deferred annuity starting at his retirement.

He will qualify for a federal income tax deduction of approximately $29,776 and will receive fixed payments of 15.3 percent in quarterly installments totaling $7,650 each year, starting at age 65, for life. In addition, $204 of each year's payments will be tax free for the first 19.9 years, the actuarial life expectancy of an individual at age 65.

He will owe no capital gains tax at the time of his gift. Instead, $814 of his annual payments from the gift annuity will be taxed as capital gain in each of the first 19.9 years of payments. If he were to sell and reinvest this property himself, he would owe tax on $40,000 of capital gain. In addition, his estate may enjoy reduced probate costs and estate taxes.

Note: This example assumes a discount rate of 7.4 percent.

LIFE INSURANCE POLICIES

Donor Benefits:

- Charitable deduction for cash value of policy
- Modest out-of-pocket cost

Life insurance provides the means by which a donor can make a handsome charitable gift at modest out-of-pocket cost. There are three versions of giving life insurance policy gifts: (1) with the charity as beneficiary of the insurance policy, (2) with the charity as owner and beneficiary of the insurance policy, and (3) with the life insurance policy as replacement for donated assets.

> *Life insurance provides the means by which a donor can make a handsome charitable gift at modest out-of-pocket cost.*

The donor may own a policy for which there is no longer a need (a policy purchased to fund college tuition for children who have long since graduated). Life insurance also provides an opportunity to make a larger gift than would normally be possible and pay for it on an installment basis through annual premiums.

Charity as Beneficiary of the Policy Only

Donor Benefits:

- Retention of ownership and control of policy
- Modest out-of-pocket cost

A donor can name a charity as the beneficiary of a life insurance policy while retaining ownership and control of the policy and having access to its cash value. As the death benefit will be a charitable gift, estate tax is

---

Table 7–2 Comparison of Immediate and Deferred Gift Annuity Payment Rates (Quarterly Payments)

Age	Immediate	Deferred to Age 65
50	5.7%	15.3%
55	6.0%	11.6%
60	6.4%	8.7%

Note: A discount rate of 7% is assumed.

avoided. However, if the donor retains ownership of the policy, no income tax charitable deduction for the premiums is allowed.

Charity as the Owner and Beneficiary of the Policy

Donor Benefits:

- Charitable deduction for cash value
- Tax deductibility for premiums if paid to charity as contributions
- Modest out-of-pocket cost

The donor can irrevocably assign ownership of an insurance policy to a charitable organization, at which time the donor is allowed an immediate federal income tax charitable deduction for the lesser of the policy's fair market value or the net premiums paid. The donor's subsequent contributions to enable the charity to pay premiums on the policy also represent charitable gifts for which a deduction is allowed. If in subsequent years the donor ceases to reimburse the charity for premiums, the charity then must decide to cash in the policy or to continue paying the premiums out of its own funds. The age and health of the insured donor would be key factors in reaching a decision on that issue.

The Policy Used for Wealth Replacement

Donor Benefits:

- Replacement of the value of assets given
- Modest out-of-pocket cost

Insurance can be used to replace the value of the gift of the assets for the benefit of the donor's heirs. The donor can utilize the income tax savings resulting from the charitable deduction and/or the increased income from a life income gift to defray the cost of the premiums. In order to avoid estate tax on the death benefit of the insurance policy, the policy must not be owned by the donor. This can be arranged by planning to have a life insurance trust purchase and own the policy or by enabling the donor's heirs to purchase and own the policy using gifts from the donor.

RETAINED LIFE ESTATE GIFTS

Donor Benefits:

- Charitable deduction for gift value
- Ability to maintain lifestyle
- Avoidance of capital gains tax
- Reduction of estate tax

With a life estate agreement, a donor transfers to a charity the title of a residence, vacation property, or farm, retaining the right to live there and use the property for life and continuing to pay all the maintenance costs. For tax purposes, the property is divided into two parts:

1. the "life estate value" of the donor's retained right to occupy the property for the donor's and/or his or her spouse's actuarial life expectancy
2. the "gift value" is the difference between the life estate value and the appraised market value of the property at the time of the gift and it determines the amount of the income tax charitable deduction. At the death of the last owner of the life estate, the possession of the property passes to the charity.

Example
A Retained Life Estate Gift to Worthy Charity

A husband and wife, aged 75 and 70, give to Worthy Charity their jointly owned personal residence under an agreement that allows them to retain the full enjoyment of the property for their lifetimes. They purchased the property many years ago for $75,000. Its current fair market value is $300,000; the house is valued at $250,000 and the lot at $50,000. Under the terms of the agreement, they will continue to maintain the property, pay the taxes, and provide for insurance protection.

In the year of the gift, the donors receive an income tax deduction of approximately $85,346 based on their ages and the value of the property (reduced by straight-line depreciation on the depreciable portion, i.e., the house). They avoid completely the tax on the capital gain of $225,000 they may have incurred if they had sold the house instead.

Note: This example assumes a discount rate of 7.4 percent.

If the donor decides to sell the property, that can be done in conjunction with the charity: the value of the remaining life estate is recalculated as of the time of the sale, taking into consideration the remaining actuarial life expectancy of the donor. The proceeds of the sale are divided proportionately between the value of the remaining life estate, which goes to the donor, and what is left over, which goes to the charity. Another option is for the donor to give the remaining value of the life estate to the charity and receive a charitable deduction for it.

The retained life estate gift option allows the donor to retain his or her lifestyle while providing for a handsome charitable gift in the future.

CHARITABLE LEAD TRUSTS

Donor Benefits:
- Gift returned to the donor or heirs at reduced tax cost

- Satisfaction of giving cash donations during lifetime

This gift option is the opposite of the life income gift, in which the donor gives assets and retains a life income. In establishing a charitable lead trust, the donor (grantor) places assets in a trust. The income from the trust goes to the charity for a fixed number of years, after which the assets return either to the donor or to others designated by the donor in the trust instrument.

A charitable lead trust is fully taxable and pays tax both on its income and capital gains, although it can deduct the amounts paid to the charitable beneficiary in accordance with its terms. Because the charitable lead trust gift option requires the family of the donor to forgo the income from the assets for a number of years, it is used primarily by wealthy individuals for whom the absence of the income does not present a problem. As this form of gift is not often encountered, you will not have to devote significant time to its study. It is, however, important to know the concept and terminology.

The principal benefit to the donor from a charitable lead trust is that it allows property to be transferred to the eventual beneficiaries at a reduced tax cost. It is particularly attractive for property in which there is a good potential for high appreciation. A charitable lead trust may be established either during the donor's life (inter-vivos) or by the donor's will (testamentary).

> *The principal benefit to the donor from a charitable lead trust is that it allows property to be transferred to the eventual beneficiaries at a reduced tax cost.*

The income to be paid to the charity is either a percentage of the trust assets as revalued annually (charitable lead unitrust) or a fixed dollar amount (charitable lead annuity trust).

At the end of the trust term, if the assets return to the donor, the trust is called a *grantor charitable lead trust*. The donor (grantor) of a grantor charitable lead trust enjoys an income tax charitable deduction, subject to the limits on deduction, for the present value of the trust's payments to charity over the term of the trust. However, the grantor is also taxed on the income paid to the charity. If the trust is funded with tax-exempt bonds, the donor will not be taxed on the income.

At the end of the trust term, if the assets are transferred to someone other than the donor, such as the donor's heirs, the trust is called a *nongrantor charitable lead trust*. With a nongrantor charitable lead trust, although the donor (grantor) does not enjoy a charitable income tax deduction, he or she receives a gift tax charitable deduction for the present value of the income stream passing to the charity.

Example
Nongrantor Charitable Lead Annuity Trust

John, age 72, has been a long-time supporter of Worthy Charity's good works. He was open to the suggestion of development director Mary Jones that he set up a planned gift that would provide major outright cash support for Worthy Charity and return the assets to his heirs at reduced tax cost.

John irrevocably transferred stock with a market value of $1,000,000 to a 20-year 6.5-percent charitable lead annuity trust and named his bank's trust department as trustee. During the trust's term, the trustee will invest the trust's assets and provide a fixed dollar amount, $65,000 each year, to Worthy Charity. The payments will continue for 20 years or until the unlikely event that the trust distributes all its assets. The payments will be made out of trust income, or trust principal if the trust income is not adequate. Additions to the trust are not permitted. If trust income during a given year exceeds the annual charitable payment, the trust pays income tax on the excess.

John will qualify for a federal gift tax deduction of approximately $487,870 and, when the trust term ends, the beneficiaries will receive all of the trust's assets. Any asset growth that occurs within the trust will be distributed to the beneficiaries free of gift or estate tax.

Note: This example assumes a discount rate of 7.4 percent.

Example
Nongrantor Charitable Lead Unitrust

When Henry, John's brother and co-enthusiast for Worthy Charity, heard of John's plan, he decided to set up a similar plan (see the example for the nongrantor charitable lead annuity trust). The main difference was that Henry wanted to be able to add to the trust after it was set up.

Henry placed $1,000,000 worth of stock in a 20-year 6.5-percent nongrantor charitable lead unitrust. The trustee will invest the unitrust's assets and pay 6.5 percent of the unitrust's current value, as revalued annually, to Worthy Charity. If the unitrust's value goes up from one year to the next, its payout increases proportionately. Likewise, if its value goes down, the amount it donates also decreases.

Henry will qualify for a gift tax deduction of approximately $508,630. This differs from John's gift tax deduction, as the IRS uses a different calculation for unitrusts. Additions to Henry's trust are permitted.

Note: This example assumes a discount rate of 7.4 percent.

BEQUESTS

Donor Benefits:

- Retention of control of assets during lifetime
- Reduction of estate tax

Bequests are the single most important source of planned gifts. They are attractive to donors who wish to retain control of their assets during their lifetimes and assist their favorite charities later. Many donors prefer the idea of voluntary philanthropy to the idea of giving involuntarily through estate taxes.

As mentioned in Chapter 4, any charity that does not have an active planned giving program can begin one simply by inviting bequests. A few of the many types of bequests are listed below (see also Appendix 7–F):

- **Bequest of a Fixed Amount.** The donor states, "I give [amount] to [name of charity] to be used for its exempt purposes."
- **Percentage Bequest.** The donor states, "I give _____ percent of my residual estate to [name of charity] to be used for its exempt purposes."
- **Specific Bequest.** The donor states, "I give [description of property] to [name of charity] to be used for its exempt purposes."
- **Residuary Bequest.** This option is used to give a charitable organization all or part of a donor's property remaining after all expenses, debts, taxes, and other bequests have been paid by the donor. The donor states, "All the rest, residue, and remainder of my estate, both real and personal, I give to [name of charity] for its exempt purposes."
- **Contingency Bequest.** This option provides for a donor's property to pass to the designated charity in the event all of the other beneficiaries have disclaimed (declined to accept) bequests or have died before the donor's demise. The donor states, "If the above-named beneficiary(ies) predecease me or disclaim any interest in [description of property], I give and bequeath my residuary estate to [name of charity] for its exempt purposes."
- **Deferred Gifts.** It is also possible to include in a donor's will many of the deferred gift options previously described. In this context, *testamentary charitable remainder trust*, *testamentary charitable lead trust*, and *testamentary charitable gift annuity* are the terms used to refer to these options.

ADDITIONAL WAYS OF MAKING PLANNED GIFTS

There are other avenues by which a donor can benefit charities with planned gifts.

Through a Community Foundation

Among the several hundred community foundations in population centers across the country, an increasing number are making their planned giving expertise available to local charities, making it unnecessary to set up such gift options as pooled income funds and charitable gift annuities. This is extremely good news to many nonprofit organizations that may see themselves as too small or too new to set up their own. An example of such an organization is the Community Foundation for Southeast Michigan (http://comnet.org/local/orgs/comfound). Charities may wish to check with their local community foundation or contact the Council on Foundations (www.cof.org) to locate the community foundation serving their area.

Through a Donor Advised Fund

An increasing number of brokerage firms and other commercial asset managers are offering "donor advised funds" structured to enable individuals to make a donation of cash or appreciated stock to a fund bearing their name, enjoy an immediate charitable deduction, and later request that the fund pay out gifts to the charities of their choice. The key word is *request*, rather than *require* that the grants be made to the specific nonprofit organizations. An example of such an arrangement is the Fidelity Charitable Gift Fund (see Appendix B), which has rapidly grown to be one of the largest charitable organizations in the country.

Both of these offer new ways to make gifts independent of the charities that may be the ultimate beneficiaries. They afford the donor an element of control that is increasingly important as newly wealthy entrepreneurs exercise their philanthropy.

Through a Supporting Organization

This is a charitable fund established within one or more public charities with the express purpose of benefiting one or more of the favorite charities of the founder, identified when the foundation is started. It affords more flexibility than a private foundation, while affording an entrepreneurial founder the opportunity to identify the foundation with his or her name, and to fund it with a family business or closely held corporation. The supporting organization's board, typically appointed by the donor, oversees the use of the assets to benefit the specified charities.

POINTS TO PONDER

- There are a great number of assets that can be used to make planned gifts. Planned giving officers must learn which assets fit best with which type of planned gift.
- A successful planned giving officer listens carefully to donors in order to uncover ways they can be helped.
- Identifying the type of gift that will benefit the donor most and at the same time benefit the organization most is the goal of every conscientious planned giving officer.

Appendix 7–A
Charitable Giving Options

Type of Gift	Example	Donor Benefits	Donor Profile
Outright gift of cash	Donor writes $100,000 check payable to charitable organization	Simplicity and ease of delivery Income tax deduction for full amount of gift	Wealthy person with spare funds
Outright gift of appreciated property	Donor transfers to charitable organization stock valued at $100,000 that donor purchased for $20,000	Income tax deduction for full value of stock Avoidance of potential tax on capital gain of $80,000	Wealthy person with highly appreciated property who is concerned about capital gains tax exposure
Bargain sale	Donor sells to charitable organization for $50,000 real estate valued at $200,000 that donor purchased for $50,000	Donor receives $150,000 income tax deduction for contributed portion of property ($150,000)	Person holding property not perceived to be readily marketable who wants an immediate cash return
Charitable remainder trust (during lifetime) (CRT)	Donor establishes trust and transfers stock worth $100,000 to trust, retaining 5 percent per year income stream for life of donor (and/or other beneficiary); upon death of donor (and/or other beneficiary), trust assets pass to charitable organization	Donor (and/or another beneficiary) receives income stream; if transferred stock was low yielding, income stream may exceed the amount of dividend income that donor had been receiving (either immediately or after retirement) Avoidance of potential capital gains tax Donor could retain control over trust investments as trustee or, if donor would prefer, someone else could be the trustee and relieve the donor of investment responsibilities Income tax deduction calculated on actuarial basis	Person holding low-yielding and/or highly appreciated property who wants income for life or supplemental retirement income

Type of Gift	Example	Donor Benefits	Donor Profile
		With certain kinds of trusts (unitrusts), donor can make additional contributions to the trust	
Charitable remainder trust (by will) (TCRT)	Donor includes trust provision in will directing that $100,000 be placed in trust for benefit of spouse during spouse's lifetime; upon spouse's death, trust assets pass to charitable organization	Estate tax marital deduction for spouse's income interest and estate tax charitable deduction for value of remainder interest Provides income stream for spouse for life Donor can select experienced trustee to manage investments for benefit of spouse	Person who is reluctant to part with assets prior to death and who wants to provide income for surviving spouse or child prior to donating gift to charitable organization
Gift annuity (immediate) (CGA)	Donor transfers appreciated stock to charitable organization in exchange for organization's agreement to pay a specified annuity to the donor (and/or another beneficiary)	Donor (and/or another beneficiary) receives income stream A portion of each annuity payment will be free from income tax Capital gains tax reduced and spread out Income tax deduction calculated on an actuarial basis	Person holding low-yielding and/or highly appreciated property who wants income for life
Gift annuity (deferred) (DCGA)	Donor transfers appreciated stock to charitable organization in exchange for organization's agreement to pay a specified annuity to the donor (and/or another beneficiary) in the future (e.g., after retirement)	All of the same benefits as with an immediate annuity, with the added benefit of providing supplemental retirement income on a tax-favored basis	Person with high earnings who wants supplemental retirement income
Remainder interest in residence or farm (RLE)	Donor transfers residence to charitable organization but retains the right to live in home for life	Income tax deduction equal to the value of charitable organization's remainder interest calculated on an actuarial basis Right to live in home for life	Person whose house is main asset and who wants to continue to live in house for life but is not concerned about preserving house for family after death

Type of Gift	Example	Donor Benefits	Donor Profile
Life insurance (charitable organization as beneficiary)	Donor names charitable organization as beneficiary of life insurance policy	Donor retains ownership of policy and has access to its cash value No federal estate tax on life insurance proceeds will be due upon donor's death because of charitable deduction	Person who wants to retain control, who wants to make contributions in manageable amounts over time, and for whom income tax deduction is not critical
Life insurance (charitable organization as owner)	Donor irrevocably assigns life insurance policy to charitable organization; each year donor contributes annual premium amount to organization to allow it to pay subsequent premiums	Income tax deduction for lesser of policy's value or net premiums paid Income tax deduction for subsequent contributions	Person who wants to make contributions in manageable amounts over time and who wants income tax deductions
Life insurance (wealth replacement)	Donor has transferred property to charitable organization and uses tax savings produced by the income tax deduction to pay premiums on life insurance policy, the proceeds of which will be roughly equivalent to the value of the gifted property	Provides funds to family beneficiaries in compensation for the property contributed to charitable organizations	Person is making a planned gift (e.g., charitable remainder trust) and at the same time wants to preserve estate for family
Outright bequest (by will)	Donor includes outright bequest of $100,000 to charitable organization in will or a bequest of a percentage of the estate	Estate tax deduction for full amount of bequest	Person who is reluctant to part with assets prior to death and who has plenty of assets for family or does not have close family
Pooled income fund (PIF)	Donor makes contribution of $5,000 to charitable organization's established pooled income fund and makes additional contributions each year	Simplicity and ease Income tax deduction each year calculated on an actuarial basis Provides income stream for life of donor and/or another beneficiary	Person of any age and any level of wealth who wants to make contributions in manageable amounts over time
Charitable lead trust (during lifetime) (CLT)	Donor establishes trust, transfers stock worth $100,000 to trust, and directs that trust is to pay charitable organization $8,000 annually for	Allows property to be transferred eventually to family beneficiaries at a low transfer tax cost	Person who has assets with high appreciation potential and whose family can forgo income from the assets for a period of time

Type of Gift	Example	Donor Benefits	Donor Profile
	15 years; at termination of trust, assets to be distributed to donor's children		
Charitable lead trust (by will) (TCLT)	Donor includes trust provision in will directing the transfer of $100,000 to trust and annual payment of $8,000 to charitable organization for 15 years; at termination of trust, assets to be distributed to donor's children	Allows property to be transferred eventually to family beneficiaries at lower transfer tax cost	Person who has assets with high appreciation potential and whose family can forgo income from the assets for a period of time

Appendix 7–B
Gifts of Appreciated Securities

Note: If the donor is considering a gift of securities that have *decreased* in value, advise him or her to sell the securities first, donate the proceeds, and take advantage of the capital loss on the next tax return.

Stock Certificates Sent by Mail. Advise the donor to send the unendorsed certificates in one envelope and the stock powers in another, omitting the charity's name. The donor's signature on the stock powers must exactly match the name on the face of the stock certificates, and must be guaranteed by a banker or broker.

Stock Certificates Delivered in Person. The donor can deliver both the unendorsed certificates and the properly signed stock powers, again omitting the name of the charity.

Stock Transferred through the Donor's Broker. A new account in the name of the charity is created at the donor's brokerage house and the ownership of the stock is transferred electronically. This is the simplest and most common procedure, because very little stock currently is held by individuals in the form of paper certificates.

Follow-up calls are helpful to avoid delays (see Contribution Date, below).

Gifts of Mutual Fund Shares present an additional challenge to the donee nonprofit organization. In most cases, these shares are held by management organizations in the account of the donor. In order to transfer ownership from the donor to the charity:

1. An account must be opened by the charity with the mutual fund management organization.

2. The donor must send a letter of instruction to the mutual fund management organization requesting that the donated shares be transferred into the charity's account.

3. The charity then must send a letter of instruction to the mutual fund management organization requesting that its new shares be sold and the proceeds be remitted to the charity.

Experience has shown that frequently, repeated telephone calls are necessary to accomplish this on a timely basis. This is particularly critical at the end of the year when the timing of the transfer of the shares into the control of the charity determines the year in which the gift has actually taken place.

The contribution date is an important factor in determining the timing and amount of the donor's charitable deduction. It is the date when the donor irrevocably relinquishes possession of the securities. This is determined by the postmark if they were mailed, by the date of delivery if they were hand-delivered, the date of the electronic transfer if they were handled by the broker, or the date of the transfer of mutual fund shares into the account of the charity.

The method of valuation of the securities also affects the charitable deduction. For listed securities, the high and the low price are averaged; the mean between the bid and ask price is used for bonds; the redemption price on the contribution date is used for mutual fund shares.

Appendix 7–C

Appreciated Securities Gift Data Sheet

1. Donor's Name:

    Address:

    City: State: ZIP:

    Phone: (Home)   (Office)

2. Participating in gift is:

    Relationship:

3. Broker's Name:

    Representative:

    Address:

    City: State: ZIP:

4. Name/description of securities (CUSIP number, if available):

5. Number of shares to be given:

6. Donor's account number:

7. Donor's taxpayer ID number:

8. Valuation of securities traded on: _____/_____/_____ (the date of irrevocable transfer from donor)

    For stocks (including mutual funds):

    > High $ Low $ Gift Value $

    For bonds:

    > Bid $ Ask $ Gift Value $

9. For Mutual Fund Gifts: Number of account opened by [Charity] to receive the donor's shares

10. Mutual Fund Organization instructed to liquidate donated shares and transfer proceeds to [Charity] on _____/_____/_____.

11. ❑ Check or electronic transfer for $ received from broker on _____/_____/_____.

12. ❑ Contribution entered into donor's record on _____/_____/_____.

Appendix 7–D

Sample Donor Information—Gifts of Real Estate

GIFTS OF REAL ESTATE TO WORTHY CHARITY

INTRODUCTION

There are important benefits in giving long-term appreciated real estate to Worthy Charity: (1) both the value of the gift and the donor's income tax deduction are the same as the full fair market value of the property (as established by appraisal), (2) the donor avoids the capital gains tax on the appreciation and selling expenses that would have to be paid if the property were sold, and (3) the donor has the satisfaction of providing endowment support to an organization he or she considers worthy of support.

The following considerations should also be taken into account by a prospective donor:

- The full market value of charitable gifts of long-term appreciated property is tax deductible. Appreciation is long term if the donor has owned the property for more than one year.
- Donors of gifts of appreciated property avoid the capital gains tax that would be incurred if the property were sold.
- Income tax deductibility of a charitable gift of long-term appreciated property is limited to 30 percent of the donor's adjusted gross income in the gift year, with a carry-over for up to five additional years for an unused deductibility (up to the same 30-percent limit in each carry-over year).
- It is normally inadvisable to make a charitable gift of property in which the donor has a capital loss (i.e., *depreciated* property). The donor should sell the property to establish a capital loss deduction and make a charitable gift of the sale proceeds.

TYPES OF REAL ESTATE

Almost any type of real estate can be given to Worthy Charity—a personal residence, farm, or ranch; commercial or industrial property; subdivision lots; unimproved land; a condominium; and so on. Because every piece of real estate is unique, and because of the different considerations that may arise for both the donor and to Worthy Charity, a donor contemplating such a gift to Worthy Charity should discuss it with the director of development in advance.

Also, because each piece of real estate has its own special characteristics, including some that may reduce its marketability or create difficult environmental issues, Worthy Charity reserves the right to accept or not accept the property as a gift.

METHODS OF GIVING REAL ESTATE

Outright Gifts

The entire property is given to Worthy Charity. If there is no mortgage or other indebtedness on the property, both the donor's gift and tax deduction are equal to the full market value, subject to the 30 percent of adjusted gross income limit noted earlier.

Gift Subject to Life Income

The property is conveyed to a life income trust for the ultimate benefit of Worthy Charity. The income of the trust is paid for life to the donor and/or to another beneficiary named by the donor. If the property is not income producing, there will be no income paid by the trust until the property can be sold by the trustee and the proceeds reinvested in income-producing assets. Depending on the donor's objectives, the trust yield can range between 5 and 7 percent under normal investment conditions.

As with an outright gift, the donor completely avoids capital gains tax liability on the appreciation of the property. However, the donor's tax deduction is only a portion of the appraised value of the property—that portion representing the discounted value of Worthy Charity's interest in the gift property when the trust terminates in the future. The deduction is computed from U.S. Treasury actuarial tables based on the ages of the life income beneficiaries and the stated payout rate of the trust.

Example. A donor, age 64, owns a tract of unimproved non–income-producing land. The appraised market value of the land is $100,000, and the donor's cost basis is $20,000, which he or she irrevocably transfers to a *flip unitrust with a makeup provision*, managed by a trustee of his or her choice (in this example, a bank trust department). Under the terms of the trust, the donor is to receive income payments each year for life of the actual net income earned by the trust prior to the sale, if any. After the sale of the property, the trust "flips" to one that pays the donor 6 percent of the market value of the trust assets as revalued each year. When the trust terminates upon the death of the last income beneficiary, the trust principal will pass to Worthy Charity.

One year after the trust is established, the trustee is able to sell the property for a net of $90,000 (after the real estate commission and other closing costs). During the year when the land was the only asset of the trust, there were no income earnings and thus no payments to the beneficiary. The trustee reinvests the $90,000 to yield at least 6 percent income including capital appreciation. Thereafter, the beneficiary receives 6 percent of the trust assets, as revalued each year.

Based on the donor's age and the 6-percent payout rate of the trust, the donor's income tax deduction is approximately $39,881. The donor also avoids the large potential capital gains tax on the $80,000 of appreciation in the property and selling expenses.

Gift Subject to Life Tenancy

A home (including a second or vacation home), a farm, or a ranch can be given to Worthy Charity subject to the right of continued tenancy by the donor and/or another individual, usually the spouse. The tenancy can be for life or a term of years. Upon termination of the tenancy, Worthy Charity will own the property outright.

A portion of the appraised value of the home, farm, or ranch is tax deductible in the gift year and is computed from U.S. Treasury actuarial tables based on the ages of the tenants. The computation is complicated by the fact that depreciation must be taken into account. The donor also avoids capital gains tax liability on the gift portion of the property.

Example. A husband and wife, aged 75 and 70, give to Worthy Charity their jointly owned personal residence under an agreement that allows them to retain the full enjoyment of the property for their lifetimes. They purchased the property many years ago for $75,000. Its current fair market value is $300,000; the house is valued at $250,000 and the lot at $50,000. Under the terms of the agreement, they will continue to maintain the property, pay the taxes, and provide for insurance protection.

In the year of the gift, the donors receive an income tax deduction of approximately $85,346 based on their ages and the value of the property (reduced by straight-line depreciation on the depreciable portion, i.e., the house). They avoid completely the tax on the capital gain of $225,000 they may have incurred if they had sold the house instead.

Because the husband and wife are the only life tenants in the property, no part of their tenancy interest will be taxable in either of their estates.

Note: This example assumes a discount rate of 7.4 percent.

What happens if the life tenants decide to give up their tenancy? In this event, (1) the value of the remaining tenancy can be given to Worthy Charity as an additional deductible gift, (2) it can be sold to the charity, or (3) the entire property can be sold jointly by Worthy Charity and the life tenants to a third party.

If the tenancy is given to Worthy Charity, the computation of its value is based on a new appraisal and the ages of the tenants at the time the tenancy is relinquished. The value of the tenancy can be given (1) outright, in which case its full value is tax deductible, or (2) subject to a life income plan (net income unitrust), in which case only a portion of the value of the tenancy is deductible. Whether the gift is outright or subject to life income, capital gains tax on the appreciation attributable to the tenancy is completely avoided.

If the tenancy is sold to Worthy Charity, the selling price will be mutually agreed upon by Worthy Charity and the life tenants, who will have a potential capital gains tax liability on their appreciation attributable to the selling price.

If the entire property is sold to a third party, the net sale proceeds will be divided proportionately between Worthy Charity (for the remainder interest) and the life tenants (for the tenancy). The life tenants will have a potential capital gains tax liability on their appreciation attributable to the tenancy portion of the sale only.

Gift of Fractional Interest

A gift of real estate need not be the entire property. A donor can make a deductible charitable gift of an "undivided fractional interest" in the property (e.g., one-half or one-fifth), providing he or she retains no substantial interest in the donated fraction. Capital gains tax liability is also avoided on the donor's appreciation in the donated fraction. After such a gift, the donor and Worthy Charity will own the property jointly as tenants in common.

A gift of fractional interest will normally apply to an outright gift. However, it can also be used to fund a life income trust if the property is to be sold immediately or is income producing. Such a gift cannot be applied to a life tenancy plan.

> **Example 1.** The donor makes a gift to Worthy Charity of a 15-percent undivided fractional interest in three building lots having an appraised market value of $100,000. The donor's income tax deduction is $15,000. Upon the sale of the property, the donor will receive 85 percent of the net proceeds and Worthy Charity will receive 15 percent. The donor will have to pay capital gains tax on his or her share of any realized gain on the sale.

> **Example 2.** The donor and his wife occupy a vacation home for four months each year. They decide to make a gift to Worthy Charity of an undivided two-thirds interest in the vacation home. The appraised value of the home is $120,000, so the donors' deductible gift is $80,000. They also avoid capital gains tax on their appreciation in the donated fraction. Be-

cause they retain a one-third ownership, they can continue to use the house for one-third of each year (four months), with Worthy Charity using it for the other eight months.

Gift of Mortgaged Property

A charitable gift of mortgaged real estate is a "bargain sale" and the donor is considered to have "sold" the property to Worthy Charity for the amount of the outstanding mortgage. The donor's deductible gift is the difference between the mortgage and the market value of the property. The donor will have a partial capital gains tax on his or her appreciation in the property attributable to the sale (amount of mortgage) but not on the gift portion of the transaction.

> **Example.** A donor in the 36-percent income tax bracket makes a gift of a vacation home to Worthy Charity. The appraised value of the property is $100,000, the donor's cost basis is $50,000, and the current outstanding mortgage is $30,000. The donor is considered to have "sold" the property to Worthy Charity for $30,000 (the value of the mortgage), thus making a deductible gift of $70,000. The donor avoids capital gains tax on his or her appreciation in the $70,000 gift but not on the appreciation attributable to the sale. Because the sale is 30 percent of the total transaction, the adjusted cost basis on the sale is $15,000 (30 percent of $50,000). The appreciation attributable to the sale is thus $15,000 ($30,000 sale minus $15,000 adjusted cost basis). The 29-percent capital gains tax is $3,000, which is far outweighed by the $25,200 tax saving on the charitable gift (36 percent of $70,000).

Note: Mortgaged real estate can be used for an outright charitable gift or a gift subject to life tenancy but not for a life income gift.

Giving Real Estate to Worthy Charity by Bequest

A donor can give real estate under his or her will either (1) outright, (2) with retained life income for a survivor, or (3) subject to life tenancy for a survivor. Although there are no *income* tax benefits in this case, the property is removed from the donor's taxable estate if the bequest is outright or is subject to life income or life tenancy solely for the surviving spouse. If someone other than the spouse is the life income beneficiary or life tenant, the beneficiary's income or tenancy interest is potentially taxable in the donor's estate.

Note: There is a special advantage in bequeathing real estate or other nonliquid property to Worthy Charity. Removing such property from one's taxable estate eliminates the possible need for a "distress" sale of the property or depletion of the liquid assets of the estate to pay the tax on the nonliquid property.

MAKING A GIFT OF REAL ESTATE TO WORTHY CHARITY

A proposed gift of real estate should be discussed with Worthy Charity's director of development. If the gift is acceptable to Worthy Charity and the value of the property is over $5,000, the donor must obtain (by law) a complete written appraisal from an independent appraiser no earlier than 60 days before the date of the gift. IRS Form 8283 (Appraisal Summary) must also be completed by the donor, the appraiser, and Worthy Charity to substantiate the donor's deduction on his or her tax return. (The appraisal itself is not submitted but must be retained by the donor.)

The donor's attorney should prepare the deed transferring the real estate to Worthy Charity or to a trust. The donor must also provide assurance of good title. The date of the closing is the date of the gift, after which Worthy Charity will have the deed recorded.

For his or her own protection, the donor should not enter into any type of binding agreement to sell the real estate to a potential buyer prior to the date of the gift. In other words, at the time of the gift, the charity should be free to sell the donated property to anyone. However, Worthy Charity will always welcome the assistance of the donor in finding a buyer after the gift has been made.

For additional information concerning gifts of real property, write or call without obligation.

Appendix 7–E
Real Estate Gift Data Sheet

Note: It is not recommended that a charity accept direct gifts of real estate, as it must bear the carrying costs and the environmental clean-up liability until the property is sold. There are resources available to assist in the safe handling of real estate gifts. Please refer to Appendix B.

Donor's Name:

Address: Telephone:

Description and location of property:

Appraised value:

Appraised by:

Date of appraisal:

      Existing mortgage: Yes   No

      Amount and terms:

      Mortgage held by:

Taxes:

      Date due:

      Year last paid:

Use of property:

Zoning classification:

Estimated annual expenses:

Percentage of ownership being donated:

Other owners on the title:

Donor agrees to arrange and pay for environmental audit:

Results of Level 1 environmental audit:

Appendix 7–F
Sample Bequest Provisions

The provisions in a will for making a gift to Worthy Charity will depend upon the type of bequest and the donor's circumstances. These sample provisions might be helpful to the donor and the donor's attorney.

UNRESTRICTED GIFT

I give to Worthy Charity, 1800 Main Street, Goodtown, USA, a [state] nonprofit corporation, the sum of $_____ [or _____% of my estate; or the property described herein] for its general purposes.

SPECIFIC LEGACY

I bequeath my home, farm, livestock, car, truck, etc., to Worthy Charity, 1800 Main Street, Goodtown, USA, a [state] nonprofit corporation.

MEMORIAL FUND

I give to Worthy Charity, 1800 Main Street, Goodtown, USA, a [state] nonprofit corporation, the sum of $_____ [or property herein described], the same to be known as "The _____ Memorial Fund." The income therefrom shall be used for its general purposes.

RESIDUARY LEGATEE

All the rest, residue, and remainder of my estate, both real and personal, I give to Worthy Charity, 1800 Main Street, Goodtown, USA, a [state] nonprofit corporation, for its general purposes.

CONTINGENCY GIFT

I devise and bequeath the residue of the property owned by me at my death, real and personal and wherever situated, to my wife (husband) _____, if she (he) survives me. If my wife (husband) does not survive me, I devise and bequeath my residuary estate to Worthy Charity, 1800 Main Street, Goodtown, USA, a [state] nonprofit corporation, for its general purposes.

FINAL CONTINGENT BENEFICIARY

I give and bequeath the residue of the property owned by me at my death, real and personal and wherever situated, in equal shares to my above named beneficiaries, if they survive me. If my above named beneficiaries do not survive me, I give and bequeath my residuary estate to Worthy Charity, 1800 Main Street, Goodtown, USA, a [state] nonprofit corporation, for its general purposes.

TESTAMENTARY CHARITABLE TRUSTS

Note: Testamentary charitable trusts may be set up (1) to provide life income to one or more individuals with the principal passing to Worthy Charity at the demise of the last income beneficiary, or (2) to provide income to Worthy Charity for a fixed time period, after which the remaining assets pass to the individuals designated.

Chapter 8

Communication: Letting the World Know about Your Program

WORDS TO WATCH FOR

- Internet
- e-mail
- allied professionals
- prospect profile
- targeted prospects
- constituency

This chapter is different from the previous ones. Instead of introducing a relatively unfamiliar topic and proceeding with general information or guidelines, it discusses a subject that is familiar to all of us: communication. Communication is so important to the success of your planned giving program that it warrants treatment in its own separate chapter.

Throughout this primer you have been strongly encouraged to establish a planned giving program (if you do not have one already) but to keep the program as simple as possible, at least until you can hire more staff.

> *Keep the program as simple as possible.*

Another point that has been stressed is the importance of being creative in your cultivation and stewardship programs. The caring for and the continual education of donors, particularly planned gift donors, can keep them interested in becoming more involved with the organization and supporting it further. In short, ongoing communication with your donors results in satisfied donors and repeat donations.

COMMUNICATING

The overall purpose of a planned giving program is to build a base of loyal donors, of course to raise money for the not-for-profit organization, and to accomplish this

by maintaining relationships with these donors. How this is accomplished varies according to the not-for-profit organization and the structure of the development department.

For the planned giving program to be effective, you, the person responsible for planned giving, need to identify, cultivate, and solicit donors who show an interest in supporting the organization with a planned gift or endowment. Even though gift planning is an integral part of the development program and its normal activities (targeting prospects, executing a direct mail campaign, etc.), it is something more. No amount of fine-tuning usual direct mail fundraising procedures alone will ensure success.

To be effective, you have to work with volunteers and staff in all departments in the organization—managers, board members, other volunteers, and allied professionals. By educating all members of the organization about planned giving, you can build credibility and trust. As the payoff, you will receive introductions to potential donors with whom you can discuss planned gifts. You must first have prospects in order to have opportunities for success.

Marketing your planned giving program both inside and outside the organization is a high priority. Your main goal should be to increase the visibility of your organization, create a positive image of its mission, communicate how you're solving your communities' needs, and publicize the opportunities for supporting it through gift giving.

Some new terms were introduced in Chapter 3: donor-focused approach and integrated fund development. Integrated fund development is a new term to better describe an organization's thinking in terms of "best for" the donor and ultimately for the charity when developing your fundraising strategy, personnel plans, and teamwork. Successful nonprofit organizations are focusing energy on developing these donor-focused fundraising plans. Keeping people within the organization up to date through an effective communication plan on the current thinking and approach to major gift fundraising will ultimately help you in your role.

COMMITMENT

Communication is not a once in a while activity casually undertaken. A communication plan must be developed with a written budget and plans to revise it periodically.

You must decide whether communication is of sufficient importance to have high priority because it takes a considerable amount of time. To understand the degree of commitment required, you need to consider these questions:

- Whom do you need to communicate with?
- Why are you communicating with them?
- What message do you want them to hear?
- When do you need to communicate your message?
- Where will you present your message?
- How will you accomplish the communication?

Each of these questions is explored in the following sections.

INSIDE THE ORGANIZATION

Interdepartmental communication has a low priority within some organizations. If this is true of your organization, you will have to push to educate specific groups about planned giving (for training guidelines, see Appendix 8–A). In particular, you need to communicate information about planned giving to

- your supervisor
- top management
- board members
- development staff
- volunteers
- others who may have contact with potential donors (alumni relations staff, program staff, financial staff, and administrative staff)

> *Interdepartmental communication has a low priority within some organizations.*

The way you communicate this information will depend upon which group you're addressing and which aspect of the program you're presenting.

Training

Training could encompass any of the following subjects:

- the general nature of planned giving
- how different departments can support the planned giving program
- future planned giving program goals
- how to communicate information about planned giving prospects
- using prospect profiles to identify clues for soliciting gifts successfully
- types of assets donors might give (see Chapter 7)
- types of gift options you offer (see Chapter 7)
- benefits donors receive from planned gifts (see Chapter 7 and Appendix 7–A)
- benefits that planned gifts provide the organization

Develop a training program. If you are not convinced training is worthwhile and a good use of some of your time and funds, conduct a survey within the organization. The survey should not be complicated or difficult. You need only a short, simple questionnaire, either verbal or written, to determine what level of understanding the members of your various groups have of estate and finance terminology. Even if you are extremely fortunate and all your colleagues have a finance or business background and are well versed in estate planning, they still need training. The additional training is to prepare them with positive statements regarding the organization's accomplishments, and of course to add how much more could be accomplished with additional resources.

Keep in mind that you have several objectives in training these groups, not just the goal of raising the level of understanding of basic terminology. One important objective is to gain as many prospects as possible, and the time you devote to training could result in reducing the time you spend qualifying new prospects.

Explaining to staff that planned gifts can help ensure the future of the organization and at the same time reflect credit on them may motivate some to retain and use the information you have given them about the planned giving program. You should inform them that major outside funding is often needed to support special programs, purchase new equipment, and build or renovate facilities.

Other less tangible benefits to the organization and staff are not necessarily of lesser importance, so keep them in mind. For one thing, the teamwork exhibited by integrated fund development to attract gifts sends a positive message to the outside world.

Internal Marketing

There are other ways to "market" or increase awareness of planned giving inside your organization. Three of the most important ways are described below.

Updates

Write short "basic info" pieces for an internal newsletter. Post information promoting your "open to staff" training sessions. Something worth considering is extending special invitations to those groups you believe have frequent contact with potential donors. Taking extra steps in the beginning can frequently provide significant benefits down the road.

Fundraising Information Materials

Share copies of printed information brochures and pamphlets with colleagues and volunteers. **These are not for them to mail to potential donors!** Their purpose is to allow people in the organization and volunteers to understand the different types of gifts you offer and the benefits for donors.

Prospect Files

Maintain a separate file for any potential donor whose name you have received and the name of the referral source. And keep the contact person, your referral source, regularly informed of any progress.

Coaching

When developing your training plans, keep in mind that training top managers, board members, and your supervisor may be more on the order of coaching. For these individuals you will likely have different objectives and expectations. Besides assisting them in increasing their understanding of planned giving, you may wish to encourage them to refer potential prospects to you or introduce them to you. You may also need them to visit donors on their own. All of these are reasonable options. Only you can determine whether they are realistic and whether they fit into your overall plan.

Consultants

Another option available to you when training high-level managers and board members is to bring in an outside consultant. Often, a consultant can have more impact at this level than you can have. Of course, you need to consider the cost, but if the end results will be substantially better than you could achieve on your own, then the investment is a good one. Again, only you can be the judge. Only you know who the participants are

and what the best course to follow is by developing an effective communication plan given your circumstances and what you are trying to accomplish.

OUTSIDE THE ORGANIZATION

Someone once said, "As long as you're talking, you can't learn anything." True words that highlight a dilemma. As a fundraiser, you must communicate, convey, explain, train, coach, and persuade. You must present your organization to the public in as many ways as are available to you, both written and verbal. On the other hand, you also need to encourage an exchange of information. You need to listen to prospective donors to find out which type of gift would be best for them to consider giving. In short, you must continuously be willing to relearn where the fine line is between speaking too much and not enough.

Unlike intraorganizational communication about planned giving, communication to potential donors and advisors almost always has been given a high priority. But it can always be improved. The audience for this communication is quite broad, consisting not only of potential prospects, prospects, current donors, and lapsed donors, but also all the allied professionals—the accountants, lawyers, trust officers, financial planners, insurance agents, and stockbrokers—who act as advisors to donors or potential donors. You will have to meet with these professionals, and it is important that you develop good working relationships with them.

Marketing and promoting your organization and communicating its mission and goals has never been more important. There are many worthwhile organizations vying for the same limited resources. Your task is fairly straightforward: connect prospects to your organization, involve them in your mission, and inspire them into planned gift donors. In order to accomplish this, you need to call upon your creative talents as well as the talents of others in your organization and of any consultants you use.

A New Means of Communication

A lot has happened in communication since the first edition of this book was published. Web fundraising isn't a should, shouldn't, or maybe I'll think about it later proposition—it's happening right now and, as ethical practitioners, we're obligated to understand this amorphous medium inside and out.

The fastest growing population of new users of e-mail and the Internet are seniors. It behooves your organization to have a Web site and a fundraising site with a link to planned giving and of course, a Web site that's attractive, educational, communicative, and dynamic. The planned giving Web site should be well linked within your organization's Web site and have multiple response devices. In addition, you will want to make certain the site meets your marketing goals and is easy to read and easy to maintain. You will need to continuously improve it and measure its effectiveness.

> *The fastest growing population of new users of e-mail and the Internet are seniors.*

Allied Professionals

Allied professionals outside the organization can be good sources for prospective donors. Help them help you—communicate your organization's case for support to them, develop working relationships with them, and educate them about planned giving. The professionals who advise donors and potential donors include the following:

- attorneys
- trust officers
- financial advisors or planners
- certified public accountants
- stockbrokers
- insurance agents

Frequently, these advisors know their client's net worth, tax situation, and real estate holdings. Consequently, they are often uniquely situated to suggest to their clients the need for a charitable gift. And, of course at the same time, they could recommend a worthy charity. Will it be yours they recommend?

How do you get to know these advisors? The answer: with a plan and persistence. Any of the following ways can be used to develop a dialogue with allied professionals.

Keep an open channel of communication with the attorney handling a donor's estate if your organization has been the beneficiary of a bequest. By doing this, you could help to ensure a timely distribution of the bequest and might also be able to develop a lasting relationship with the attorney and that may possibly attract other charitable gifts on the basis of his or her recommendation.

Compile a list of local estate and financial planning advisors. Keep them informed of your organization's activities through your newsletter or by the other means you use in promoting your organization and its mission. Let them know about any significant gifts you have

received. That and similar information could bring your organization to mind when they are in a position to recommend a worthy charity to their clients.

Develop a plan to cultivate these advisors. Often, they lack comprehensive information about different types of planned gifts, and so you can assist them by teaching them what you know. Help them to help you and all will be served.

Establish an advisory committee. First, ask board members and other sources to assist in compiling a list of allied professionals to ask to a breakfast or lunch where the various planned gift options would be discussed. This advisory committee could also arrange other educational offerings, such as estate planning seminars or workshops open to potential prospects and selected allied professionals (who can present themselves in the role of good citizens and receive free advertising for the knowledge they dispense).

Join a national professional organization, such as the local council of the National Committee on Planned Giving. At the meetings, select the best of the allied professionals to cultivate.

Of course, the purpose for these strategies is to have your organization and its mission made known to as many prospects as possible and to present the options that planned giving can offer to satisfy potential donors' needs. Keep in mind that these advisors want something, too—if you try to help them build or expand their client base and income opportunities, all will be served. It's important for you to consistently communicate that your organization is a problem solver, and that you provide a unique and valuable service to the community.

External Marketing

Marketing is now quite a buzzword in the not-for-profit world, and it purposefully has not been the primary term used in this chapter. Recently the definition of marketing has been expanded to include end results. That is to say, if marketing is effective, it will cause a transaction to occur. If a transaction does not occur, marketing has not occurred. In other words, if a fundraiser's marketing does not eventually result in a sufficient number of leads to produce contributions to the organization, the fundraiser is not really marketing (Berg and Shiffman 1996).

What are the current marketing materials that are going to your prospects? Are they consistent with other marketing materials that go out from the organization? Are you getting the right results or are you just getting statistics? The number of responses you receive from your mailings and the number of nice conversations you have with prospects will be all you can quantify in the beginning of your program, but eventually these will not be sufficient means to measure results. You must look at all possible options. If what you are doing is ultimately not bringing in enough real prospects and realized gifts, then you need to assess what is wrong. Of course, you have to keep in mind planned giving takes a longer cultivation time than other types of fundraising. Nevertheless, you must have a means of measuring your marketing efforts.

The final test of marketing is the number of gifts that ultimately result from *all* your communication efforts inside and outside the organization to promote the organization's mission and broadcast its needs. This includes the training and coaching you or a consultant has provided, the working relationships you have developed with allied professionals, the marketing materials you have been able to mail, and all the cultivation efforts you have been involved with. Not to be forgotten is your creative stewardship of past and current planned gift donors. In the final analysis, any or all of these efforts, when fine-tuned, can bring you success.

> *The final test of marketing is the number of gifts that ultimately results from all your communication efforts.*

Any new program you take on requires a specific plan or road map so you know where you are going and know how to measure whether you have accomplished your goals. Prior to communicating your gift planning message, whether inside or outside the organization, you must set specific goals and objectives you wish to achieve within a reasonable time frame. In addition, you must set priorities and guides for managing your time. Your new program will require you to be very focused. You are your own best guide as to the specifics necessary to accomplish the goals of your individual program. As you know, if you set your priorities, manage your time, and stay focused, you can accomplish a lot.

POINTS TO PONDER

- Training and coaching carried out in a collegial atmosphere can foster the kind of teamwork and coordination between departments and members of an organization that sends a strong message to prospects and potential donors and makes the organization seem more attractive to them and its mission seem more important.
- Educating members of your organization about planned giving is one important way of increasing the pool of potential prospects.
- The time spent communicating and listening to prospects for clues to their needs can be a test of patience; however, a gift could be your reward for such patience.

REFERENCE

Berg, L., and R. Shiffman. 1996. Marketing for planned gifts: Breaking the rules. *Planned Giving Today* 7, no. 2:1, 8–9.

Appendix 8–A
Training Guidelines

INTERNAL STAFF TRAINING

1. Training preparation is the first step.
   - Why should you train staff and volunteers?
     - so they can help you by "uncovering" prospects
     - so you will have to spend less time qualifying prospects
   - Who needs to be trained? Anyone who comes in contact with prospects, including
     - development staff
     - executive officers
     - trustees or board members
     - volunteers
     - others
       - financial or business office staff
       - personnel staff
   - What do they need to know?
     - how planned giving can help ensure the charity's future
     - how planned giving can help the charity's donors
     - how prospects typically identify themselves in conversation
     - what financial terms and simple estate planning terms mean
     - information about the gift options offered by the charity
   - Participants should want training for the following reasons:
     - Planned gifts benefit the charity by funding programs, endowments, new buildings, and equipment.
     - Knowledgeable and well-trained staff convey a positive message about the charity and can help donors achieve their goals.

2. You need to decide on the training program format and find out about the groups you will be training.
   - According to one suggested format, the training sessions should be
     - held monthly
     - 60 to 90 minutes in length
     - open to all
     - run in an informal roundtable style
   - You need to determine what the participants know. How do you find out their general knowledge and skill level?
     - Their earlier careers will give you a clue.
     - Knowing their current positions might also help.
     - Survey the participants to gain additional information.
   - What do you want the participants to do?
     - They need to let you know the names of their prospects.
     - They should assist in cultivating prospects.
     - Many of them might be able to introduce you to prospects.

3. Different groups have different characteristics and need different training.
   - The development staff
     - should be "people people"
     - can identify prospects
     - can cultivate prospects
     - should know basic terminology
     - need to know some gift options and benefits for donors
     - need to know how to refer prospects to you and make introductions if appropriate
   - You need to find out the characteristics and capabilities of the executive officers and trustees or board members.

– Are they "people people"?
– Can they identify prospects?
– Do they know basic terminology?
– Do they have contacts with prospects?
– Will they introduce prospects to you?

• You need to find out the characteristics and capabilities of volunteers, program directors, business office staff, etc.
– Are they "people people"?
– Do they come in contact with potential donors?
– What is their level of knowledge of business or estate terms?
– Do they know clues to look for in talking with potential donors?
– Do they know how to refer potential donors to you?

4. What should you include in their training?
• Development staff (fundraisers) need to know
– the benefits for the organization of the various gift options
– the benefits for the donors
– financial and estate planning terminology
– the gift options and when each is appropriate
– how and when to refer prospects to you
• Nonfundraisers need to know
– how to recognize a prospect (what clues to look for)
– what questions to ask
– how to refer prospects to you (set up appointments, call you ASAP, make an introduction)

5. You need to remember these guidelines:
• Work to increase your knowledge and comfort level with the planned giving subject matter.
• Determine the level of information each training group needs to know—your goal is to help them help you.
• Interact with the training session participants.
• Allow time for questions.
• Training takes time—but is worthwhile for you and the people you are training.

Chapter 9

International Planned Giving

The United States has a unique tradition of broad-based individual and community support for charitable institutions. Representatives of overseas universities, museums, refugee care organizations, and other charities often express their admiration for U.S. philanthropy. Unlike other countries, the tax system in the United States encourages individual donations to charitable organizations. Foreign charitable organizations simply do not receive the same kind of public support and must rely on support from their governments.

> *The United States has a unique tradition of broad-based individual and community support for charitable institutions.*

INTER-NATION GIVING

Not-for-profit organizations throughout the world are beginning to recognize and do something about problems associated with individuals in one country making charitable gifts to organizations in another. One reason is that in recent years much closer ties have developed between American citizens and foreign nations and between American businesses and foreign businesses, as indicated by these facts:

- Many charities now cooperate on global issues like disaster relief, hunger, and disease prevention.
- Investment barriers have been reduced for U.S. citizens who are investing in overseas markets, and at the same time an increasing number of foreign nationals are investing in U.S. stocks and bonds.
- Many foreign nationals come to the United States for medical treatments that are unavailable in their home countries.
- American universities are attracting an increasing number of foreign students, and these students often

maintain close ties with their alma maters after they return to their own countries (Bigelow and George 1994).

THE BEGINNINGS OF CHANGE

As a result of the increased interest in inter-nation gift giving, several changes are taking place:

- The European Association for Planned Giving was established.
- The United Kingdom's tax codes have become more charity friendly.
- There is increased pressure on foreign lawmakers to make their tax codes more charity friendly.
- Some U.S. organizations have established foundations in other countries, making it possible for gifts to be received in those other countries.
- Some overseas charities have established affiliations with U.S. charitable organizations to help U.S. citizens who wish to support those overseas charities (Green 1996).
- A World Wide Web site now contains an international directory of more than 5,000 charities that have their own sites on the Web and also lists publications and other resources for people interested in management, fundraising, and legal issues related to not-for-profit organizations (*The Chronicle of Philanthropy* 1996).

For the gift planning community, the most important development is the increased worldwide pressure being brought to bear by individuals and organizations. Laws are made by most governments in response to public need, and changes in laws to better facilitate inter-nation giving no doubt will occur in response to such demands by individuals and organizations. Fundraisers are uniting to address the methods of facilitating gifts. For example, the Canadian Association of Gift Planners (CAGP) was formed in 1994; it is a counterpart to the National Committee on Planned Giving in the United States and is an added voice in the call for change.

By last year the CAGP had over 1,000 members. The Canadians have used the roundtable format as one means of developing and expanding the phenomenal growth of their association over the past four years. As their membership has grown, so too has the "Leave a Legacy" program, a community-based effort that encourages people from all walks of life to make gifts from their estates to the nonprofit organization of their choice.

An individual or organization just entering the rewarding field of planned giving might well be able to take advantage of the increasingly interrelated network of global charitable support. Worldwide philanthropy and inter-nation giving is growing. There is nothing to expect except improvement. These are very exciting times, indeed!

REFERENCES

Bigelow, B., and C. George. 1994. The new frontier: Planned gifts across international borders. *Charitable Gift Planning News* 12, no. 9: 4–8.

The Chronicle of Philanthropy. 1996. On-line directory for charities worldwide. *The Chronicle of Philanthropy*, 4 April: 36.

Greene, S. 1996. Making friends in America. *The Chronicle of Philanthropy*, 13 June: 29–31.

Part II

Planned Giving: Getting Started Right

In this section of the book you will learn how to start a planned giving program from scratch or revitalize a flagging one. Part II will take you from your first step—preparing a thoughtful road map for the program—through organizing the resources to start, designing a marketing plan, and managing the gifts. It can be a rewarding journey for you, your donors, and your organization, especially if you avoid the pitfalls, which is what the following chapters are intended to help you do.

Chapter 10
Preparing Your Action Plan

The board of trustees of Worthy Charity, recognizing that the organization must increase its endowment in order to ensure its survival, has decided to embark on a planned giving program. They have asked you to prepare the plan to get the program started successfully and to distribute it to the members in time for the plan to be considered at the next board meeting.

In this chapter you will learn how to create a plan that shows your organization what should be done before they do it so that when they do it they'll do it right the first time (see Appendix 10–A). It should be brief, simple, and readable, and should answer these questions in conversational language:

- Where are we are now?
  1. What is our present situation?
  2. How did we get to this point?
  3. What problem do we want to solve?
- Where do we want to go?
  1. What should the program do?
  2. When should we start?
- How do we get there?
  1. What specific steps should we take?
  2. When should we take them?
  3. Who should be responsible?
  4. How much will it cost?
  5. What results should we expect?

Assume that the readers of your plan will be the organization's trustees, staff members, and perhaps, volunteers.

THE PLAN

Introduction to Planned Giving

Begin with a discussion of planned giving so the reader understands why the plan was prepared. The following sample explanation can be used as a guide:

What is planned giving? Planned giving is concerned with present and future gifts that require more specialized expertise than that required for gifts of outright cash. There are a variety of types of planned gifts: outright gifts, life income gifts, gifts of income only, gifts of a retained life estate, and bequests. Numerous kinds of assets can be used: cash, bonds, stock, real estate, livestock, timber, mineral rights, life insurance policies, royalty, and tangible personal property.

The largest gifts tend to be bequests and life income plans. Planned gifts are usually made out of a donor's assets rather than from current income. Often these gifts come from individuals who have never viewed themselves as being in a position to part with cash, therefore, they represent a new group of prospects. Frequently, the discussion of planned gifts leads to an outright gift.

> *Often these gifts come from individuals who have never viewed themselves as being in a position to part with cash.*

Worthy Charity's initial planned giving program need not require the laborious identification of potential donors, extensive cultivation of promising prospects, and face-to-face solicitation. With an effective education program, our planned giving prospects will identify themselves and ask for further information. They will be expecting our follow-up calls. As our program matures, Worthy Charity should dedicate increased resources to the cultivation of planned giving prospects.

Why is planned giving important to Worthy Charity . . . and to its donors? Planned giving provides additional ways to encourage donor funding, because you are working in partnership with your donors to help them structure gifts that will benefit themselves and their families as well as Worthy Charity. You are providing a new and important service to your constituents. Often this beneficial partnership can produce much larger gifts than ever anticipated.

Planned gifts are usually made out of the donors' assets rather than their current income. Some planned gift options can provide immediate funds for our charitable purposes, while with others the financial benefits to Worthy Charity will be deferred. Planned gifts can maximize benefits to our donors as well as to their families by using assets in creative ways, to possibly increase lifetime income and provide substantial savings in income and estate taxes.

The important point is that planned gifts will expand options for our donors, options that allow them to take care of personal, family, and financial needs while providing support for Worthy Charity. Planned giving is a vital part of any comprehensive development program, because it can substantially enhance the giving capacity of donors.

Because planned giving often involves decisions about major assets affecting the financial plans of older donors, the period of consideration often lasts many months. Thus, the payoff from establishing a planned giving program will not be immediate. However, as more people realize that they can include Worthy Charity in their estate plans and can make life income gifts, we will see the volume of planned gifts increase—and many of the gifts will come from people who have previously given little or nothing. Further, by establishing a bequest or legacy society, we will be able to develop a group of donors who are committed to the goals of Worthy Charity.

Experience has shown that a consistent education program based on a clear statement of mission and supported by prompt and accurate response efforts will yield an increasing number of bequest intentions and irrevocable gift plans over time.

Where We Are Now: The Situation Assessment

To give the reader a full understanding of why the board has decided to start a planned giving program at this time, paint a brief but compelling picture of the organization and its need to build endowment. Your description should portray the situation in such a way that a busy reader can quickly grasp the need for change.

Background

Write a thumbnail sketch of the history of the organization, outlining the reasons why donors have felt compelled to support its mission. Highlight the characteristics of the organization that make it a good candidate for planned giving. The list might look like this:

- Significant portion of the membership is in the 55 and older age category
- Long history of good works
- Recipient of previous bequests or other planned gifts
- Well known in the community

Do not be dismayed if your organization lacks some of these characteristics. There are ways to develop planned gifts even if yours is a relatively new organization. For ideas, refer to "Selecting the Gift Options To Be Offered" in Chapter 11 and the first steps for starting a new program in Chapter 4.

Publications

To show the ways in which the organization is reaching its potential donors, briefly describe the publications (newsletters, Web site, annual appeals, event notices, and pamphlets), indicate the number of people receiving them, and note the methods of distribution. This step is helpful in determining the best way of educating potential donors about planned giving.

Development Program

To show why the board has decided that a planned giving program is needed to round out the development potential of the organization, outline the ways in which the organization is now raising money and indicate the funds raised from each activity. Include

- annual giving
- special events
- direct mail
- Web site
- e-mail
- capital campaigns
- government funding
- United Way funding
- foundation grants
- corporate contributions

Summary

Summarize the situation and repeat the board's call for action. All you need is a statement like this:

> In summary, Worthy Charity, as reflected by the decision of the Board of Trustees on [date],
>
> - needs to increase contributions from individuals,
> - recognizes that the offering of planned giving options can increase the potential for the organization to raise money, and
> - intends to establish a planned giving program on September 1, 2xxx.

Where We Want To Go

In this section you briefly define the goal of the plan: the establishment of the planned giving program by a certain date in the future. You might say something as simple as this:

> "Start Worthy Charity's planned giving program on September 1, 2xxx."

How We Get There: Setting Up the Program

Gift Options To Be Offered

List the gift options and their attributes (see Chapter 7), define the order in which they will be introduced, and describe the rationale behind the schedule.

The Communications Plan

Outline the specific methods by which you will educate your potential donors about the features and benefits of planned giving. Chapter 12 describes how to reach out to your potential donors and to the audience inside your organization.

The Proposed Budget

List the costs of establishing and administering the planned giving program for both the startup phase and the mature phase (see Chapter 11). The cost elements will probably include these:

- staff
- publications
- training
- promotion
- professional fees
- recognition society
- software
- office space and equipment
- asset management fees

How We Know We're Getting There: Measuring Results

Because planned giving produces gifts that do not materialize for years, perhaps decades, it is extremely important to design measures other than "dollars received" for demonstrating the progress of the program. The basic strategy is to keep track of those activities that, if done well, will surely result in dollar gifts. Consider this sample "Measuring Results" section:

> As the monetary gifts resulting from Worthy Charity's planned giving program will be received in the future, we will begin by measuring those activities that will lead to their realization and other indicators of the program's potential:
>
> - number of planned giving intentions affirmed by board members
> - number of planned giving newsletters or direct mail pieces sent
> - number of inquiries received
> - number of follow-up phone calls made
> - number of will intentions received
> - number of Worthy Charity Legacy Society members
> - number and dollar amount of irrevocable gift commitments made
> - number and dollar amount of realized bequests, annuities, and trusts

Appendix 10–A
Guide to Writing a Plan

1. Introduction: Planned giving.
   - What is it? [Chapter 1]
   - Why it is important to the organization?
   - How can it benefit the donors? [Chapter 7]
2. Where are we now? Situation assessment.
3. Where do we want to go? Direction and goal.
4. How do we get there?
   - Who are the potential donors? [Chapter 12]
   - How do we reach them? [Chapters 8, 12]
   - What options do we give them? [Chapters 4, 7]
   - How do they let us know they are interested? [Chapter 12]
   - What do we do then?
   - How do we explain the options to them?
   - How do we "close" gifts?
   - How do we recognize the donors?
   - How do we follow up to develop future gifts?
   - How do we invest gifts to be able to pay a lifetime of checks? [Chapter 13]
   - How much will the program cost?
   - How do we integrate planned giving into the organization's entire fundraising program? [Chapter 3]
5. How do we know we're getting there? Measuring results.
6. Expectations: Building the pipeline for major future support.

Chapter 11

Organizing To Begin the Planned Giving Program

In this chapter you will learn how to maximize the effectiveness of the planned giving program through workload planning, training, software selection, use of financial and legal professionals, and teaming up with your local community foundation.

PLANNING FOR PHASED GROWTH

Check Your Image

The IRS requires that public charities over a certain size annually file a "Return of Organization Exempt from Income Tax" Form 990 (see Appendix D). This form provides an opportunity to outline the accomplishments of the organization. As it is available on the Web to potential donors, it is extremely important that it be viewed as a public relations opportunity for the organization. A check on the contents of your Form 990 is highly recommended. It can yield handsome results as your charity is compared to others. (See GuideStar in Appendix B under Web Sites.)

The Startup Phase

This is the trial period for the program. It is important that the cost of the initial "investment" for the organization be held to a minimum, as the payback, in terms of gifts received, will begin in the future. Cost restraint can be achieved by controlling the major expense items: salary and publications.

Salary expense can be minimized by engaging the services of a planned giving consultant on an hourly or contract basis rather than hiring a full-time planned giving officer. Utilize the advice and software support of the consultant to help with marketing, coaching, and donor consulting (see Appendix B).

The program can usually be handled on a part-time basis by a responsible staff member with the support of a specialist. With the knowledge gained by working with the specialist, the staff member will be a candidate for the planned giving officer position when the organization enters the mature phase of the program.

Publication expense can be minimized during the startup period by using the organization's newsletter to "piggyback" planned giving articles and examples. Information on gifts sent in response to inquiries generated by the newsletter can be obtained from organizations specializing in planned giving marketing materials (see Appendix B). Small quantities of materials should be ordered, as the inquiries will be relatively few and the "shelf life" of such materials tends to be limited owing to legislative changes. The turnaround time for receiving additional materials is usually short.

The Mature Phase

Once the planned giving program has proven itself (through increased numbers of gift commitments, legacy society members, and gifts received), the organization may wish to expand the program by adding a full-time planned giving officer and the necessary administrative and software support. At that point the organization may already have established its own pooled income fund and charitable gift annuity structure.

STAFFING

The individual who is assigned the responsibility of starting the planned giving program should

- have a good knowledge of planned giving
- be a good listener and be attuned to planned giving clues (see Exhibit 3–1)
- have a talent for conversing empathetically with older people
- be familiar with the mission and good works of the organization
- be capable of attending to details

This individual's principal duties will include

- answering inquiries from potential donors
- sending prescribed information materials in response to inquiries
- telephoning to follow up on the mailing of information materials
- bringing a planned giving consultant in on a conference call basis when potential donors are interested in detailed discussions of the various options
- maintaining records of contacts with prospective and actual donors
- handling donor recognition and enrollment in the legacy society
- compiling records of planned giving activities

In some organizations this individual is also responsible for producing the newsletter or other development communications and is in fact the chief development person.

SELECTING THE GIFT OPTIONS TO BE OFFERED

Your organization may wish to take a step-by-step approach and phase in the various options as you build the necessary foundations to support them.

Bequests require little preparation other than reminding donors to consider your organization in their estate plans. The next level of effort is to give them an opportunity to request bequest language naming your organization. A third level is to admit them to membership in your **legacy society**. (See Chapter 12 for more ideas.)

After establishing procedures to handle them, encourage **outright gifts of appreciated securities** (see Chapter 13 for information on managing gifts).

Once your methods of handling inquiries, sending response literature, and following up with gift counseling are in place, you will be in position to promote **life income trusts, gifts of life insurance, lead trusts, retained life estate arrangements,** and other gift options.

The final step: offer **pooled income fund** gifts and **charitable gift annuities** as soon as you have arranged for their setup and administration, and gotten any necessary regulatory approvals.

PLANNING THE WORKLOAD

In the beginning, your planned giving program will occupy only a minor portion of a single staff person's time. As there will not be many responses to any particular planned giving newsletter article, there will not be much follow-up activity required. Each response, however, is worthy of close individual attention, as it has the potential to yield a major gift.

The two controlling factors that can be used to adjust the volume of inquiries are (1) the size and frequency of each mailing of planned giving information and (2) the content of the offer of information to be requested.

The Size and Frequency of the Mailings

A rough rule of thumb is that the response to any one mailing will be in the range of .1 to .2 percent. That means that if you send out 5,000 pieces of mail, you will probably only get 5 to 10 responses. If you send out 25,000 pieces of mail, you will probably get 25 to 50 responses.

Keep a sharp eye on the number of inquiries resulting from a partial mailing. Calculate the response rate. The response volume can then be predicted for the remainder of the mailing and the staff workload can be forecast. By increasing, decreasing, or spacing out the number of pieces to be mailed, your staff's time commitment can be adjusted accordingly.

The Content of the Offer

An offer of more specific information will yield a smaller number of responses but the level of interest in donating will on average be higher, allowing you to focus your staff's attention on a group that is more likely to

---

A Low-Expense, High-Yield Offer of Information

Worthy Charity Newsletter carries an article about a life income gift plan, with a specific illustration of the gift. Included is a response card for requesting further information about "The gift to Worthy Charity that saves taxes three ways and pays a life income." Response information on life income gifts would be sent only to those who have requested it, followed by a phone call "to get your thoughts about it."

A High-Expense, Low-Yield Offer of Information

A newsletter article offers a general booklet on tax-advantaged giving to Worthy Charity. Many more inquiries would be received by Worthy Charities—perhaps too many, at least for the startup phase of the program. Valuable staff time would be devoted to the individual follow-up calls, and the level of interest of most respondents might be quite low. This type of offer will make more sense when the program has matured and the administrative support has expanded.

yield completed planned gifts. For more ideas about the offer of information and the handling of inquiries, please refer to Chapter 12.

TRAINING

Plan to present planned giving workshops for board members, staff, and volunteers to explain

- how the planned giving program can benefit the organization
- what the features of the program are
- how each person can help ensure the program's success

More information on conducting these workshops is contained in Chapter 12.

TELEPHONES AND VOICE MAIL

In addition to your publications, Web site, and e-mail, your telephones are your organization's window to the world and to its donors. There are several steps that you can take to ensure that your telephone communications are welcoming and helpful.

> *Your publications, Web site, and telephones are your organization's windows to the world and its donors.*

The person answering your telephone should be well briefed on the program, its value to the organization, and the methods for obtaining further information about the program. A script in a three-ring notebook near the telephone can save time and allow the information giver to deal with questions in a more assured manner.

Make certain that you have a voice mail system that is welcoming and user friendly. Systems with intricate successive decision requirements ("If you wish to reach A, press 4") can be virtually impenetrable for some older people.

Get an incoming 800 number if your constituency is beyond your local telephone area. A startup 800 number for a small organization is quite affordable and can yield handsome results by encouraging potential donors to call you with questions.

Use spiral-bound multiple-part telephone message pads. Each message notation can be torn off and placed in the donor's file, while the carbon copy that remains in the book provides a chronological trail of your communications with no added effort.

The next chapter describes in more detail the unique and surprising power of the telephone in negotiating planned gifts.

COMPUTER SOFTWARE

How do we respond to inquiries? Where is that follow-up letter? An up-to-date version of word processing software can increase an organization's efficiency in producing, editing, storing, and retrieving planned giving information for use in responding to potential donors.

Who said what when? What's the next step? To keep track of the information about and communications with planned giving prospects and donors, you should establish a contact management database (see Appendix B for a list of planned giving management software programs).

What are the details of the plan? The deduction? The cash flow? The alternatives? As the volume of the inquiries from prospective donors increases, the organization may find it cost-effective to invest in software that produces gift examples. Such software provides calculations, descriptions, diagrams, and charts to help explain specific gifts to donors and advisors. In addition it can add to an organization's planned giving Web site pages, the ability for the donor to do his or her own gift calculations. Most software suppliers provide a telephone support service for gift planners. (For contact information, please refer to Appendix B.)

WORKING WITH ALLIED PROFESSIONALS

Financial and legal professionals can be helpful in obtaining referrals to your program. Be aware, however, of the potential conflicts of interest. Once the word gets around that you are starting a planned giving program, you will be approached with offers of assistance. Some of the would-be advisors may be members of your board of trustees. It is important to realize that they may not be specialists in charitable gift planning and that their principal agenda may be to increase their client lists and sell their services or products. Keep them informed about the gift options you are offering. They can best help the organization by referring individuals already among their clientele who may be interested in the mission of your organization. (This issue is discussed further in Chapter 14.)

HOW COMMUNITY FOUNDATIONS CAN HELP

When a not-for-profit organization is getting started in planned giving, the cost of setting up and administrating pooled income funds and charitable gift annuities can present a hurdle that might delay the offering of these popular gift options. Your local community foundation may be willing to let your organization use its pooled income funds and charitable gift annuities to ultimately benefit your organization, saving you the setup and administrative charges. Nationwide there are more than four hundred community foundations that function as conduits through which donors' funds can pass to local charities.

Contact the Council on Foundations (see Appendix B) for information about the community foundation closest to you. A phone call to that foundation can then tell you whether it has a pooled income fund and charitable gift annuity arrangement and if your organization would qualify to share it. Later, as your gift volume grows, you may wish to establish your own pooled income funds and charitable gift annuities. (See Chapter 13 for detailed information on managing gifts.)

Appendix 11–A

Case Study: The Development of a Planned Giving Program

This is how a real organization, let's call it "Worthy Conservation," got started in planned giving.

Worthy, established 50 years ago, has a membership of 15,000 individuals interested in the protection of the many species and habitats of the world's oceans. Many of them are older than 55. Although Worthy Conservation has received cash donations from its membership over the years, the principal funding of its programs has been through foundation grants. Occasionally, Worthy has been the beneficiary of bequests, even though they were not solicited.

Worthy's board, concerned about its dependence on foundation grants, decided to establish a planned giving program to tap the transfer of the trillions of dollars that will pass from one generation to the next over the next several decades. Not wishing to incur the expense of adding a planned giving professional to its staff at this point, Worthy retained the services of a planned giving specialist who, working at an hourly rate, would help it get started on a cost-effective basis.

The recommendations of the planned giving specialist addressed

- the members and their potential for planned gifts
- how they can be most effectively reached with planned giving information
- which planned gift options to offer and when
- how the gifts should be screened to avoid accepting those that may be more expensive than they're worth
- how gifts of stock, life income plans, and insurance policies could be handled
- guidelines for the establishment and prudent management of Worthy's endowment:
  1. what gifts should go into it
  2. how it could be effectively invested

3. what monies could be withdrawn for use by Worthy's programs
- the coaching of board members, staff, and volunteers to show how each of them can contribute to the success of the major/planned giving program
- the establishment of a legacy society to recognize and honor those who have committed to make planned gifts to further Worthy's mission

Following the plan, Worthy Conservation

- added planned giving promotional material to its existing newsletter and Web site at minimum incremental expense and immediately began receiving expressions of interest from its members
- answered inquiries with brief information booklets about the requested gift plan
- made follow-up phone calls to get the donors' thoughts about the information they had requested.

During the conversation with a donor, if the staff person was asked detailed questions, a further conference call was arranged to include the planned giving specialist. As a result of the conference call, the specialist would develop a written illustration of the gift for the staff person to send to the donor to share with his or her advisor. In this manner, the gift process was moved toward fruition.

The results for Worthy Conservation included the following:

- Within several months of commencing the promotion, Worthy began to receive outright gifts of appreciated stock, offers of gifts of real estate, inquiries about life income options (charitable gift annuities, charitable remainder trusts), and requests from donors who had included Worthy in their estate plans to be added to Worthy's legacy society.

- After 18 months, Worthy could justify the addition of a planned giving officer to its staff, as the increasing volume of committed gift plans indicated a strong future flow of gift income from matured gifts.
- Within three years, Worthy began to receive the cash from realized bequests and matured life income plans. This is not surprising, as people tend to revisit their estate plans in the event of failing health. In this case, Worthy stood in a much better position to be included in those plans because of their repeated planned giving promotion.

Because of the addition of planned gift options to their major gift program, Worthy Conservation not only feels more comfortable with its broader sources of funding, but its donors have found new ways to help Worthy carry out its mission by utilizing the win-win opportunities offered by planned gifts.

Chapter 12
Marketing Planned Giving

WHY "MARKETING"?

When we employ marketing techniques, we focus upon the **needs** of the donors rather than upon the **names** of the planned gift options. It helps us to avoid the problem experienced by the tragic hero of this marketing tale:

The World's Greatest Dog Bone
The president of a famous dog food company was approached one day by his wildly enthusiastic vice-president of production.

"Boss, we've developed the most fantastic dog bone in the world! The highest grade ingredients and the most authentic shape ever devised! We'll sweep the market!"

The president carefully examined the product, considered the many years of production experience that had gone into its development, and immediately agreed to a full-scale advertising and production program.

What were the results? Dismal! In fact, the product was a crushingly expensive failure that nearly put the company out of business.

Why?

Because they'd never tried it on the dogs!

They had neglected the all-important ingredient of marketing success: finding out the needs and wants of their market. In their enthusiasm over their technical expertise, they had taken a *product-centered* rather than a *need-sensitive* approach.

Gift planners are in the business of offering gift options that meet the special needs of their donors. To be successful, they have to determine the nature of those needs in order to select the right gift plans to discuss with the donor.

Marketing Principles Applied to Planned Giving

- Determine the *needs* of the donor.
- Select the gift option that meets those *needs*.
- Discuss the *benefits* of the gift chosen.

Here is an example of a **product-centered** statement:

> Worthy Charity offers charitable remainder trusts, charitable gift annuities, and pooled income funds.

Then there is the kind of statement that entails a **need-sensitive** approach:

> Worthy Charity offers gift plans that can help you to save taxes three ways while getting a lifetime income and giving major support to Worthy Charity.

Which will sell better? The need-sensitive approach wins every time!

WHO ARE THE POTENTIAL DONORS?

Q. Who are the potential donors?

A. Anyone who cares about what you are doing to change lives for the better!

The 55 and older age group is the primary market for planned giving. Why? Because this demographic group has the greatest concentration of wealth. It has been estimated that this group represents one-quarter of the population, one-half of discretionary spending, and three-quarters of all household assets.

The next several decades will see the largest intergenerational transfer of money ever, estimated at $6 to $11 trillion. Most of the wealth accumulated since World War II will pass to the next generation. The charities that have discovered how to utilize planned giving to tap into this huge conduit of funds will have taken a major step toward ensuring their future.

A recent survey of the donors of planned gifts to a major university yielded a surprising result: many of the donors had a record of only modest gifts to the annual fund and quite a few were "never givers." The conclusion: many people do not view themselves as being in a position to part with cash. Donors of planned gifts represent a new and different group than those who are on your organization's rolls as faithful annual givers. Planned giving presents an organization with an opportunity to expand its base of donors.

The Needs of Donors

Donors' needs are as individual as the donors themselves. Here are a few of them:

- Donors may wish to pass on the torch and at the same time communicate their values to future generations.
- Many donors want to give something back. They recognize their good fortune and wish to help a worthy cause.
- Some donors, facing uncertainties in investments and health, like the idea of an assured income.
- Donors like to feel united with others who share their values.
- Some donors seek recognition. They want the community to know that they have been successful enough to be able to donate a building, an X-ray machine, a library section, or a scholarship.
- Making a substantial gift can be, for some donors, a meaningful way to remember a loved one.

Tax Savings

Are tax savings the prime gift motivator?

No, *charitable intent* is the prime motivator. People typically give to an organization because they believe in what it is doing to change others' lives for the better. Tax benefits and income streams are merely icing on the cake.

> *People typically give to an organization because they believe in what it is doing to change others' lives for the better.*

Your organization will be successful in attracting planned gifts if it has

- done a good job in carrying out its mission
- told people about its mission effectively
- given potential donors a clear understanding of planned gifts
- given potential donors an easy way to ask for more information
- established the type of dialogue with donors that leads to gift closure

OUTREACH: COMMUNICATING WITH DONORS

The outreach strategy has four major components:

- **Educate** to promote self-identification and inquiry.
- **Respond** immediately and encourage dialogue.
- **Illustrate** the gift and move toward closure.
- **Recognize** and cultivate the donor to increase the chance of further gifts.

Education

The Message

Describe the features and benefits of each gift in nontechnical language and give a specific illustration. It is extremely important to provide a response mechanism (response card, e-mail form, 800 telephone number) with which the potential donors can identify themselves by asking for further information. Include a space for the name, address, and telephone number for future contact (see Exhibit 4–2).

The information about planned gifts can be included in newsletters, Web sites, brochures, advertisements, and handouts.

Newsletters

The most cost-effective way of spreading the word is to utilize your organization's newsletter. Publicizing the planned giving information can be done at modest added expense. If your organization does not have a newsletter, consider starting one. The essential ingredient in cultivating donors for planned gifts is to keep them informed about your good works and future plans. A newsletter is an effective way to tell the story.

Georgetown University, to publicize its planned giving program, started *Legacy*, a newsletter whose content was 50 percent planned giving information and 50 percent happenings at the university related to planned gifts. Each issue included a response card and an envelope addressed to the director of gift planning by name and marked "Confidential." The mailings were carefully timed to avoid conflicting with the annual giving campaign.

The university-oriented material was written by the development staff, while the writing, layout, printing, addressing, and mailing of the planned giving materials was handled by a supplier of planned giving marketing materials from its offices in the Midwest (see Appendix B for a list of suppliers).

Legacy was mailed to approximately 14,000 alumni aged 55 and older, and 25 to 30 responses (approximately two-tenths of one percent) were received after each mail drop. These response cards contained check-off blocks asking for further information and/or confirming that the senders had included the university in their estate plans (see Exhibit 4–2). By the end of two years, the university had admitted 150 members to the newly established Legacy Society and had begun signing up donors for life income gifts.

The response rate was surprisingly high (usually one-tenth of one percent is regarded as a successful return), and the gift giving started sooner than the three-year norm experienced by similar organizations. Perhaps it was because the alumni and parents had not recently been contacted by the university about the planned gift opportunities.

Web Sites

The fastest growing segment of Web users is seniors, many of whom use the medium to communicate with their grandchildren. It is not surprising that an increasing number of nonprofit organizations are utilizing the Web to promote planned giving. Some are making available the calculation of planned gifts to potential donors in the privacy of their own personal computers.

A well-designed Web site with frequent links to "ask for more information" e-mail forms can pay handsome dividends by providing a cost-effective method to get in contact with potential donors.

Brochures

Accompanied by a personal cover letter, commercially obtained brochures can be used to send to people requesting further information. They can be inexpensively personalized with your organization's logo or can be entirely tailor-made, depending on your budget.

You can begin with a modest supply, as you will not get many responses from any given mailing. Brochures can also be used as handouts at events. If your organization's budget does not allow for brochures, gift information can be condensed to single-page format.

Advertisements

Gift planning information can be condensed into an advertisement as small as one-eighth of a page, and the advertisement can be printed in your newsletter and used as a mailing insert or a handout at appropriate events (see Exhibit 12–1). The important thing is to include a way for interested readers to respond—by calling or

Exhibit 12–1 Sample Advertisement

> **Did you know**
> that you can make a gift to Worthy Charity,
> save taxes twice,
> and get back a life income?
> Well, you can!
>
> **Life Income Gifts**
>
> Your life income gifts to Worthy Charity pay dividends. There are several options to choose from, depending on your age, your needs, and the way you fund your gift. A life income gift provides the following benefits:
>
> - An income for the lifetime of the donor and/or the donor's spouse
> - A charitable income tax deduction
> - An opportunity to establish an endowed fund in your name or in the name of a loved one
> - Avoidance of capital gains taxes on gifts of appreciated property
> - Membership in the Worthy Charity Codicil Club
> - A reduction in federal estate taxes
>
> When you plan your giving to Worthy Charity, you know that you are contributing to the increased well-being of our community.
>
> **Please call us at 1–800–123–4567 to request further information about LIFE INCOME GIFTS.**

sending in a reply requesting further information (see Exhibit 4–2).

Workshops for Potential Donors

Seminars and workshops are extremely useful outreach tools. If well planned, they can be directed toward potential donors as well as staff, board members, and volunteers.

One strategy for holding down the cost of workshops is to join forces with a locally known estate planning attorney and contribute illustrations of planned charitable gifts.

> Tip: *A low-key approach is advisable.*

Discuss gifts to "the charity of your choice" rather than to your organization by name, but have information about your organization's planned gifts in the handout packet. Of course, include ways of getting further information from your organization and have a signup sheet for further follow-up.

In-House Workshops

Dissertation on the need for in-house planned giving workshops:

If they ain't up *on it, they're* down *on it!*

In order for your organization to win in the battle to attract individual gifts, you need to help staff, board members, and volunteers overcome their reticence to talk about planned giving with potential donors. No doubt, planned giving terminology is intimidatingly complex. Further, solicitors of gifts may feel pressure to bring in "today money" rather than "tomorrow money" and may fear that if the donors hear about planned gifts they will not make outright contributions. Try to allay this fear. Experience has shown that people who make planned gift commitments are far more likely to make subsequent outright gifts because of their increased sense of involvement with the goals of the charity.

Build your team of gift solicitors in the following ways:

- Use workshops to encourage everybody in the organization to feel comfortable talking about planned gift opportunities, to teach them how to listen for clues when talking with donors, and how to bring in planned giving expertise to close gifts.
- Include planned giving as part of the orientation given to new board and staff members and volunteers.
- Distribute copies of planned giving promotional materials to everyone concerned with fundraising. Encourage their reactions and questions.
- Make sure that all planned giving donor materials offer the opportunity to enclose cash donations (see Exhibit 4–2).
- Conversely, all cash donation solicitation materials should include a check-off block for requesting planned giving information.
- Solicitors of major gifts should be ready to offer planned giving alternatives as a fallback position in the event the donor is not comfortable making an outright gift. Planned giving can be a way of making a larger gift than the donor might ever have thought possible.
- Give credit for soliciting and closing planned gifts to any member of your organization's "family" who helps.

Help board members, staff, and volunteers to feel knowledgeable about planned giving. Show them how they can help the program to be successful in developing the kind of major support needed to ensure the future of the organization. Some of the most effective ambassadors are individuals who have a special dedication to their organization.

Remember, solicitors do not have to use the technical names of the gift options. "We have a gift plan that saves taxes twice and pays a life income" does the job! It can be effective to bring in someone from outside the organization to help with the training (see Appendix 8–A).

Workshop Agenda
Conversational Planned Giving at Worthy Charity
- How planned giving can help ensure the future of Worthy Charity
- How planned giving helps Worthy Charity's donors
- Gift illustrations
- Planned giving clues to listen for
- Role-playing
- Success stories and "near misses"

Responding to Inquiries

A key element in any planned giving communication is the prompt handling of inquiries.

Phone or e-mail *immediately* when you receive response cards or e-mail inquiries. You now have the opportunity to concentrate your attention on these few select individuals, any one of whom might make a gift many times the size of your entire annual fund income. If you have stored the text of a cover letter in your computer, with a few keystrokes you can send it and the illustrative materials on their way. A quick response tells people that they are special and that they really count.

A follow-up call or e-mail message should be made no later than seven or eight working days after you have sent information to a potential donor so that it is still fresh in the donor's mind. After you thank the donor for his or her interest, ask for the donor's thoughts about the materials requested. Listen carefully for clues that can reveal the donor's needs (see Exhibit 3–1). This can help you identify the gift plan most likely to be appealing to the donor. Be understanding and informative but never pushy. "Here are some thoughts for your consideration . . ."

> *Be understanding and informative, but never pushy.*

Once a gift option is selected, you can more fully describe the features and benefits of that option. When the questions become detailed ("What is my deduction for that?" "What are my options regarding income?"), offer to call back at a convenient time so that your planned giving specialist can be part of the conversation. With the specialist joining you in a conference call, you can discuss the detailed questions that have arisen and examine the pros and cons of alternative gift plans.

From Gift Illustration to Closing

The Specific Gift Illustration

The specialist can prepare a written gift illustration incorporating the donor's specific information and send it to you, along with sample gift documents. Add a cover letter in which you encourage the donor to share the information with his or her advisor, and end with the all-important "I'll phone shortly to get your thoughts about this." (See Appendix 12–A for sample response letters.) Time spent with a potential planned gift donor is an investment that can pay off handsomely in major support for your organization.

Donor Visits . . . by Telephone

Using the telephone is a cost-effective way to contact donors on a very personal basis regardless of their location or your travel budget. Experience has shown that many people are more comfortable discussing their assets, estate plans, and hopes and desires over the telephone than they are sitting face to face with an unfamiliar individual in their office or living room.

Closing the Gift

The next follow-up call should seek the donor's reactions to the gift illustration and sample documents that you sent. Offer to discuss questions with the donor's advisor. Bear in mind that many otherwise experienced accountants and estate planning attorneys may not be conversant with planned giving. Encourage the donor to have the advisor call you directly with questions, as the advisor can then be armed with the answers when he or she next consults with the donor. Your planned giving specialist can help by joining the telephone conversation.

When the donor says, "Well, I understand, and I'd like to do one of those," then signs the documents and sends the assets to your organization or to his or her trustee (if the gift involves a trust), the gift can be considered closed. At that point, you congratulate yourself and your team for a job well done and get on with the next steps: acknowledging the gift, recognizing the donor, and establishing a cultivation plan to develop future gifts.

Person-to-Person Visits

When your planned giving program matures and the budget and staff have expanded, it can be quite effective to visit personally with good planned giving prospects to bring them up to date on the organization's good works and to move them toward donating a planned gift.

Donor Recognition

To give each planned giving donor a sense of belonging and to provide your organization with a pool of com-mitted donors, establish a legacy society. Select an appropriate name (the American Red Cross calls its legacy society the Codicil Club; Georgetown University calls its society the Georgetown University Legacy Society). Involving board members in the name selection process helps enhance their involvement in the program.

You may wish to present each new legacy society member with a suitable certificate and a recognition pin to help spread the word about the society.

The most important function of a legacy society is to give people the opportunity to let you know that they have included your organization in their estate plans. Admit to membership people who have informed you that you are in their will and those who have committed to an irrevocable gift plan. To have some evidence of intent, some organizations ask for a copy of the appropriate page of the donor's will. However, this can be seen as an unwarranted invasion of privacy and has no lasting meaning, as one's will is revocable until death. If people tell you that your organization is in their estate plan, they are less likely to remove it when they revise their wills. The increasing membership in the society will provide a demonstration of the progress of your planned giving program.

The members of the legacy society are prime prospects for additional planned or outright gifts. An increased interest in outright contributions occurs frequently as planned giving donors become more emotionally committed to the goals of your organization. In this way, planned giving enhances outright giving.

Something To Get the Ball Rolling

A university planned giving officer was in the process of arranging a retained life estate gift involving a $750,000 house that would eventually be used to fund a scholarship program. The donor called to say that it was getting close to the end of the year and she realized that the gift could not be put into place that rapidly—therefore she was putting a check for $100,000 in the mail to "get the ball rolling."

THE KICKOFF OF YOUR PROGRAM

Once you have your communications plan, planned giving expertise, and gift administration in place, you are ready to publicize that your organization is now offering creative ways for donors to ensure that its mission will be carried out for many years in the future. This notification might take the form of an announcement in your newsletter and Web site, together with examples of the kinds of gifts that you will be offering, and a description of the legacy society. The announcement should be accompanied, as should all communications regarding planned giving, by a means of requesting further information. Once the response cards start coming in, you reply with your prepared information, begin answering questions, and your program is underway!

Experience has shown that a **consistent education program** based on a **clear statement of mission**, and supported by a **prompt and accurate response effort** will yield an increasing number of bequest intentions and irrevocable gift plans over the months and years ahead.

The Eternal Buggy Whip
If the buggy whip makers had realized that they were in the business of filling a *transportation* need, they might still be going . . . making accelerator pedals!

In Memory Of . . .
One of the first calls received at Georgetown University after it started a planned giving newsletter was from the attorney of an 80-year-old woman whose son had been tragically killed in an accident while an undergraduate many years ago. She set up a charitable gift annuity that would pay her a dependable income until her death, after which the assets would be used to create a scholarship fund in her son's name.

Appendix 12–A

Sample Response Letters

Response to check-off block: **"I have made a provision in my will for Worthy Charity."**

DATE

Dear_____:

Thanks for confirming that you have made a provision for Worthy Charity in your will. It has been said that a will is the ultimate expression of a person's values. We are deeply grateful that you have chosen this manner in which to help Worthy Charity carry out your wishes.

It is my great pleasure to welcome you into the Legacy Society that has been established to recognize and honor those who, through their thoughtfulness and generosity, have made a Legacy Gift: a will provision or an irrevocable gift plan that provides a life income for the donor and a later gift of the assets to Worthy Charity for the purpose you designate.

Your Legacy Society membership certificate will be presented to you in the near future.

Enclosed is *Planned Giving*, which describes some gift plans that can yield a life income as well as major tax savings to the donor. I'll phone you shortly to get your views on this information and to answer any questions you might have.

With best wishes,

Mary Jones
Director of Development

Enclosure: *Planned Giving*

Response to check-off block: **"Please send me information about a gift to Worthy Charity that I can live in for the rest of my life."**

DATE

Dear_____:

Thank you for your inquiry about the gift you can live in for the rest of your life.

A gift of your residence or farm, retaining the right for you and your spouse to live in it for the remainder of your lives, gives you the satisfaction of providing major support for Worthy Charity without changing your lifestyle. In addition, you get a handsome charitable deduction that can give you major tax savings.

There is further information starting on page 3 of the enclosed *Gifts of Real Estate to Worthy Charity*, along with an example of the tax benefits.

I'm also sending you *Planned Giving*, which describes some gift plans that can yield a life income as well as the avoidance of income, capital gains, and estate taxes.

Thanks for the opportunity to share these gift options with you. I'll phone shortly to get your thoughts about this information and to answer any questions you might have.

With best wishes,

Mary Jones
Director of Development

Enclosures: *Gifts of Real Estate to Worthy Charity*; *Planned Giving*

Response to check-off block: **"Please send me information about the gift to Worthy Charity that saves taxes twice and can provide a life income."**

DATE

Dear_____:

Thanks for your inquiry regarding a gift to Worthy Charity that can save taxes twice and can provide a life income to you and your family.

When you make a gift of securities that have increased in value, not only do you enjoy a significant charitable deduction for the year in which you make the gift, but the capital gains tax can be delayed or avoided completely.

I'm sending you *Planned Giving*, which describes some gift plans that can yield a *life income* as well as *major tax savings*.

They are truly "win-win" scenarios, because you get major financial benefits along with the satisfaction of knowing you have helped Worthy Charity build for the future.

Those who have been thoughtful and generous enough to provide for Worthy Charity's future, either through a bequest or an irrevocable gift plan, will be eligible for membership in the Legacy Society. I look forward to welcoming you into that distinguished group.

I'll phone shortly to get your thoughts about this information and to answer any questions you might have.

Sincerely,

Mary Jones
Director of Development

Enclosure: *Planned Giving*

Response to check-off block: **"Please send me sample Worthy Charity bequest language."**

DATE

Dear_____:

Thanks for your inquiry concerning bequests to Worthy Charity.

I'm enclosing sample language for bequest provisions, which can save you time in discussing the matter with your attorney.

Those who have been thoughtful and generous enough to provide for Worthy Charity's future, either by means of a bequest or an irrevocable gift plan, will be eligible for membership in the Legacy Society. I look forward to welcoming you into that distinguished group.

I'm also sending you *Planned Giving*, which describes some gift plans that can yield a life income as well as major tax savings to the donor.

I'll phone shortly to get your views on this information and to address any questions you might have.

With best wishes,

Mary Jones
Director of Development

Enclosures: *Sample Bequest Provisions; Planned Giving*

Chapter 13
Managing the Gifts

If you have done all the right things to get your program started, eventually your organization will begin receiving gifts. Handling them in a sound manner is something that will endear you to the donors and contribute to the wise financial management of the charity. To manage gifts well, you must answer a number of questions:

- How do you evaluate proffered gifts to make certain they will be truly beneficial to the organization, and how do you diplomatically decline to accept those that are not?
- How should a donor be advised to send stock certificates so they arrive safely?
- Should your organization hold or sell the stock?
- How do you set up an investment policy for your endowment to ensure that the hard-won gifts are well invested?
- What are your organization's guidelines for dipping into the endowment funds?
- Who actually prepares timely and accurate life income checks and tax reports for the donors?
- How do you account for and give credit to donors for future gift commitments?
- How can the planned giving program mesh with the other fundraising efforts of the organization?

You will learn how to tackle these questions and other management issues in this chapter.

ESTABLISHING A SOUND GIFT ACCEPTANCE POLICY

Some gifts are not suitable for acceptance by a charitable organization. These include gifts that may result in

- a drain on the organization in the form of carrying costs and/or staff time

- liability for environmental cleanup
- risk of investment portfolio loss
- embarrassment in donor relations

To provide for consistency in the handling and evaluation of gifts and to avoid embarrassment when you must decline a gift, adopt a policy that can serve as a guide to members of the organization. It should describe the standards by which the various kinds of gifts are to be evaluated for acceptance and should allow for some flexibility in handling each case. (Refer to the sample gift acceptance policy in Appendix 13–A.)

DEVELOPING AN EFFECTIVE ENDOWMENT FUND POLICY

Do not be intimidated by the word *endowment*. It is the organization's nest egg, which, if wisely managed, will yield a dependable stream of operating funds through the years. What needs to be agreed upon are the rules that govern which gifts go into it, how you invest it, what you plan to take out of it and under what circumstances.

Acquisition

What gifts go into the endowment fund?
Suggestion: The proceeds of planned gifts and such major outright gifts as are clearly designated for endowment.

Investment

How should the endowment be invested?
Suggestion: 70 percent of the fund should be invested in stocks and 30 percent in fixed income investments. This strategy enables the organization to take advantage of the growth potential in a well-selected stock portfolio. With fixed income investments (bonds), the income stream is dependable, but the principal will lose purchasing value

each year by an amount equal to the annual inflation rate. Over the years, the growth in the market value of common stocks has exceeded the annual loss from inflation.

Spending

What portion of income and/or principal should be used for operating expenses and under what circumstances?

Suggestion: Make annual withdrawals for operating expenses. Instead of defining withdrawals in terms of interest from bonds and dividends from stocks, consider setting a withdrawal target based on a percentage of the total market value of the portfolio as revalued each year. Make it a conservative proportion, say 3 to 4 percent, so that the remaining nest egg has a chance to grow.

If the organization has a reasonable cash flow at present, consider deferring withdrawals until a future date to build up the fund. Then, withdrawals can be phased: only take out dividends and interest for a few years, then add the modest capital withdrawals of the "total return" method later.

ARRANGING FOR INVESTMENT ADVICE

Endowment Fund

When the nest egg fund is relatively small, consider putting it in a no-load mutual fund managed by one of the proven top-line companies until it gets to the size where searching out a bank or other professional investment manager would be economical.

Pooled Income Funds and Charitable Gift Annuities

Select a bank, investment manager, or community foundation that specializes in the management of such charitable funds (see Appendix B).

Charitable Remainder or Charitable Lead Trusts

Encourage the donor to select a bank or trustee in which he or she has confidence. Because of the heavy legal responsibilities associated involved with acting in a fiduciary capacity, it is not advisable for a smaller institution to act as trustee. (See Chapter 14 to learn about avoiding this and other potential pitfalls.)

PREPARING CHECKS AND TAX REPORTS FOR A LIFETIME

These technical and exacting donor-related tasks associated with pooled income funds and charitable gift annuities should be handled by a bank or other organization with a proven record of administering planned gifts.

Promptness and accuracy are critical to the maintenance of good donor relations. Caution is advised in the selection process, as some banks are just getting into the charitable fund field and may not have the depth of expertise you need. Ask for a bank's specific experience with the management of pooled income funds and charitable gift annuities, and personally ask the references about the bank's accuracy, promptness, and donor-friendliness.

Some charities have the income checks sent directly to them for forwarding to their donors. This gives them the opportunity to see the checks before they are sent out and to include notes and other cultivation materials in the envelopes. The downside of this practice is that it must be handled promptly to avoid delay in payment.

CREDITING OF GIFTS: REALITY AND PERCEPTION

Each gift is credited or recorded in the organization's formal accounting records, and it is also publicly credited to the donor as a way of recognizing the donor's generosity.

The accounting rules set by the Financial Accounting Standards Board (FASB) are quite rigid. On the other hand, the practices for crediting gifts for donor recognition purposes vary quite widely. Some ways of publicly crediting gifts can be misleading to potential donors and damaging to the organization's overall fundraising effort. If, for example, a charity reports bequest intentions and life income gifts at their face value and adds the dollars to their gift totals, potential donors may conclude that the organization has already received the money. They could easily be discouraged from making gifts as a result, because it would appear their funds were not needed. Moreover, in the event of a capital campaign, such illusory dollars are simply not available to build that new wing on the hospital.

To avoid the possibility of misperception, consider reporting planned gifts in a separate category clearly labeled as *commitments for future gifts*. Consider running a "two-bucket" campaign: one bucket for cash and the other for such commitments.

> *Consider running a "two-bucket" campaign: one bucket for cash and the other for future commitments.*

SUBSTANTIATING GIFTS FOR THE DONOR'S TAX RECORDS

In 1993, the IRS increased the documentation required to claim certain charitable deductions. If a donor's gift is in excess of $250, in addition to the usual canceled check, the donor must produce a receipt from the charity documenting the

- nature of the payment
- amount of the payment
- value of goods or services (if any) received by the donor in return

Generally, the amount of the charitable deduction would be the initial amount of the gift less the value of the goods or services received. In the case of a life income gift such as a pooled income fund contribution, the deduction would be the face amount of the gift received less the present value of the income stream that the donor will get in return.

Example

Assume that Mrs. Smith, aged 65, makes a $10,000 gift for a charitable gift annuity of 7 percent and that a discount rate of 7.4 percent is in effect at the time of the gift. Her charitable deduction would be $10,000.00 less $6,272 (the present value of the $700 annual income stream for 19.9 years—the life expectancy of a 65-year-old individual in the actuarial tables used by the IRS—expressed as "present value" by discounting at 7.4%), or $3,728. The charity would indicate in their receipt to Mrs. Smith that the value of the goods or services that she received in exchange for her gift is $6,272 and that the "gift value" for charitable deduction purposes is $3,728.

Encouraging note: The highly complex calculations to produce this example can be accomplished with a few keystrokes when using planned giving computer software. Please refer to Appendix B for a list of software vendors.

Appendix 13–A
Sample Gift Acceptance Policy

Cash

- Checks should be made payable to Worthy Charity rather than to an individual who represents Worthy Charity.

Publicly Traded Securities

- Readily marketable securities, such as those traded on a stock exchange, can be accepted by Worthy Charity.
- Gift securities are to be sold immediately. Avoid the temptation to play the market. For gift crediting and accounting purposes, the value of the securities is the average of the high and low on the date of the gift.

Closely Held Securities

- Non–publicly traded securities may be accepted after consultation with the Treasurer's Office and/or Office of the General Counsel. The fair market value of the securities must be determined by a "qualified" appraiser.
- Prior to acceptance, Worthy Charity should explore methods of immediate liquidation of the securities through redemption or sale.
- No commitment for repurchase or sale of closely held securities should be made prior to completion of the gift of the securities, as the transaction might be viewed by the IRS as a sale rather than a gift, with adverse tax consequences for the donor.

Real Estate

- Gifts of real estate should be reviewed by the Gift Acceptance Committee before acceptance.

- The donor should be responsible for obtaining and paying for an appraisal of the fair market value and an environmental audit of the property.
- Prior to presentation to the Gift Acceptance Committee, a member of the staff must conduct a visual inspection of the property. If the property is located in a geographically isolated area, a local real estate broker can substitute for a member of the staff in conducting the visual inspection.
- Property that is encumbered by a mortgage should not be accepted.

Life Insurance

- Worthy Charity should accept a life insurance policy as a gift only when it is named as the owner and beneficiary of the policy.

Tangible Personal Property

- Gifts of tangible personal property to Worthy Charity should have a use related to the charity's tax-exempt purpose.
- Gifts of jewelry, artwork, collections, equipment, and software may be accepted after approval by the Gift Acceptance Committee.
- Such gifts of tangible personal property defined above shall be used by or sold for the benefit of Worthy Charity.
- Worthy Charity must follow all IRS requirements in connection with disposing of gifts of tangible personal property and filing of appropriate tax reporting forms.

Charitable Gift Annuities

- Worthy Charity will pay annuity rates as currently suggested by the American Council on Gift Annuities.

- There shall be no more than two beneficiaries for a charitable gift annuity.
- The minimum gift accepted to establish a charitable gift annuity is $10,000.
- No income beneficiary for a charitable gift annuity shall be younger than 50 years of age.

Deferred Gift Annuities

- There will be no more than two beneficiaries for a deferred gift annuity.
- The minimum gift accepted to establish a deferred gift annuity is $10,000.
- No income beneficiary for a deferred gift annuity shall be younger than 40 years of age.

Pooled Income Funds

- Administrative fees shall be paid from the income earned on the pooled income fund.

- No income beneficiary in the fund shall be younger than 55 years of age.
- No more than two income beneficiaries may be named.
- The minimum initial contribution to the fund shall be $10,000. Additional gifts may be added for amounts beginning at $1,000.

Charitable Trusts

- Worthy Charity does not act as trustee. The administration of these trusts should be performed by a bank trust department or other trustee selected by the donor.

Bequests

- Worthy Charity should refuse to accept (disclaim) any bequest that might prove to be more of a cost than a benefit.

Chapter 14
Avoiding Pitfalls

There are a number of traps for the unwary in planned giving. Some can sap your staff resources and leave you with nothing to show for your efforts, some can enmesh your organization in conflicts of interest, and still others may cause your organization to needlessly delay starting a planned giving program. In this chapter you will learn to recognize these problems and take timely steps to avoid them. See Appendix 14–A for a list of model standards of practice for charitable gift planners. These standards, if followed, will also help you skirt various pitfalls.

"ALL I NEED IS YOUR MAILING LIST"

Situation

Your planned giving program is getting underway and you get a call from someone who is a volunteer for Worthy Charity and also an insurance professional. He has an idea to help you develop donors for the new program: conduct an estate planning seminar for your best prospects. He offers to run the meeting, as he "has had considerable experience with estate planning matters." To get the ball rolling, he asks for your list of major donors so that he can help you select the invitees for the seminar. He carries influence with several of your board members. Should you accept his offer?

Discussion

Once the word gets around that your organization is promoting a planned giving program, you may receive tempting offers of assistance from charming, articulate, and gregarious insurance salespeople and stockbrokers. Some may be board members or volunteers. Caution is in order, as their primary agenda may be to increase their client base rather than assist you in developing planned gifts.

Example

Recently, a university medical center agreed to put on an estate planning seminar as a service for its major donor prospects. They arranged a well-attended meeting conducted by an advisory board member who was an insurance professional. He subsequently vigorously hounded the seminar attendees—to sell insurance! The medical center lost support from a considerable number of the participants, who felt that their time and goodwill had been abused.

> Tip: *If you are staging an estate planning seminar, enlist the aid of a well-regarded local trust and estate attorney and be very protective of your organization's mailing list.*

WRITE THE WILL AND PAY THE PIPER

Situation

You are discussing bequest provisions with a wealthy potential donor who tells you that she wants to include Worthy Charity in her estate plans. As she has no attorney, she asks you to have the charity draft her will. You feel that it could probably result in a major bequest to Worthy Charity. Should you arrange it?

Discussion

For a charity to draft a donor's will represents a conflict of interest. It makes the organization vulnerable to possible accusations by disgruntled heirs that undue influence was exerted on the donor.

> Tip: *If the donor has no attorney, give her a list of three or four known to be dependable. The names should be in alphabetical order.*

"WE HAVEN'T GOT THE STAFF TO MAKE VISITS"

Situation

The trustees of Worthy Charity have experience in the techniques of major gift development. Although they know that planned giving could tap an important source of support for Worthy Charity, they have been putting off considering whether to start a planned giving program. "If planned gifts are anything like outright gifts, we simply don't have the staff to make it happen."

Discussion

Personal meetings, so important and effective in developing major outright cash gifts, are not always necessary in planned giving. Indeed, many individuals are not comfortable talking about their assets, estate plans, hopes, fears, and desires in a face-to-face discussion with a stranger in their office or living room. Once they have learned about the options through literature that they have requested, studied, and discussed with their advisors, they will usually freely discuss them over the telephone.

Later, when the planned giving program matures, the organization will have the staff and budget to support person-to-person visits, which can be an extremely important element of stewardship and a means of moving gifts to fruition.

Example
The planned giving officer of a large university received a call from a lady in a Midwestern city. "Now's the time!" she said. When the mystified planned giving officer asked her to explain, she reminded him that two years previously she had checked off a block on a change of address form requesting further information about a life income gift to the university. She explained that she had recently retrieved the letter and booklet from her desk, had discussed the planned gift with her attorney, and had decided to proceed. She was sending $75,000 worth of stock to set up a pooled income fund that would eventually be the basis of a scholarship program to be named in memory of her deceased husband. The gift planning officer had never met this donor, nor many of the others who established planned gifts at the university.

Do not let the fact that your organization lacks sufficient staff for personal visits stand in the way of your starting a planned giving program. If potential donors are sold on your charity and its mission, once they have learned that they can help themselves and, at the same time, contribute more to your organization than they ever thought possible, you can often arrange gifts from them over the telephone without needing to make personal visits.

> **Tip:** *You can make visits by telephone!*

GIFTS THAT ARE TOO EXPENSIVE

Situation

A donor proposes to give Worthy Charity a residential rental property that he has had trouble selling. It cannot be used for your charitable purposes, is encumbered by a mortgage, is occupied by tenants, and is in need of substantial repairs to make it marketable.

Discussion

Worthy Charity would be required to pay the taxes, mortgage, insurance, and upkeep of the property, including the repairs to make it salable. Staff time would be required to administer the rents, or an agent would have to be retained, adding further expense. By the time the property is sold, the value of the gift would have been seriously eroded, along with Worthy Charity's already thinly stretched resources.

> **Tip:** *Diplomatically decline to accept a gift whose cost, either in money or in staff time, may be more than its value to the charity.*

"HERE'S THE STOCK . . . DON'T SELL IT FOR FIVE YEARS!"

Situation

The planned giving officer of Worthy Charity is discussing a potential gift of XYZ.com stock with Henry, a long-time volunteer and supporter of Worthy's mission. "This stock has gone up dramatically, and will be even more valuable to Worthy if you hold onto it for five years."

Discussion

Worthy Charity's gift acceptance policy is to immediately sell gifted stock to realize its value at the time rather than to "play the market." The planned giving officer should tell the donor that there is a risk of loss of the charitable deduction if a donor does not relinquish control over the asset given, diplomatically suggesting that the donor is in the best position to follow this stock and perhaps donate its increased value later. Hopefully, there may be other stock that Henry could consider donating at this time.

> Tip: *Avoid accepting a gift with strings attached that could put the charity at risk of loss and jeopardize the donor's charitable deduction.*

GIFTS THAT NEED AN ENVIRONMENTAL CLEANUP

Situation

Worthy Charity accepted the generous outright gift of a sizable tract of land close to the city. It had formerly been one of the most successful manufacturing plants in the area but had become outdated. As it was situated directly in the path of urban growth, the charity thought the land could be a valuable source of endowment. Hopes were dashed, however, when an environmental inspection showed severe and pervasive contamination that threatened the local water supply. Worthy Charity was sued for the cleanup cost, which far exceeded the assets of the organization.

Discussion

The current environmental protection laws make the owner of contaminated property responsible for the cost of the removal of the hazardous condition. The charity needed to protect itself by asking the right questions before accepting the gift.

> Tip: *Before accepting a real estate gift, require the owner to obtain and pay for an appropriate environmental inspection and make certain that the audit shows no environmental problems.*

THE FANTASTIC RETURN SEEKER

Situation

Worthy Charity receives a phone call from an individual who says she is representing a donor who shall remain nameless for the present. Her client, aged 70, has been offered an 8.5-percent return on a charitable gift annuity by another charity. "A $350,000 gift is yours if you can match that rate," as her client "is a great admirer of the good works of your charity." You check the table of rates suggested by the American Council on Gift Annuities and find that 6.9 percent is the maximum rate recommended for an annuitant at age 70. Should you encourage Worthy Charity to offer the extra incentive to get the gift?

Discussion

You may get such a call from a financial planner who is "shopping the market" for the charity offering the best annuity payment for his or her client. The suggested rates published by the American Council on Gift Annuities are based on conservative assumptions combined with careful analysis of actuarial factors and current market interest rates. As a result, the rates are financially sound for a charitable organization to offer. It is doubtful that a donor who really cares about your organization would insist upon a practice that would put it at financial risk.

> Tip: *Stick to the annuity payment rates suggested by the American Council on Gift Annuities. They are conservatively developed and the vast majority of American charities use them as maximums.*

"WE'RE TOO NEW TO HAVE A PLANNED GIVING PROGRAM"

Situation

Worthy Charity, a five-year-old organization, has been postponing the start of a planned giving program because its board feels the charity has not had enough of a track record to inspire a donor to make a gift that might not come to fruition for many years.

Discussion

In this case, the trustees of Worthy Charity are passing up the opportunity to build the pipeline of future support that can ensure the future of the organization.

> Tip: *If the question of the future viability of the organization is raised by a potential planned giving donor, explain that his or her legal advisor can add language to a will or charitable trust to the effect that the trustee or executor can be empowered to direct the gifted assets to another charitable organization if yours is not operating at the time of transfer.*

GIFT ANNUITIES AREN'T FOR EVERYONE

Situation

You are establishing a planned giving program for Worthy Charity, whose mission is to raise funds for medical research. As all of the donations (with the exception of a small part reserved for overhead) are used for its programs, Worthy Charity has not accumulated reserve funds. When evaluating the broad range of planned gifts to offer, you identify the charitable gift annuity option as an attractive one, particularly for older donors, because of the higher payment rates. Should gift annuities be part of your "starting lineup"?

Discussion

The payment of income (the annuity) for life is the contractual obligation of the charity that undertakes to offer charitable gift annuities. The payments are backed by all the assets of the organization. Several states require periodic reports highlighting the assets used to back charitable gift annuities. As Worthy Charity has yet to build an endowment reserve, it would be unwise to put the medical research programs at risk for the payment of annuities.

> Tip: *Start your planned giving program with gift options appropriate for your organization. When the endowment fund has been built up through whichever gift options you are offering, then consider adding the attractive charitable gift annuity to your offerings. Check with your local community foundation, as it may offer its charitable gift annuity structure to nonprofit organizations in your area.*

ACTING AS TRUSTEE

Situation

As a result of your thoughtful cultivation, a prospective donor tells you that, although she likes the benefits of establishing a $250,000 charitable remainder unitrust, she balks at the idea of paying the legal fees to set up the trust and the trustee fees for administering it. She has heard that some charities will act as trustee without these fees and asks you if Worthy Charity will act in this capacity for her.

Discussion

Some organizations are large enough to support their own asset management organizations and offer fee concessions. The legal restrictions for acting in a position of trust (fiduciary capacity) are exacting, and the staff costs are considerable. Your organization could act in a trustee role, with a bank as co-trustee, but the fees would not go away. If your charity decides to foot these bills, they will act as a cash drain until the assets are finally transferred, perhaps many years later.

You could offer the donor the pooled income fund, as it is a trust already established by your organization and the donor's funds could be placed into it. There would be no additional legal or trustee fees payable by the donor. An "off the shelf" plan, the pooled income fund may not offer quite the flexibility of an individually designed unitrust, but it puts your organization into contention for the gift and may very well meet the needs of your donor.

> Tip: *Keep it simple at the start of your planned giving program! You can add bells and whistles as your organization gains size and experience.*

"PLANNED GIVING IS TOMORROW. WE NEED THE MONEY NOW."

Situation

A major grant has not been renewed, and at the next meeting of the board of trustees someone brings up the idea of getting a planned giving program started. Some trustees argue that the need for outright funds is so pressing that the charity's personnel and resources are stretched too thin to handle both outright and planned giving. The majority agree with them.

Discussion

The board's focus on outright cash support is quite understandable under the circumstances. However, one of the basic responsibilities of a trustee is to plan for the future stability of the organization as well as for its current programs. To build a pipeline of future money through planned giving is to help ensure the continuation of the charity by reducing its dependence on the fluctuations in annual contributions and the vagaries of government, foundation, and corporate grant giving.

> Tip: *Consider starting a planned giving program in an economical manner by outsourcing the needed expertise to a specialist on an hourly or retainer basis. The organization can then match its staff investment to the increase in gift income as it occurs.*

CONCLUSION

In Part I, the broad background of fundraising has been described and the special role that planned giving plays in attracting major gifts to charitable organizations has been highlighted. Part II has given you a step-by-step method of starting a successful planned giving program from scratch. We have provided a realistic plan for you to launch a cost-effective and growth-oriented program for your organization. For those who are considering embarking upon a gift planning career, we have shared a number of the ingredients for success in this rewarding field. Our experience has been one of great personal satisfaction in helping donors enjoy the broad benefits from charitable giving, and at the same time providing life-sustaining financial support for the organization's mission. We wish the best of success to you and your organizations.

Appendix 14–A

Model Standards of Practice for the Charitable Gift Planner

PREAMBLE

The purpose of this statement is to encourage responsible charitable gift planning by urging the adoption of the following Standards of Practice by all who work in the charitable gift planning process, including charitable institutions and their gift planning officers, independent fundraising consultants, attorneys, accountants, financial planners, and life insurance agents, collectively referred to hereafter as "Gift Planners."

This statement recognizes that the solicitation, planning, and administration of a charitable gift is a complex process involving philanthropic, personal, financial, and tax considerations, and as such often involves professionals from various disciplines whose goals should include working together to structure a gift that achieves a fair and proper balance between the interests of the donor and the purposes of the charitable institution.

I. Primacy of Philanthropic Motivation

The principal basis for making a charitable gift should be a desire on the part of the donor to support the work of charitable institutions.

II. Explanation of Tax Implications

Congress has provided tax incentives for charitable giving, and the emphasis in this statement on philanthropic motivation in no way minimizes the necessity and appropriateness of a full and accurate explanation by the Gift Planner of those incentives and their implications.

III. Full Disclosure

It is essential to the gift planning process that the role and relationships of all parties involved, including how and by whom each is compensated, be fully disclosed to the donor. A Gift Planner shall not act or purport to act as a representative of any charity without the express knowledge and approval of the charity, and shall not, while employed by the charity, act or purport to act as a representative of the donor, without the express consent of both the charity and the donor.

IV. Compensation

Compensation paid to Gift Planners shall be reasonable and proportionate to the services provided. Payments of finders fees, commissions, or other fees by a donee organization to an independent Gift Planner as a condition for the delivery of a gift are never appropriate. Such payments lead to abusive practices and may violate certain state and federal regulations. Likewise, commission-based compensation for Gift Planners who are employed by a charitable institution is never appropriate.

V. Competence and Professionalism

The Gift Planner should strive to achieve and maintain a high degree of competence in his or her chosen area, and shall advise donors only in areas in which he or she is professionally qualified. It is a hallmark of professionalism for Gift Planners that they realize when they have reached the limits of their knowledge and expertise, and as a result, should include other professionals in the process. Such relationships should be characterized by courtesy, tact, and mutual respect.

VI. Consultation with Independent Advisers

A Gift Planner acting on behalf of a charity shall in all cases strongly encourage the donor to discuss the proposed gift with competent independent legal and tax advisers of the donor's choice.

VII. Consultation with Charities

Although Gift Planners frequently and properly counsel donors concerning specific charitable gifts without the prior knowledge or approval of the donee organization, the Gift Planner, in order to ensure that the gift will accomplish the donor's objectives, should encourage the donor, early in the gift planning process, to discuss the proposed gift with the charity to whom the gift is to be made. In cases where the donor desires anonymity, the Gift Planner shall endeavor, on behalf of the undisclosed donor, to obtain the charity's input in the gift planning process.

VIII. Explanation of Gift

The Gift Planner shall make every effort, insofar as possible, to ensure that the donor receives a full and ac-

curate explanation of all aspects of the proposed charitable gift.

IX. Full Compliance

A Gift Planner shall fully comply with and shall encourage other parties in the gift planning process to fully comply with both the letter and spirit of all applicable federal and state laws and regulations.

X. Public Trust

Gift Planners shall, in all dealings with donors, institutions, and other professionals, act with fairness, honesty, integrity, and openness. Except for compensation received for services, the terms of which have been disclosed to the donor, they shall have no vested interest that could result in personal gain.

Appendix A
Glossary of Planned Giving Terms

accountability. The responsibility of an institution to provide a full public accounting of financial affairs.

accumulated deficiencies. These occur during the administration of a charitable remainder unitrust (net income plus makeup) when the income actually earned by the trust is less than the percentage of the net fair market value of the trust assets. These deficiencies can be made up in future years when the trust actually earns more than the percentage of the fair market value of the trust assets.

actuarial tables. Actuarial, life expectancy, and other tables issued by the U.S. Treasury Department for use in calculating tax deductions for gifts made through trusts and by contract.

adjusted gross income. Amount of income remaining after the expenses of earning that income have been deducted.

administrator. The personal representative appointed by the probate court to settle the estate of a person who dies without a will.

annual fund drive. The annual program for soliciting current gifts for a charity.

annuitant. The person receiving annual or more frequent payments from a gift annuity.

annuity payments. The annual or more frequent payment of principal and interest to an annuitant or to his or her beneficiary.

annuity trust. *See* **charitable remainder annuity trust.**

appreciated property. Property with a value greater than the cost basis.

assignment form. Separate from a certificate, this form is used in transferring ownership of securities from one party to another. The stock certificate does not have to be signed when this form is used. Also called a *stock power*.

bargain sale arrangement. A method whereby a person can sell appreciated property to a charity at a lower price than the fair market value, with the charity realizing the difference as a gift.

beneficiary. One named in a will, trust, or other legal document to receive an interest in the assets.

bequest. A gift made by will.

bequest society. A group organized by a charity to recognize and honor those who have committed to including the charity in their estate plans. *See* **legacy society.**

blue sky laws. State laws regulating securities within that particular state.

board of trustees. The policy-making body of a not-for-profit institution.

cash surrender value. The amount of money received by a policyholder from a life insurance company when the holder surrenders a policy for cash prior to the maturity date.

charitable estate planning. Estate planning that includes a provision for a charitable institution to receive a portion of the person's assets

charitable gift annuity. *See* **gift annuity agreement.**

charitable income tax deduction. The amount a donor can deduct from a federal income tax return for a gift to a qualified charity.

charitable income trust. *See* **reversionary living trust.**

charitable lead trust. A trust that is irrevocable for a term of years, with the income being paid to the charity during this term. There is a provision for the property to revert back to the trustor or heirs at the end of the term.

charitable remainder annuity trust. A trust created by the Tax Reform Act of 1969. It provides for a donor to transfer property to a trustee subject to the donor's right to receive a fixed percentage of the initial fair market value of the property for as long as he or she lives. Whatever remains in the trust at the donor's death becomes the property of the beneficiary institution.

charitable remainder interest. The amount expected to be received by a charity from a charitable remainder trust at the death of the trustor.

charitable remainder unitrust. A trust created by the Tax Reform Act of 1969. It is similar to the charitable remainder annuity trust in many ways, except that the income is a percentage of the fair market value of the property determined annually.

CLT. *See* **charitable lead trust.**

codicil. An addition or amendment to a person's will.

commemorative gift. A gift made in remembrance of one or more individuals.

common disaster. A situation in which husband and wife die under circumstances where it is impossible to determine who died first.

corpus. The amount of principal in a trust.

cost basis. The original cost of property plus improvements and other expenses paid by the owner during the period of ownership.

CRAT. *See* **charitable remainder annuity trust.**

CRUT. *See* **charitable remainder unitrust.**

database. Usually refers to a computer-based file with information on donors or prospects.

DCGA. *See* **deferred payment gift annuity.**

death benefit. Proceeds of a life insurance policy paid to a beneficiary of the policy at the death of the policyholder.

deferred gift. A gift that is made now whereby the charitable organization does not benefit until some time in the future according to conditions stated in a contract.

deferred payment gift annuity. A gift annuity agreement issued by a qualified charity providing for payments to the beneficiary to commence at a future date and to continue for life.

direct mail fundraising. A method of soliciting gifts for a charity via mail.

discount rate. The interest rate used to convert the payments from a life income gift, such as a charitable remainder trust, into its present value, which is then deducted from the market value of the asset gifted, to arrive at the charitable deduction for the gift.

director of development. The officer of a charity who has responsibility for the institution's total fund development program.

dividends. The amount of money paid each year on a life insurance policy or share of stock to the policyholder or the shareholder.

donor advised fund. A charitable fund maintained within a public charity structured to enable a person to make a donation of cash or appreciated stock to a fund bearing his or her name, enjoy an immediate charitable deduction and later request that the fund pay out gifts to the charities of their choice.

donor classification. The separation of a donor list into groups, with divisions determined by the previous yearly amount of gifts made by each donor.

donor profile. A composite profile of an institution's donors or classes of donors.

donor prospect. A person believed to be a potential donor to a charity.

endowment. A pool of property held by a charity and invested to provide an annual income for the institution.

estate planning. Planning for the management of all of an individual's assets for the benefit of this person and his or her heirs.

ex-donor file. Names of donors who have ceased giving to an institution.

executor. The personal representative (male) named in a will to settle the testator's estate.

executrix. The personal representative (female) named in a will to settle the testator's estate.

fair market value. Amount of money a willing buyer will pay a willing seller for property.

FASB 116, 117. Rules dealing with the treatment that a nonprofit organization must use in its accounting for a life income gift, such as a charitable remainder trust.

feasibility study. A careful investigation of an institution's operation and structure to determine whether or not the institution should launch new programs, such as a planned giving program.

federal estate tax. The tax imposed on the transfer of property to others at death, payable from the corpus of the estate.

federal gift tax. The tax imposed on the transfer of property during the lifetime of the donor. This tax is paid by the donor.

federal income tax. The tax on an individual's income.

flip. An event, which must be beyond the control of the donor, that changes a net income unitrust to a straight unitrust.

FLIPCRUT. A charitable remainder unitrust with a "flip" provision.

FLIP NIMCRUT. A net income charitable remainder unitrust with a "flip" provision.

Form 990 Return of Organization Exempt from Income Tax. An IRS-required form on which a nonprofit organization must report its activities.

401(k). *See* **qualified retirement plan.**

five-year carry-forward rule. A federal income tax provision that permits a donor to carry over into the five succeeding tax years any amount of a gift that exceeds the deductible amount in the year the gift is made.

501(c)(3). A not-for-profit organization, contributions to which are deductible for federal income tax purposes.

503(b). *See* **qualified retirement plan.**

gift annuity agreement. An agreement in which a donor makes a gift to a charity that in turn provides stipulated annual payments for life to one or two persons.

grantor. The creator of a trust or other legal instrument.

guardian. A person appointed or approved by the court to look after the personal interests of another person.

income only withdrawals. Restricting periodic withdrawals from an endowment fund to the dividends and interest earned from the investments.

in perpetuity. To be held in the same form forever.

insurance trust. A trust consisting of life insurance policies or proceeds.

intestate. Dying without a will.

IRA. Individual retirement account. *See* **qualified retirement plan.**

irrevocable living trust. A trust that cannot be revoked by the trustor.

Keogh. *See* **qualified retirement plan.**

laws of descent and distribution. State laws controlling distribution of property when a person dies without a will.

lead trust. *See* **charitable lead trust.**

legacy. Distribution of property by a will.

legacy society. A group organized by a charity to recognize and honor those who have committed to including the charity in their estate plans, either by a bequest or other planned gift.

life estate agreement. An agreement between a donor and a charity in which the donor deeds a personal residence or farm to a charity but reserves the right to use or reside on the property for life. Can also include personal vacation property. Also called a **retained life estate.**

life expectancy. The actuarial estimate of the number of years a person will live from any given age.

life income trust. A plan whereby gift assets are placed in a trust for the lifetime(s) of one or more income beneficiaries.

liquidity. Cash or readily marketable investments available to pay the cost of estate settlement.

long-term capital gains. The capital appreciation realized from the sale of property (stocks, bonds, land, etc.) that the seller has owned more than 12 months.

marketing plan. A comprehensive plan used in obtaining gift income from donors that has the approval of the board of trustees and is committed to writing.

matured bequest. A bequest to a charity is considered "matured" when the gift is actually received by the charity.

matured charitable remainder trust. A charitable remainder trust is matured when trust assets are finally delivered to the charitable institution after the death of the last income beneficiary.

memorial gift. A gift to a charity in memory of a deceased person.

net income plus makeup unitrust. Same as a net income unitrust, except for the provision that the payments may exceed the stated percentage up to but not exceeding the amount required to make up any accumulated deficiencies for prior years, that is, years in which the trust earned less than the stated percentage. *See also* **charitable remainder unitrust, net income unitrust,** and **accumulated deficiencies.**

net income unitrust. A variation of the charitable remainder unitrust that provides that the trustee must pay the donor or other designated beneficiaries an amount equal to a fixed percentage of the net fair market value of the trust assets (not to be less than 5 percent), determined annually, or the actual income earned, whichever is less.

NIMCRUT. *See* **net income plus makeup unitrust.**

ordinary income property. Property that produces income taxed at the owner's regular income tax rate.

owner and beneficiary. The charitable institution that has control and possession of a life insurance policy during the life of an insured person. The institution is designated to become the irrevocable charitable beneficiary at the individual's death.

phonathon. A telephone campaign soliciting gifts.

PIF. *See* **pooled income fund.**

planned giving. The making of charitable gifts other than outright cash. Involves considering the effect of the gift on the donor's estate.

planned giving consultant. A person who consults with the management of an institution on better ways to secure more and larger planned gifts.

pledges. An amount of money a person promises to give over an extended period of time.

pooled income fund. A trust funded by a number of donors, each retaining an income for life. Each donor is paid a pro rata share of the trust earnings. Each donor's portion of the principal becomes the property of the charity at the death of the donor.

powers of appointment. Contractual power given by one person to another to make legal decisions on behalf of the person granting such powers. Also referred to as *powers of attorney.*

primary beneficiary. The first person named to receive the proceeds of a will.

private foundation. A foundation created by a person during life or at death through a will for the purpose of receiving assets to be distributed to public charities in the future.

probate. The "proving" of a will. When a person dies, the will is taken to the probate court to prove that the will is indeed that person's last will and testament.

prospect file. The names of people who are motivated to give to a charity, have the money or property to give,

and have confidence in the charity. Usually part of a charity's database.

qualified retirement plan. A retirement plan that qualifies for special tax treatment. Examples include IRAs, Keoghs, 401(k)s, and 503(b)s.

realized capital gain. The amount of money received from the sale of property in excess of the original amount paid for the property.

remainder. The amount remaining in a trust after income payments have ended.

remainderman. The person or institution receiving the assets of a trust upon the death of the trustor.

residuary clause. A clause in the will that bequeaths or devises property, which is not specifically bequeathed or devised earlier in the will.

residue. Property left for the final beneficiaries named in a will after all other bequests have been paid.

response device. A coupon or card included in an advertisement or a direct mail mailing package for the convenience of the recipient in requesting more information or indicating that a gift is being made to the charity. Also called *response mechanism.*

retained life estate. The gift of one's home or farm but with retention of the right of the donor and spouse to live there for life.

retained life income plans. Planned gifts that provide a gift to a charity but retain for the donor or others the right to the income earned on the assets for life.

revenue ruling. A statement defining the IRS's position regarding certain tax questions.

reversionary living trust. A trust that is irrevocable for a term of years, with the income being paid to the charity during this term. There is a provision for the property to revert back to the trustor at the end of the term. *See* **charitable lead trust.**

revocable living trust. A trust that may be revoked at any time by the trustor (with a reasonable advance warning of the intention to revoke the trust).

rights of survivorship. The ownership rights held by an individual whose partner in ownership of property is no longer living.

RLE. *See* **retained life estate.**

secondary beneficiary. Person named in a life insurance policy to receive the proceeds should the primary beneficiary predecease him or her. (May also refer to an institution.)

segregated portfolio. A separate investment account covering the assets of a trust or special investment fund.

settlement costs. The costs of settling an estate.

short-term charitable trust. *See* **reversionary living trust.**

special needs trust. A category of trust in common usage as a device for protecting individuals under a disability. Such a trust is an irrevocable trust giving the trustee discretion to apply income and principal for the benefit of the disabled individual.

state inheritance tax. A tax on a person's right to receive property at the death of another person. The tax is paid to the state of residence of the decedent or to the state where any real property transferred is located.

straight unitrust. A separate trust from which a fixed percentage of the net fair market value of the trust assets, as determined annually, must be paid to a designated beneficiary or beneficiaries for life or a number of years not to exceed 20.

supporting organization. A charitable fund established within one or more public charities with the express purpose of benefiting one or more of the favorite charities of the founder, identified when the foundation is started.

survivorship gift annuity. A gift annuity that provides income payments to a second beneficiary surviving the first beneficiary. The payments are made to both parties while they are both alive, then to the surviving beneficiary for the remainder of his or her life.

suspect file. The names of people who have requested information on ways to make planned gifts to a charity.

target marketing. The directing of a marketing plan to a select group of people possessing certain similar characteristics that increase the probability of their responding to the plan.

tax-exempt bonds. Bonds issued by a municipality, the income from which is usually exempt from federal tax.

tax-exempt status. Refers to the fact that a not-for-profit corporation is exempted from paying taxes because of its charitable activities.

telethon. A television campaign for gifts.

term life. A life insurance policy that is purchased for a term of years. If the person dies during this term, the beneficiary receives the face amount of the policy. The policy expires at the end of the stated number of years.

testamentary gifts. Gifts made through a will.

testamentary trust. A trust created by a provision in a person's will.

testator. The person making a will.

tier structure. Represents the way in which an income beneficiary must report for tax purposes the income generated by a charitable remainder annuity trust or unitrust. It gives the order in which the income is reported as earned by the trust. The tier is as follows: (1) ordinary income, (2) capital gains, (3) tax-exempt or "other" income, and (4) return of principal.

tithes. The giving of 10 percent of one's income to a charitable institution. Tithing is a practice found in the Bible.

total return withdrawals. The concept of making periodic withdrawals from an endowment fund based on income generated by the assets plus capital gains.

treasury regulations. The regulations issued by the U.S. Treasury Department that interpret code sections passed by Congress.

treasury tables. Actuarial, life expectancy, and other tables issued by the U.S. Treasury Department for use in calculating tax deductions for gifts made through trusts and by contract.

trust. An arrangement whereby property is held by an individual or institution for the benefit of others.

trustee. The person or institution legally responsible for carrying out the terms of the trust.

trust instrument. The legal document that provides operating instructions for a trustee in carrying out the terms of a trust.

trust officer. The person in a trust company who is responsible for the administration of property of which the trust company is trustee.

trustor. The person creating a trust. Also called *grantor.*

trust principal. The assets of a trust.

twenty-percent institution. A person may give and deduct up to 20 percent of his or her adjusted gross income to a private foundation, which is referred to as a 20-percent institution.

unitrust. *See* **charitable remainder unitrust.**

unrealized capital gain. The difference between the current fair market value of some property and the original cost basis. The gain is not realized until the property is sold.

unrelated business income rules. Rules that govern the taxability of income generated from a trade or business activity unrelated to the primary purpose for which the charity gained its tax-exempt status.

wealth replacement. A gift plan in which a life insurance policy is acquired and placed into an insurance trust to replace assets for the donor's heirs.

will. A legal instrument disposing of a person's property at the time of his or her death.

wills clinic. A presentation on wills to a group of people interested in the subject of wills.

wills emphasis program. An annual direct mail solicitation emphasizing the use of wills in making charitable gifts.

Appendix B
Resources

BOOKS

Arthur Andersen & Co. 1999. *Tax economics of charitable giving.* 13th ed. Chicago: Arthur Andersen & Co., Tel. no. 800-872-2454, Web site: www.arthurandersen.com. Technical resource for charitable giving transactions.

Ashton, D. Forthcoming. *The complete guide to planned giving: Everything you need to know to compete successfully for major gifts.* 3rd ed. This edition, a major revision, is planned for release in 2001. For more information, contact the author at 617-472-9316.

Giving USA. AAFRC Trust for Philanthropy, 25 W. 43rd Street, New York, NY 10036. Updated annually. Provides statistical information and trends in philanthropy.

Howe, F. 1991. *The board member's guide to fund raising: What every trustee needs to know about raising money.* San Francisco: Jossey-Bass.

Jordan, R., and K. Quynn. 2000. *Planned giving: Management, marketing, and law.* 2d ed. New York: Wiley.

CONSULTANTS

Barrett Planned Giving, Inc., Richard D. Barrett, President, 2000 L Street, N.W., Suite 200, Washington, DC 20036, Tel. nos. 800-332-9132 and 202-416-1667, e-mail: BarrettPln@cs.com, Web site: www.BarrettPlannedGiving.com. Provides marketing, coaching, and telephone donor consulting services.

Estes Associates, Ellen G. Estes, L.L.B, planned giving consultant, 41 Spoke Drive, Woodbridge, CT 06525, Tel. no. 203-393-3159, e-mail: ellen.estes@juno.com. Provides full range of planned giving consulting services.

Gift Planning Associates, Richard Lamport, Principal, 223 Clipper Street, San Francisco, CA 94114, Tel. no. 415-970-2380, Fax: 415-970-2383, e-mail: Giftplanner1@cs.com. Provides full range of planned giving consulting services.

John Brown, Limited, Inc., John J. Brown, President, 46 Grove Street, P.O. Box 296, Peterborough, NH 03458-0296. Tel. no. 603-924-3834, e-mail: jblnh@aol.com, Web site: jblnh.com. Provides full range of planned giving consulting services.

Planned Giving Resources, James B. Potter, P.O. Box 8300, Alexandria, VA 22306, Tel. no. 703-799-8300, Web site: www.pgresources.com. Telephone consulting in the area of planned giving. Specializing in charitable gift annuities.

Planned Giving Services, Frank Minton, President, 3147 Fairview Avenue East, Suite 200, Seattle, WA 98102, Tel. no. 206-329-8144, e-mail: Plangiv@aol.com, Web site: www.plannedgivingservices.com. Offers full range of planned giving consulting services, including handling of Canada-U.S. cross-border gifts.

Ware Development Consulting, Molly E. Ware, CFRE, Principal, 220 S. Alfred Street, Alexandria, VA 22314, Tel. no. 703-549-7548, e-mail: molware@aol.com. Offers development and planned giving program assessments, coaching, and training workshops for staff and board.

Winton Smith & Associates, Winton Smith, Jr., Owner, 2670 Union Extended, Suite 1200, Memphis, TN 38112, Tel. no. 800-727-1040, e-mail: winton@wintonsmith.com. Provides full range of planned giving consulting services.

GIFT MANAGEMENT

Fidelity Charitable Gift Fund, 82 Devonshire Street H4D, Boston, MA 02109, Tel. no. 800-682-4438, Web site: www.charitablegift.org. Provides pooled income fund and donor advised fund services.

Fiduciary Trust Company International. Tel. no. 800-632-2350. Provides planned gift fiduciary and administrative services.

First Union National Bank, Charitable Funds Services, Two First Union Center, CMG-10, 301 South Tryon Street, Charlotte, NC 28288-1159, Tel. no. 704-374-6025. Provides planned gift fiduciary and administrative services.

Hemingway & Reinhardt, Inc., 4 Park Avenue, Swarthmore, PA 19081, Tel. no. 610-544-4545. Provides administrative support for planned giving programs.

Kaspick & Company, 555 University Avenue, Palo Alto, CA 94301, Tel. no. 650-322-5477, Fax: 650-854-9023, also Four Liberty Square, 6th Floor, Boston, MA 02109, Tel. no. 617-357-0575, Fax: 617-357-0573, e-mail: info@kaspick.com, Web site: www.kaspick.com. Provides planned gift administrative, asset management, and consulting services.

Mellon Private Capital Management, Boston Safe Deposit and Trust Company, One Boston Place, Boston, MA 02108-4402, Tel. no. 800-842-2354. Provides planned gift fiduciary and administrative services.

Real Estate For Charities, Chase V. Magnuson, President, 3164 Vista Rica, Carlsbad, CA 92009, Tel. no. 714-815-8889, e-mail: Chasemagnuson@msn.com, Web site: www.realestateforcharities.com. Helps nonprofit organizations sell real estate.

State Street Global Advisors, Janie Wilson, Principal, 225 Franklin Street, 23rd Floor, Boston, MA 02110, Tel. no. 617-664-3199, e-mail: janie_wilson@ssga.com. Provides planned gift fiduciary and administrative services.

Vanguard Charitable Endowment Program, P.O. Box 3075, Southeastern, PA 19398-9917, Tel. no. 888-383-4483, Web site: www.vanguardcharitable.org. Provides donor advised fund services.

Wachovia Charitable Funds Management, 100 North Main Street, Winston-Salem, NC 27150, Tel. no. 800-462-7159. Provides planned gift fiduciary and administrative services.

MARKETING MATERIALS

Future Focus, 101 Gregory Lane, Suite 52, Pleasant Hill, CA 94523, Tel. nos. 800-737-3437 and 925-686-3212, Fax: 925-686-3217, e-mail: mail@futurefocus.net, Web site: www.futurefocus.net. Provides planned giving Web site design services.

Pentera, Inc., Andre R. Donikian, President, 8650 Commerce Park Place, Suite G, Indianapolis, IN 46268, Tel. no. 317-875-0910. Provides direct mail, Web site, consulting, and training services in the planned giving area.

Robert F. Sharpe & Co., Inc., 5050 Poplar Avenue, Memphis, TN 38157-1212, Tel. nos. 901-680-5300 and 800-238-3253, Web site: www.rfsco.com. Provides direct mail, Web site, consulting, and training services in the planned giving area.

R&R Newkirk Co., 8695 S. Archer, Suite 10, Willow Springs, IL 60480, Tel. no. 888-342-2375, Fax: 708-839-9207, Web site: www.rrnewkirk.com. Provides planned gift publications, response booklets, consulting, training, and the *Charitable Giving Tax Service*, a planned giving resource manual.

The Stelter Company, 10435 New York Avenue, Des Moines, IA 50322, Tel. no. 800-331-6881, Fax: 515-278-5851, Web site: www.stelter.com. Provides a wide range of printed and Web site promotional material.

VirtualGiving.com, Viken Mikaelian, Co-founder, 66 Witherspoon Street, Suite 390, Princeton, NJ 08542, Tel no. 877-244-8464. Provides planned giving Web site design.

Young-Preston Associates, Inc., P.O. Box 280, 55 McIntosh Road, Cloverdale, VA 24077, Tel no. 800-344-5701, Web site: www.youngpreston.com. Provides planned giving seminars, newsletters, donor-accessed Web newsletters, and printed booklets.

MEMBERSHIP ORGANIZATIONS

American Council on Gift Annuities, 2401 Cedar Springs, Dallas, TX 75201, Tel. no. 214-720-4774, Web site: www.acga-web.org. A volunteer organization consisting of the representatives of charities throughout the United States. Sponsors a conference every three years dealing with a broad range of charitable issues. Reviews and recommends appropriate gift annuity rates.

Association of Fundraising Professionals (AFP), 1101 King Street, Alexandria, VA 22314, Tel. no. 703-684-0410, Web site: www.afp.org. Provides fundraising education, training, and advocacy. Local chapters in major cities.

Canadian Association of Gift Planners, P.O. Box 4084, Edmonton, AB T6E 4S8, Canada, Tel. nos. 780-430-9494 or 888-430-9494, Fax: 780-438-4837, Web site: www.cagp-acpdp.org. The Association brings together professionals from various disciplines to ensure that the gift planning process achieves a fair and proper balance between the interests of donors and the aims and objectives of registered charitable organizations in Canada in accordance with the Association's Standards of Professional and Ethical Practice.

Council for the Advancement and Support of Education (CASE), 1307 New York Avenue, N.W., Washington, DC 20005-4701, Tel. no. 202-328-2273, Web site: www.case.org. Offers conferences by region throughout the United States in all areas of fundraising. Publishes *Currents* magazine.

Council on Foundations, 1828 L Street, N.W., Washington, DC 20036-3926, Tel. no. 202-466-6512, Web site: www.cof.org. Professional organization for private, corporate, and community foundations. Provides information on local community foundations.

European Association for Planned Giving (EAPG), Museum House, 25 Museum St., London WC1A 1PL, U.K., Tel. no. +44 (0)20 7323 1587, Fax: +44 (0)20 7631 0029, e-mail: planned.giving@netway.co.uk, Web site: www.plannedgiving.co.uk. To advance the development of planned giving in Europe, EAPG provides a network for professional advisors involved in the structuring of charitable gifts and charity and other non-government organization (NGO) fundraisers. EAPG focuses on current developments in areas such as major gift planning and legacies, charitable and private trusts planning, differing estate and gift tax and succession rules, and cross-border charity fundraising issues.

National Committee on Planned Giving (NCPG), 310 N. Alabama, Suite 210, Indianapolis, IN 46204-2103, Tel. no. 317-269-6274, Web site: www.ncpg.org. The national professional association of gift planners, with a constituency consisting of 110 local councils with approximately 12,000 individual members. It maintains resource lists of planned giving service providers and training opportunities and publishes *Gift Planning Update,* a bimonthly newsletter.

NEWSLETTERS, PERIODICALS, AND LISTSERVS

Charitable Gift Planning News, Jerry J. McCoy, LL.B LL.M and Terry L. Simmons, JD., LLM, publishers, P.O. Box 551606, Dallas, TX 75355-1606, Tel. no. 214-328-4244, e-mail: carolcgpn@aol.com. Published monthly. Helpful update on the legal side of planned giving.

The Chronicle of Philanthropy, 1255 23rd Street, N.W., Washington, DC 20037, Tel. no. 202-466-1200, Web site: http://philanthropy.com. Widely read biweekly with articles on all aspects of fundraising. Date book section lists training events. Directory of services.

Contributions, P.O. Box 338, Medfield, MA 02052-0338, Tel. no. 508-359-0019,
Fax: 508-359-2703, e-mail: Contrib@ziplink.net, Web site: www.contributionsmagazine.com.
Published bimonthly with articles about all aspects of fundraising.

GIFT-PL. Tel. no. 317-269-6274, Web site: www. ncpg.org. An e-mail distribution list (listserv) to which more than 1,000 gift planners and allied professionals

subscribe worldwide. It is sponsored by the National Committee on Planned Giving.

The Journal of Gift Planning, published by the National Committee on Planned Giving, 233 McCrea, Suite 400, Indianapolis, IN 46225, Tel. no. 317-269-6274.

The Planned Gifts Counselor, Published by Practical Publishing, LLC, P.O. Box 970367, Orem, UT 84097, Tel. no. 877-PGC-0499.

Planned Giving Today, G. Roger Schoenhals, publisher, 100 Second Avenue South, Edmonds, WA 98020-8436, Tel. no. 800-525-5748, Fax: 425-744-3838, Web site: www.pgtoday.com. Published monthly.

Taxwise Giving, Conrad Teitell, publisher, 13 Arcadia Road, Old Greenwich, CT 06870, Tel. no. 203-637-4553.

The Tidd Letter, Jonathan G. Tidd, publisher, 9 Beaver Brook Road, W. Simsbury, CT 06092, Tel. no. 203-651-8937.

SOFTWARE

ACT! Interact Commerce Corporation, 8800 N. Gainey Center Drive, Suite 200, Scottsdale, AZ 85258, Tel. no. 480-368-3700, Fax: 480-368-3799, Web site: www.act.com, e-mail: actinfo@interactcommerce.com. Computer database software designed to assist in the tracking of contacts.

Blackbaud, Inc., 2000 Daniel Island Drive, Charleston, SC 29492-7541, Web site: www.blackbaud.com. Provides software for planned giving management.

Comdel, Inc., 1601 Carmen Drive, Suite 103, Camarillo, CA 93010, Tel. no. 805-987-0565. Provides Crescendo software for planned giving management and Web sites promoting planned gifts.

P G Calc, Inc., Gary M. Pforzheimer, President, 129 Mount Auburn Street, Cambridge, MA 02138, Tel. no. 888-474-2252, Web site: www.pgcalc.com. Provides software for planned giving management and Web sites promoting planned gifts.

WEB SITES

Community Foundation for Southeast Michigan, 333 West Fort Street, Detroit, MI 48226, Tel. no. 313-961-6675, Web site: http://comnet.org/local/orgs/comfound. Shows how a community foundation offers planned giving.

Council on Foundations. Web site: www.cof.org. Information on community foundations.

GuideStar, Philanthropic Research, Inc., 427 Scotland Street, Williamsburg, VA 23185, Tel. no. 757-229-4631, Web site: www.guidestar.org. Provides a free, searchable database of the programs and finances of more than 600,000 U.S. nonprofit organizations.

OTHER RESOURCES

National Charities Information Bureau (NCIB), 19 Union Square West, New York, NY 10003, Tel. no. 212-929-6300, Web site: www.ncib.org. A "watch-dog" organization that evaluates charities' fundraising and management practices.

Philanthropic Advisory Service. Web site: www.bbb.org/about/pas.asp. Created by the Better Business Bureau, this Web site is a resource of information on nonprofit organizations that solicit gifts.

Planned Giving Design Center. Web site: www.pgdc.net. Helps charitable organizations create strategic alliances with legal, tax, and financial services professionals in their communities who have the capacity to influence philanthropy.

Appendix C
Sample Gift Instruments

Note: The following forms are merely guides to the preparation of legal instruments. Legal documents should be prepared only by lawyers who are conversant with the specific circumstances of their individual clients and the applicable state laws. Donors should **always** be counseled to consult their advisors.

SAMPLE ANNUITY TRUST FORMS PREPARED BY THE IRS

IRS FORM: REV. PROC. 89-21

SECTION 4. SAMPLE CHARITABLE REMAINDER ANNUITY TRUST

On this _____ day of _____, I, _____ (hereinafter referred to as "the Donor"), desiring to establish a charitable remainder annuity trust, within the meaning of Rev. Proc. 89-21 and section 664(d)(1) of the Internal Revenue Code (hereinafter referred to as "the Code") hereby create the _____ Charitable Remainder Annuity Trust ("the Trust") and designate _____ as the initial Trustee.

1. Funding of Trust. The Donor transfers to the Trustee the property described in Schedule A, and the Trustee accepts such property and agrees to hold, manage, and distribute such property of the Trust under the terms set forth in this Trust instrument.

2. Payment of Annuity Amount. The Trustee shall pay to [a living individual] (hereinafter referred to as "the Recipient") in each taxable year of the Trust during the Recipient's life an annuity amount equal to [at least 5] percent of the net fair market value of the assets of the Trust as of this date. The annuity amount shall be paid in equal quarterly amounts from income and, to the extent income is not sufficient, from principal. Any income of the Trust for a taxable year in excess of the annuity amount shall be added to principal. If the net fair market value of the Trust assets is incorrectly determined, then within a reasonable period after the value is finally determined for federal tax purposes, the Trustee shall pay to the Recipient (in the case of an undervaluation) or receive from the Recipient (in the case of an overvaluation) an amount equal to the difference between the annuity amount(s) properly payable and the annuity amount(s) actually paid.

3. Proration of the Annuity Amount. In determining the annuity amount, the Trustee shall prorate the same on a daily basis for a short taxable year and for the taxable year of the Recipient's death.

4. Distribution to Charity. Upon the death of the Recipient, the Trustee shall distribute all of the then principal and income of the Trust (other than any amount due Recipient or Recipient's estate under paragraphs 2 and 3, above) to _____ (hereinafter referred to as the Charitable Organization). If the Charitable Organization is not an organization described in sections 170(c), 2055(a), and 2522(a) of the Code at the time when any principal or income of the Trust is to be distributed to it, then the Trustee shall distribute such principal or income to such one or more organizations described in sections 170(c), 2055(a), and 2522(a) as the Trustee shall select in its sole discretion.

5. Additional Contributions. No additional contributions shall be made to the Trust after the initial contribution.

6. Prohibited Transactions. The income of the Trust for each taxable year shall be distributed at such time and in such manner as not to subject the Trust to tax under section 4942 of the Code. Except for the payment of the annuity amount to the Recipient, the Trustee shall not engage in any act of self-dealing, as defined in section 4941(d), and shall not make any taxable expenditures, as defined in section 4945(d). The Trustee shall not make any investments that jeopardize the charitable purpose of the Trust, within the meaning of section 4944, or retain any excess business holdings, within the meaning of section 4943.

7. Successor Trustee. The Donor reserves the right to dismiss the Trustee and to appoint a successor Trustee.

8. Taxable Year. The taxable year of the Trust shall be the calendar year.

9. Governing Law. The operation of the Trust shall be governed by the laws of the State of _____. However, the Trustee is prohibited from exercising any power or discretion granted under said laws that would be inconsistent with the qualification of the Trust under section 664(d)(1) of the Code and the corresponding regulations.

10. Limited Power of Amendment. The Trust is irrevocable. However, the Trustee shall have the power, acting alone, to amend the Trust in any manner required for the sole purpose of ensuring that the Trust qualifies and continues to qualify as a charitable remainder annuity trust within the meaning of section 664(d)(1) of the Code.

11. Investment of Trust Assets. Nothing in this Trust instrument shall be construed to restrict the Trustee from investing the Trust assets in a manner that could result in the annual realization of a reasonable amount of income or gain from the sale or disposition of Trust assets.

IN WITNESS WHEREOF _____ and [TRUSTEE] by its duly authorized officer have signed this agreement the day and year first above written.

_____

[DONOR]

_____

[TRUSTEE]

By _____

[ACKNOWLEDGMENTS, WITNESSES, ETC.]

SECTION 4. SAMPLE INTER VIVOS CHARITABLE REMAINDER ANNUITY TRUST: TWO LIVES, CONSECUTIVE INTERESTS

On this _____ day of _____, I, _____ (hereinafter referred to as "the Donor"), desiring to establish a charitable remainder annuity trust, within the meaning of section 4 of Rev. Proc. 90-32 and section 664(d)(1) of the Internal Revenue Code (hereinafter referred to as "the Code") hereby create the _____ Charitable Remainder Annuity Trust and designate _____ as the initial Trustee. [ALTERNATE OR SUCCESSOR TRUSTEES MAY ALSO BE DESIGNATED IF DESIRED.]

1. Funding of Trust. The Donor transfers to the Trustee property described in Schedule A, and the Trustee accepts such property and agrees to hold, manage, and distribute such property of the Trust under the terms set forth in this Trust instrument.

2. Payment of Annuity Amount. In each taxable year of the Trust, the Trustee shall pay to [a living individual] during his or her lifetime and, after his or her death, to [a living individual] (hereinafter referred to as "the Recipients") for such time as he or she survives, an annuity amount equal to [at least 5] percent of the net fair market value of the assets of the Trust as of the date of this Trust. The annuity amount shall be paid in equal quarterly amounts from income and, to the extent that income is not sufficient, from principal. Any income of the Trust for a taxable year in excess of the annuity amount shall be added to principal. If the net fair market value of the Trust assets is incorrectly determined, then within a reasonable period after the value is finally determined for federal tax purposes, the Trustee shall pay to the Recipients (in the case of an undervaluation) or receive from the Recipients (in the case of an overvaluation) an amount equal to the difference between the annuity amount(s) actually paid.

3. Payment of Federal Estate Taxes and State Death Taxes. The lifetime annuity interest of the second Recipient will take effect upon the death of the first Recipient only if the second Recipient furnishes the funds for payment of any federal estate taxes or state death taxes for which the Trustee may be liable upon the death of the first Recipient. [THIS PROVISION IS MANDATORY ONLY IF ALL OR A PORTION OF THE TRUST MAY BE SUBJECT TO SUCH TAXES ON THE DEATH OF THE FIRST RECIPIENT.]

4. Proration of the Annuity Amount. In determining the annuity amount, the Trustee shall prorate the same on a daily basis for a short taxable year and for the taxable year ending with the survivor Recipient's death.

5. Distribution to Charity. Upon the death of the survivor Recipient, the Trustee shall distribute all of the then principal and income of the Trust (other than any amount due either of the Recipients or their estates under the provisions above) to _____ (hereinafter referred to as "the Charitable Organization"). If the Charitable Organization is not an organization described in sections 170(c), 2055(a), and 2522(a) of the Code at the time when any principal or income of the Trust is to be distributed to it, then the Trustee shall distribute such principal or income to such one or more organizations described in sections 170(c), 2055(a), and 2522(a) as the Trustee shall select in its sole discretion.

6. Additional Contributions. No additional contributions shall be made to the Trust after the initial contribution.

7. Prohibited Transactions. The Trustee shall make distributions at such time and in such manner as not to subject the Trust to tax under section 4942 of the Code. Except for the payment of the annuity amount to the Recipients, the Trustee shall not engage in any act of self-dealing, as defined in section 4941(d), and shall not make any taxable expenditures, as defined in section 4945(d). The Trustee shall not make any investments that jeopardize the charitable purpose of the Trust, within the meaning of section 4944 and the regulations thereunder, or retain any excess business holdings, within the meaning of section 4943(c).

8. Taxable Year. The taxable year of the Trust shall be the calendar year.

9. Governing Law. The operation of the Trust shall be governed by the laws of the State of _____. The Trustee, however, is prohibited from exercising any power or discretion granted under said laws that would be inconsistent with the qualification of the Trust under section 664(d)(1) of the Code and the corresponding regulations.

10. Limited Power of Amendment. The Trust is irrevocable. The Trustee, however, shall have the power, acting alone, to amend the Trust in any manner required for the sole purpose of ensuring that the Trust qualifies and continues to qualify as a charitable remainder annuity trust within the meaning of section 664(d)(1) of the Code.

11. Investment of Trust Assets. Nothing in this Trust instrument shall be construed to restrict the Trustee from investing the Trust assets in a manner that could result in the annual realization of a reasonable amount of income or gain from the sale or disposition of Trust assets.

IN WITNESS WHEREOF _____ and [TRUSTEE] by its duly authorized officer have signed this agreement the day and year first above written.

_____

[DONOR]

_____

[TRUSTEE]

By _____
[ACKNOWLEDGMENTS, WITNESSES, ETC.]

IRS FORM: REV. PROC. 90-32

SECTION 5. SAMPLE INTER VIVOS CHARITABLE REMAINDER ANNUITY TRUST: TWO LIVES, CONCURRENT AND CONSECUTIVE INTERESTS

On this _____ day of _____, I, _____ (hereinafter referred to as "the Donor"), desiring to establish a charitable remainder annuity trust, within the meaning of section 5 of Rev. Proc. 90-32 and section 664(d)(1) of the Internal Revenue Code (hereinafter referred to as "the Code") hereby create the [NAME] Charitable Remainder Annuity Trust and designate _____ as the initial Trustee. [ALTERNATE OR SUCCESSOR TRUSTEES MAY ALSO BE DESIGNATED IF DESIRED.]

1. Funding of Trust. The Donor transfers to the Trustee property described in Schedule A, and the Trustee accepts such property and agrees to hold, manage, and distribute such property of the Trust under the terms set forth in this Trust instrument.

2. Payment of Annuity Amount. In each taxable year of the Trust, the Trustee shall pay to [a living individual] and [a living individual] (hereinafter referred to as "the Recipients"), in equal shares during their lifetimes, an annuity amount equal to [at least 5] percent of the net fair market value of the assets of the Trust as of the date of this Trust. Upon the death of the first of the Recipients to die, the survivor Recipient shall be entitled to receive the entire annuity amount. The annuity amount shall be paid in equal quarterly amounts from income and, to the extent that income is not sufficient, from principal. Any income of the Trust for a taxable year in excess of the annuity amount shall be added to principal. If the net fair market value of the Trust assets is incorrectly determined, then within a reasonable period after the value is finally determined for federal tax purposes, the Trustee shall pay to the Recipients (in the case of an undervaluation) or receive from the Recipients (in the case of an overvaluation) an amount equal to the difference between the annuity amount(s) properly payable and the annuity amount(s) actually paid.

3. Payment of Federal Estate Taxes and State Death Taxes. The lifetime annuity interest of the survivor Recipient will continue in effect upon the death of the first Recipient to die only if the survivor Recipient furnishes the funds for payment of any federal estate taxes or state death taxes for which the Trustee may be liable upon the death of the first Recipient to die. [THIS PROVISION IS MANDATORY ONLY IF ALL OR A PORTION OF THE TRUST MAY BE SUBJECT TO SUCH TAXES ON THE DEATH OF THE FIRST RECIPIENT TO DIE.]

4. Proration of the Annuity Amount. In determining the annuity amount, the Trustee shall prorate the same on a daily basis for a short taxable year and for the taxable year ending with the survivor Recipient's death.

5. Distribution to Charity. Upon the death of the survivor Recipient, the Trustee shall distribute all of the then principal and income of the Trust (other than any amount due either of the Recipients or their estates under the provisions above) to _____ (hereinafter referred to as "the Charitable Organization"). If the Charitable Organization is not an organization described in sections 170(c), 2055(a), and 2522(a) of the Code at the time when any principal or income of the Trust is to be distributed to it, then the Trustee shall distribute such principal or income to such one or more organizations described in sections 170(c), 2055(a), and 2522(a) as the Trustee shall select in its sole discretion.

6. Additional Contributions. No additional contributions shall be made to the Trust after the initial contribution.

7. Prohibited Transactions. The Trustee shall make distributions at such time and in such manner as not to subject the Trust to tax under section 4942 of the Code. Except for the payment of the annuity amount to the Recipients, the Trustee shall not engage in any act of self-dealing, as defined in section 4941(d), and shall not make any taxable expenditures, as defined in section 4945(d). The Trustee shall not make any investments that jeopardize the charitable purpose of the Trust, within the meaning of section 4944 and the regulations thereunder, or retain any excess business holdings, within the meaning of section 4943(c).

8. Taxable Year. The taxable year of the Trust shall be the calendar year.

9. Governing Law. The operation of the Trust shall be governed by the laws of the State of _____. The Trustee, however, is prohibited from exercising any power or discretion granted under said laws that would be inconsistent with the qualification of the Trust under section 664(d)(1) of the Code and the corresponding regulations.

10. Limited Power of Amendment. The Trust is irrevocable. The Trustee, however, shall have the power, acting alone, to amend the Trust in any manner required for the sole purpose of ensuring that the Trust qualifies and continues to qualify as a charitable remainder annuity trust within the meaning of section 664(d)(1) of the Code.

11. Investment of Trust Assets. Nothing in this Trust instrument shall be construed to restrict the Trustee from investing the Trust assets in a manner that could result in the annual realization of a reasonable amount of income or gain from the sale or disposition of Trust assets.

IN WITNESS WHEREOF _____ and [TRUSTEE] by its duly authorized officer have signed this agreement the day and year first above written.

_____

[DONOR]

_____

[TRUSTEE]

By _____
[ACKNOWLEDGMENTS, WITNESSES, ETC.]

IRS FORM: REV. PROC. 90-32

SECTION 6. SAMPLE TESTAMENTARY CHARITABLE REMAINDER ANNUITY TRUST: ONE LIFE

All the rest, residue and remainder of my property and estate, real and personal, of whatever nature and wherever situated [ALTERNATIVELY, IF NOT A RESIDUARY BEQUEST, DESCRIBE OR IDENTIFY THE BEQUEST], I give, devise and bequeath to my Trustee in trust. It being my intention to establish a charitable remainder annuity trust within the meaning of section 7 of Rev. Proc. 90-32 and section 664(d)(1) of the Internal Revenue Code (hereinafter referred to as "the Code"), such Trust shall be known as the _____ Charitable Remainder Annuity Trust and I hereby designate _____ as the initial Trustee. [ALTERNATE OR SUCCESSOR TRUSTEES MAY ALSO BE DESIGNATED IF DESIRED.]

1. Payment of Annuity Amount. In each taxable year of the Trust, the Trustee shall pay to [a living individual] (hereinafter referred to as "the Recipient") during the Recipient's life an annuity amount equal to [at least 5] percent of the initial net fair market value of the assets passing in trust as finally determined for federal tax purposes, provided, however, that the payout percentage (as adjusted to reflect the timing and frequency of the annuity payments) shall not exceed the percentage that would result in a 5 percent probability that the Trust corpus will be exhausted before the death of the Recipient determined as of the date of my death (or the alternate valuation date, if applicable). [NOTE: THE PRECEDING SENTENCE IS ONE MEANS OF AVOIDING DISALLOWANCE OF THE CHARITABLE DEDUCTION WITH RESPECT TO A CHARITABLE REMAINDER ANNUITY TRUST FOR WHICH THERE IS A GREATER THAN 5 PERCENT PROBABILITY THAT THE TRUST CORPUS WILL BE EXHAUSTED BEFORE THE DEATH OF THE ANNUITANT. SEE REV. RUL. 77-374, 1977-2 C.B. 329.] The annuity amount shall be paid in equal quarterly amounts from income and, to the extent that income is not sufficient, from principal. Any income of the Trust for a taxable year in excess of the annuity amount shall be added to principal. If the net fair market value of the Trust assets is incorrectly determined, then within a reasonable period after the value is finally determined for federal tax purposes, the Trustee shall pay to the Recipient (in the case of an undervaluation) or receive from the Recipient (in the case of an overvaluation) an amount equal to the difference between the annuity amount(s) properly payable and the annuity amount(s) actually paid.

2. Deferral Provision. The obligation to pay the annuity amount shall commence with the date of my death, but payment of the annuity amount may be deferred from such date until the end of the taxable year of the Trust in which occurs the complete funding of the Trust. Within a reasonable time after the end of the taxable year in which the complete funding of the Trust occurs, the Trustee must pay to the Recipient (in the case of an underpayment) or receive from the Recipient (in the case of an overpayment) the difference between: (1) any annuity amounts actually paid, plus interest, compounded annually, computed for any period at the rate of interest that the federal income tax regulations under section 664 of the Code prescribe for the Trust for such computation for such period; and (2) the annuity amounts payable, plus interest, compounded annually, computed for any period at the rate of interest that the federal income tax regulations under section 664 prescribe for the Trust for such computation for such period.

3. Proration of the Annuity Amount. In determining the annuity amount, the Trustee shall prorate the same on a daily basis for a short taxable year and for the taxable year ending with the Recipient's death.

4. Distribution to Charity. Upon the death of the Recipient, the Trustee shall distribute all of the then principal and income of the Trust (other than any amount due the Recipient or the Recipient's estate under the provisions above) to _____ (hereinafter referred to as "the Charitable Organization"). If the Charitable Organization is not an organization described in sections 170(c) and 2055(a) of the Code at the time when any principal or income of the Trust is to be distributed to it, then the Trustee shall distribute such principal or income to such one or more organizations described in sections 170(c) and 2055(a) as the Trustee shall select in its sole discretion.

5. Additional Contributions. No additional contributions shall be made to the Trust after the initial contribution. The initial contribution, however, shall be deemed to consist of all property passing to the Trust by reason of my death.

6. Prohibited Transactions. The Trustee shall make distributions at such time and in such manner as not to subject the Trust to tax under section 4942 of the Code. Except for the payment of the annuity amount to the Recipient, the Trustee shall not engage in any act of self-dealing, as defined in section 4941(d), and shall not make any taxable expenditures, as defined in section 4945(d). The Trustee shall not make any investments that jeopardize the charitable purpose of the Trust, within the meaning of section 4944 and the regulations thereunder, or retain any excess business holdings, within the meaning of section 4943(c).

7. Taxable Year. The taxable year of the Trust shall be the calendar year.

8. Governing Law. The operation of the Trust shall be governed by the laws of the State of _____. The Trustee, however, is prohibited from exercising any power or discretion granted under said laws that would be inconsistent with the qualification of the Trust under section 664(d)(1) of the Code and the corresponding regulations.

9. Limited Power of Amendment. The Trustee shall have the power, acting alone, to amend the Trust in any manner required for the sole purpose of ensuring that the Trust qualifies and continues to qualify as a charitable remainder annuity trust within the meaning of section 664(d)(1) of the Code.

10. Investments of Trust Assets. Nothing herein shall be construed to restrict the Trustee from investing the Trust assets in a manner that could result in the annual realization of a reasonable amount of income or gain from the sale or disposition of Trust assets.

IN WITNESS WHEREOF _____ and [TRUSTEE] by its duly authorized officer have signed this agreement the day and year first above written.

_____

[DONOR]

_____

[TRUSTEE]

By _____
[ACKNOWLEDGMENTS, WITNESSES, ETC.]

SECTION 7. SAMPLE TESTAMENTARY CHARITABLE REMAINDER ANNUITY TRUST: TWO LIVES, CONSECUTIVE INTERESTS

All the rest, residue and remainder of my property and estate, real and personal, of whatever nature and wherever situated [ALTERNATIVELY, IF NOT A RESIDUARY BEQUEST, DESCRIBE OR IDENTIFY THE BEQUEST], I give, devise and bequeath to my Trustee in trust. It being my intention to establish a charitable remainder annuity trust within the meaning of section 7 of Rev. Proc. 90-32 and section 664(d)(1) of the Internal Revenue Code (hereinafter referred to as "the Code"), such Trust shall be known as the _____ Charitable Remainder Annuity Trust and I hereby designate _____ as the initial Trustee. [ALTERNATE OR SUCCESSOR TRUSTEES MAY ALSO BE DESIGNATED IF DESIRED.]

1. Payment of Annuity Amount. In each taxable year of the Trust, the Trustee shall pay to [a living individual] during his or her lifetime, and after his or her death, to [a living individual] (hereinafter referred to as "the Recipients"), for such time as he or she survives, an annuity amount equal to [at least 5] percent of the initial net fair market value of the assets passing in trust as finally determined for federal tax purposes, provided, however, that the payout percentage (as adjusted to reflect the timing and frequency of the annuity payments) shall not exceed the percentage that would result in a 5 percent probability that the Trust corpus will be exhausted before the death of the survivor Recipient determined as of the date of my death (or the alternate valuation date, if applicable). [NOTE: THE PRECEDING SENTENCE IS ONE MEANS OF AVOIDING DISALLOWANCE OF THE CHARITABLE DEDUCTION WITH RESPECT TO A CHARITABLE REMAINDER ANNUITY TRUST FOR WHICH THERE IS GREATER THAN 5 PERCENT PROBABILITY THAT THE TRUST CORPUS WILL BE EXHAUSTED BEFORE THE DEATH OF THE ANNUITANT. SEE REV. RUL. 77-374, 1977-2 C.B. 329.] The annuity amount shall be paid in equal quarterly amounts from income and, to the extent that income is not sufficient, from principal. Any income of the Trust for a taxable year in excess of the annuity amount shall be added to principal. If the net fair market value of the Trust assets is incorrectly determined, then within a reasonable period after the value is finally determined for federal tax purposes, the Trustee shall pay to the Recipients (in the case of an undervaluation) or receive from the Recipients (in the case of an overvaluation) an amount equal to the difference between the annuity amount(s) properly payable and the annuity amount(s) actually paid.

2. Deferral Provision. The obligation to pay the annuity amount shall commence with the date of my death, but payment of the annuity amount may be deferred from such date until the end of the taxable year of the Trust in which occurs the complete funding of the Trust. Within a reasonable time after the end of the taxable year in which the complete funding of the Trust occurs, the Trustee must pay to the Recipients (in the case of an underpayment) or receive from the Recipients (in the case of an overpayment) the difference between: (1) any annuity amounts actually paid, plus interest, compounded annually, computed for any period at the rate of interest that the federal income tax regulations under section 664 of the Code prescribe for the Trust for such computation for such period; and (2) the annuity amounts payable, plus interest, compounded annually, computed for any period at the rate of interest that the federal income tax regulations under section 664 prescribe for the Trust for such computation for such period.

3. Proration of the Annuity Amount. In determining the annuity amount, the Trustee shall prorate the same on a daily basis for a short taxable year and for the taxable year ending with the survivor Recipient's death.

4. Distribution to Charity. Upon the death of the survivor Recipient, the Trustee shall distribute all of the then principal and income of the Trust (other than any amount due either of the Recipients or their estates, under the provisions above) to _____ (hereinafter referred to as "the Charitable Organization"). If the Charitable Organization is not an organization described in sections 170(c) and 2055(a) of the Code at the time when any principal or income of the Trust is to be distributed to it, then the Trustee shall distribute such principal or income to such one or more organizations described in sections 170(c) and 2055(a) as the Trustee shall select in its sole discretion.

5. Additional Contributions. No additional contributions shall be made to the Trust after the initial contribution. The initial contribution, however, shall be deemed to consist of all property passing to the Trust by reason of my death.

6. Prohibited Transactions. The Trustee shall make distributions at such time and in such manner as not to subject the Trust to tax under section 4942 of the Code. Except for the payment of the annuity amount to the Recipients, the Trustee shall not engage in any act of self-dealing, as defined in section 4941(d), and shall not make any taxable expenditures, as defined in section 4945(d). The Trustee shall not make any investments that jeopardize the charitable purpose of the Trust, within the meaning of section 4944 and the regulations thereunder, or retain any excess business holdings, within the meaning of section 4943(c).

7. Taxable Year. The taxable year of the Trust shall be the calendar year.

8. Governing Law. The operation of the Trust shall be governed by the laws of the State of _____. The Trustee, however, is prohibited from exercising any power or discretion granted under said laws that would be inconsistent with the qualification of the Trust under section 664(d)(1) of the Code and the corresponding regulations.

9. Limited Power of Amendment. The Trustee shall have the power, acting alone, to amend the Trust in any manner required for the sole purpose of ensuring that the Trust qualifies and continues to qualify as a charitable remainder annuity trust within the meaning of section 664(d)(1) of the Code.

10. Investments of Trust Assets. Nothing herein shall be construed to restrict the Trustee from investing the Trust assets in a manner that could result in the annual realization of a reasonable amount of income or gain from the sale or disposition of Trust assets.

IN WITNESS WHEREOF _____ and [TRUSTEE] by its duly authorized officer have signed this agreement the day and year first above written.

_____

[DONOR]

_____

[TRUSTEE]

By _____
[ACKNOWLEDGMENTS, WITNESSES, ETC.]

IRS FORM: REV. PROC. 90-32

SECTION 8. SAMPLE TESTAMENTARY CHARITABLE REMAINDER ANNUITY TRUST: TWO LIVES, CONCURRENT AND CONSECUTIVE INTERESTS

All the rest, residue and remainder of my property and estate, real and personal, of whatever nature and wherever situated [ALTERNATIVELY, IF NOT A RESIDUARY BEQUEST, DESCRIBE OR IDENTIFY THE BEQUEST], I give, devise and bequeath to my Trustee in trust. It being my intention to establish a charitable remainder annuity trust within the meaning of section 8 of Rev. Proc. 90-32 and section 664(d)(1) of the Internal Revenue Code (hereinafter referred to as "the Code"), such Trust shall be known as the [NAME] Charitable Remainder Annuity Trust and I hereby designate [TRUSTEE'S NAME] as the initial Trustee. [ALTERNATE OR SUCCESSOR TRUSTEES MAY ALSO BE DESIGNATED IF DESIRED.]

1. Payment of Annuity Amount. In each taxable year of the Trust, the Trustee shall pay to [a living individual] and [a living individual] (hereinafter referred to as "the Recipients"), in equal shares during their lifetimes, an annuity amount equal to [at least 5] percent of the initial net fair market value of the assets passing in trust as finally determined for federal tax purposes, provided, however, that the payout percentage (as adjusted to reflect the timing and frequency of the annuity payments) shall not exceed the percentage that would result in a 5 percent probability that the Trust corpus will be exhausted before the death of the survivor Recipient determined as of the date of my death (or the alternate valuation date, if applicable). [NOTE: THE PRECEDING SENTENCE IS ONE MEANS OF AVOIDING DISALLOWANCE OF THE CHARITABLE DEDUCTION WITH RESPECT TO A CHARITABLE REMAINDER ANNUITY TRUST FOR WHICH THERE IS A GREATER THAN 5 PERCENT PROBABILITY THAT THE TRUST CORPUS WILL BE EXHAUSTED BEFORE THE DEATH OF THE ANNUITANT. SEE REV. RUL. 77-374, 1977-2 C.B. 329.] Upon the death of the first of the Recipients to die, the survivor Recipient shall be entitled to receive the entire annuity amount. The annuity amount shall be paid in equal quarterly amounts from income and, to the extent that income is not sufficient, from principal. Any income of the Trust for a taxable year in excess of the annuity amount shall be added to principal. If the net fair market value of the Trust assets is incorrectly determined, then within a reasonable period after the value is finally determined for federal tax purposes, the Trustee shall pay to the Recipients (in the case of an undervaluation) or receive from the Recipients (in the case of an overvaluation) an amount equal to the difference between the annuity amount(s) properly payable and the annuity amount(s) actually paid.

2. Deferral Provision. The obligation to pay the annuity amount shall commence with the date of my death, but payment of the annuity amount may be deferred from such date until the end of the taxable year of the Trust in which occurs the complete funding of the Trust. Within a reasonable time after the end of the taxable year in which the complete funding of the Trust occurs, the Trustee must pay to the Recipients (in the case of an underpayment) or receive from the Recipients (in the case of an overpayment) the difference between: (1) any annuity amounts actually paid, plus interest, compounded annually, computed for any period at the rate of interest that the federal income tax regulations under section 664 of the Code prescribe for the Trust for such computation for such period; and (2) the annuity amounts payable, plus interest, compounded annually, computed for any period at the rate of interest that the federal income tax regulations under section 664 prescribe for the Trust for such computation for such period.

3. Proration of the Annuity Amount. In determining the annuity amount, the Trustee shall prorate the same on a daily basis for a short taxable year and for the taxable year ending with the survivor Recipient's death.

4. Distribution to Charity. Upon the death of the survivor Recipient, the Trustee shall distribute all of the then principal and income of the Trust (other than any amount due either of the Recipients or their estates under the provisions above) to _____ (hereinafter referred to as "the Charitable Organization"). If the Charitable Organization is not an organization described in sections 170(c) and 2055(a) of the Code at the time when any principal or income of the Trust is to be distributed to it, then the Trustee shall distribute such principal or income to such one or more organizations described in sections 170(c) and 2055(a) as the Trustee shall select in its sole discretion.

5. Additional Contributions. No additional contributions shall be made to the Trust after the initial contribution. The initial contribution, however, shall be deemed to consist of all property passing to the Trust by reason of my death.

6. Prohibited Transactions. The Trustee shall make distributions at such time and in such manner as not to subject the Trust to tax under section 4942 of the Code. Except for the payment of the annuity amount to the Recipients, the Trustee shall not engage in any act of self-dealing, as defined in section 4941(d), and shall not make any taxable expenditures, as defined in section 4945(d). The Trustee shall not make any investments that jeopardize the charitable purpose of the Trust, within the meaning of section 4944 and the regulations thereunder, or retain any excess business holdings, within the meaning of section 4943(c).

7. Taxable Year. The taxable year of the Trust shall be the calendar year.

8. Governing Law. The operation of the Trust shall be governed by the laws of the State of _____. The Trustee, however, is prohibited from exercising any power or discretion granted under said laws that would be inconsistent with the qualification of the Trust under section 664(d)(1) of the Code and the corresponding regulations.

9. Limited Power of Amendment. The Trustee shall have the power, acting alone, to amend the Trust in any manner required for the sole purpose of ensuring that the Trust qualifies and continues to qualify as a charitable remainder annuity trust within the meaning of section 664(d)(1) of the Code.

10. Investment of Trust Assets. Nothing herein shall be construed to restrict the Trustee from investing the Trust assets in a manner that could result in the annual realization of a reasonable amount of income or gain from the sale or disposition of Trust assets.

IN WITNESS WHEREOF _____ and [TRUSTEE] by its duly authorized officer have signed this agreement the day and year first above written.

_____
[DONOR]

_____
[TRUSTEE]

By _____
[ACKNOWLEDGMENTS, WITNESSES, ETC.]

SAMPLE UNITRUST FORMS PREPARED BY THE IRS

IRS FORM: REV. PROC. 89-20

SECTION 4. SAMPLE CHARITABLE REMAINDER UNITRUST

On this _____ day of _____, I, _____ (hereinafter referred to as "the Donor"), desiring to establish a charitable remainder unitrust, within the meaning of Rev. Proc. 89-20 and section 664(d)(2) of the Internal Revenue Code (hereinafter referred to as "the Code") hereby create the _____ Charitable Remainder Unitrust and designate _____ as the initial Trustee.

1. Funding of Trust. The Donor transfers to the Trustee the property described in Schedule A, and the Trustee accepts such property and agrees to hold, manage and distribute such property of the Trust under the terms set forth in this Trust instrument.

2. Payment of Unitrust Amount. The Trustee shall pay to [a living individual] (hereinafter referred to as "the Recipient") in each taxable year of the Trust during the Recipient's life a unitrust amount equal to [at least 5] percent of the net fair market value of the assets of the Trust valued as of the first day of each taxable year of the Trust (the "valuation date"). The unitrust amount shall be paid in equal quarterly amounts from income and, to the extent that income is not sufficient, from principal. Any income of the Trust for a taxable year in excess of the unitrust amount shall be added to principal. If the net fair market value of the Trust assets is incorrectly determined, then within a reasonable period after the value is finally determined for federal tax purposes, the Trustee shall pay to the Recipient (in the case of an undervaluation) or receive from the Recipient (in the case of an overvaluation) an amount equal to the difference between the unitrust amount properly payable and the unitrust amount actually paid.

3. Proration of the Unitrust Amount. In determining the unitrust amount, the Trustee shall prorate the same on a daily basis for a short taxable year and for the taxable year of the Recipient's death.

4. Distribution to Charity. Upon the death of the Recipient, the Trustee shall distribute all of the then principal and income of the Trust (other than any amount due Recipient or Recipient's estate, under paragraphs 2 and 3, above) to _____ (hereinafter referred to as "the Charitable Organization"). If the Charitable Organization is not an organization described in sections 170(c), 2055(a), and 2522(a) of the Code at the time when any principal or income of the Trust is to be distributed to it, then the Trustee shall distribute such principal or income to such one or more organizations described in sections 170(c), 2055(a), and 2522(a) as the Trustee shall select in its sole discretion.

5. Additional Contributions. If any additional contributions are made to the Trust after the initial contribution, the unitrust amount for the year in which the additional contribution is made shall be [THE SAME PERCENTAGE AS IN PARAGRAPH 2] percent of the sum of (a) the net fair market value of the Trust assets as of the first day of the taxable year (excluding the assets so added and any income from, or appreciation on, such assets) and (b) that proportion of the value of the assets so added that was excluded under (a) that the number of days in the period that begins with the date of contribution and ends with the earlier of the last day of the taxable year or the Recipient's death bears to the number of days in the period that begins on the first day of such taxable year and ends with the earlier of the last day in such taxable year or the Recipient's death. In the case where there is no valuation date after the time of contribution, the assets so added shall be valued at the time of contribution.

6. Prohibited Transactions. The income of the Trust for each taxable year shall be distributed at such time and in such manner as not to subject the Trust to tax under section 4942 of the Code. Except for the payment of the unitrust amount to the Recipient, the Trustee shall not engage in any act of self-dealing, as defined in section 4941(d), and shall not make any taxable expenditures, as defined in section 4945(d). The Trustee shall not make any investments that jeopardize the charitable purpose of the Trust, within the meaning of section 4944, or retain any excess business holdings, within the meaning of section 4943.

7. Successor Trustee. The Donor reserves the right to dismiss the Trustee and to appoint a successor Trustee.

8. Taxable Year. The taxable year of the Trust shall be the calendar year.

9. Governing Law. The operation of the Trust shall be governed by the laws of the State of _____. However, the Trustee is prohibited from exercising any power or discretion granted under said laws that would be inconsistent with the qualification of the Trust under section 664(d)(2) of the Code and the corresponding regulations.

10. Limited Power of Amendment. The Trust is irrevocable. However, the Trustee shall have the power, acting alone, to amend the Trust in any manner required for the sole purpose of ensuring that the Trust qualifies and continues to qualify as a charitable remainder unitrust within the meaning of section 664(d)(2) of the Code.

11. Investment of Trust Assets. Nothing in this Trust instrument shall be construed to restrict the Trustee from investing the Trust assets in a manner that could result in the annual realization of a reasonable amount of income or gain from the sale or disposition of Trust assets.

IN WITNESS WHEREOF _____ and [TRUSTEE] by its duly authorized officer have signed this agreement the day and year first above written.

_____

[DONOR]

_____

[TRUSTEE]

By _____
[ACKNOWLEDGMENTS, WITNESSES, ETC.]

IRS FORM: REV. PROC 90-30

SECTION 4. SAMPLE INTER VIVOS CHARITABLE REMAINDER UNITRUST: TWO LIVES, CONSECUTIVE INTERESTS

On this _____ day of _____, I, _____ (hereinafter referred to as "the Donor"), desiring to establish a charitable remainder unitrust, within the meaning of section 4 of Rev. Proc. 90-30 and section 664(d)(2) of the Internal Revenue Code (hereinafter referred to as "the Code") hereby create the _____ Charitable Remainder Unitrust and designate _____ as the initial Trustee. [ALTERNATE OR SUCCESSOR TRUSTEES MAY ALSO BE DESIGNATED IF DESIRED.]

1. Funding of Trust. The Donor transfers to the Trustee the property described in Schedule A, and the Trustee accepts such property and agrees to hold, manage, and distribute such property of the Trust under the terms set forth in this Trust instrument.

2. Payment of Unitrust Amount. In each taxable year of the Trust, the Trustee shall pay to [a living individual] during his or her lifetime, and after his or her death to [a living individual] (hereinafter referred to as "the Recipients"), for such time as he or she survives, a unitrust amount equal to [at least 5] percent of the net fair market value of the assets of the Trust valued as of the first day of each taxable year of the Trust (the "valuation date"). The unitrust amount shall be paid in equal quarterly amounts from income and, to the extent that income is not sufficient, from principal. Any income of the Trust for a taxable year in excess of the unitrust amount shall be added to principal. If for any year the net fair market value of the Trust assets is incorrectly determined, then within a reasonable period after the value is finally determined for federal tax purposes, the Trustee shall pay to the Recipients (in the case of an undervaluation) or receive from the Recipients (in the case of an overvaluation) an amount equal to the difference between the unitrust amount properly payable and the unitrust amount actually paid.

3. Payment of Federal Estate Taxes and State Death Taxes. The lifetime unitrust interest of the second Recipient will take effect upon the death of the first Recipient only if the second Recipient furnishes the funds for payment of any federal estate taxes or state death taxes for which the Trustee may be liable upon the death of the first Recipient. [THIS PROVISION IS MANDATORY ONLY IF ALL OR A PORTION OF THE TRUST MAY BE SUBJECT TO SUCH TAXES ON THE DEATH OF THE FIRST RECIPIENT.]

4. Proration of the Unitrust Amount. In determining the unitrust amount, the Trustee shall prorate the same on a daily basis for a short taxable year and for the taxable year ending with the survivor Recipient's death.

5. Distribution to Charity. Upon the death of the survivor Recipient, the Trustee shall distribute all of the then principal and income of the Trust (other than any amount due either of the Recipients or their estates under the provisions above) to _____ (hereinafter referred to as "the Charitable Organization"). If the Charitable Organization is not an organization described in sections 170(c), 2055(a), and 2522(a) of the Code at the time when any principal or income of the Trust is to be distributed to it, then the Trustee shall distribute such principal or income to such one or more organizations described in sections 170(c), 2055(a), and 2522(a) as the Trustee shall select in its sole discretion.

6. Additional Contributions. If any additional contributions are made to the Trust after the initial contribution, the unitrust amount for the year in which the additional contribution is made shall be [THE SAME PERCENTAGE AS IN PARAGRAPH 2] percent of the sum of (a) the net fair market value of the Trust assets as of the valuation date (excluding the assets so added and any income from, or appreciation on, such assets) and (b) that proportion of the fair market value of the assets so added that was excluded under (a) that the number of days in the period that begins with the date of contribution and ends with the earlier of the last day of the taxable year or the date of death of the survivor Recipient bears to the number of days in the period that begins on the first day of such taxable year and ends with the earlier of the last day in such taxable year or the date of death of the survivor Recipient. In the case where there is no valuation date after the time of contribution, the assets so added shall be valued as of the time of contribution.

7. Prohibited Transactions. The Trustee shall make distributions at such time and in such manner as not to subject the Trust to tax under section 4942 of the Code. Except for the payment of the unitrust amount to the Recipients, the Trustee shall not engage in any act of self-dealing, as defined in section 4941(d), and shall not make any taxable expenditures, as defined in section 4945(d). The Trustee shall not make any investments that jeopardize the charitable purpose of the Trust, within the meaning of section 4944 and the regulations thereunder, or retain any excess business holdings, within the meaning of section 4943(c).

8. Taxable Year. The taxable year of the Trust shall be the calendar year.

9. Governing Law. The operation of the Trust shall be governed by the laws of the State of _____. The Trustee, however, is prohibited from exercising any power or discretion granted under said laws that would be inconsistent with the qualification of the Trust under section 664(d)(2) of the Code and the corresponding regulations.

10. Limited Power of Amendment. The Trust is irrevocable. The Trustee, however, shall have the power, acting alone, to amend the Trust in any manner required for the sole purpose of ensuring that the Trust qualifies and continues to qualify as a charitable remainder unitrust within the meaning of section 664(d)(2) of the Code.

11. Investment of Trust Assets. Nothing in this Trust instrument shall be construed to restrict the Trustee from investing the Trust assets in a manner that could result in the annual realization of a reasonable amount of income or gain from the sale or disposition of Trust assets.

_____

[DONOR]

_____

[TRUSTEE]

By _____
[ACKNOWLEDGMENTS, WITNESSES, ETC.]

IRS FORM: REV. PROC. 90-30

SECTION 5. SAMPLE INTER VIVOS CHARITABLE REMAINDER UNITRUST: TWO LIVES, CONCURRENT AND CONSECUTIVE INTERESTS

On this _____ day of _____, I, _____ (hereinafter referred to as "the Donor"), desiring to establish a charitable remainder unitrust, within the meaning of section 5 of Rev. Proc. 90-30 and section 664(d)(2) of the Internal Revenue Code (hereinafter referred to as "the Code") hereby create the _____ Charitable Remainder Unitrust and designate [TRUSTEE'S NAME] as the initial Trustee. [ALTERNATE OR SUCCESSOR TRUSTEES MAY ALSO BE DESIGNATED IF DESIRED.]

1. Funding of Trust. The Donor transfers to the Trustee the property described in Schedule A, and the Trustee accepts such property and agrees to hold, manage, and distribute such property of the Trust under the terms set forth in this Trust instrument.

2. Payment of Unitrust Amount. In each taxable year of the Trust, the Trustee shall pay to [a living individual] and [a living individual] (hereinafter referred to as "the Recipients"), in equal shares during their lifetimes, a unitrust amount equal to [at least 5] percent of the net fair market value of the assets of the Trust (the "valuation date"). Upon the death of the first of the Recipients to die, the survivor Recipient shall be entitled to receive the entire unitrust amount. The unitrust amount shall be paid in equal quarterly amounts from income and, to the extent that income is not sufficient, from principal. Any income of the Trust for a taxable year in excess of the unitrust amount shall be added to principal. If for any year the net fair market value of the Trust assets is incorrectly determined, then within a reasonable period after the value is finally determined for federal tax purposes, the Trustee shall pay to the Recipients (in the case of an undervaluation) or receive from the Recipients (in the case of an overvaluation) an amount equal to the difference between the unitrust amount properly payable and the unitrust amount actually paid.

3. Payment of Federal Estate Taxes and State Death Taxes. The lifetime unitrust interest of the survivor Recipient will continue in effect upon the death of the first Recipient to die only if the survivor Recipient furnishes the funds for payment of any federal estate taxes or state death taxes for which the Trustee may be liable upon the death of the first Recipient to die. [THIS PROVISION IS MANDATORY ONLY IF ALL OR A PORTION OF THE TRUST MAY BE SUBJECT TO SUCH TAXES ON THE DEATH OF THE FIRST RECIPIENT TO DIE.]

4. Proration of the Unitrust Amount. In determining the unitrust amount, the Trustee shall prorate the same on a daily basis for a short taxable year and for the taxable year ending with the survivor Recipient's death.

5. Distribution to Charity. Upon the death of the survivor Recipient, the Trustee shall distribute all of the then principal and income of the Trust (other than any amount due either of the Recipients or their estates under the provisions above) to _____ (hereinafter referred to as "the Charitable Organization"). If the Charitable Organization is not an organization described in sections 170(c), 2055(a), and 2522(a) of the Code at the time when any principal or income of the Trust is to be distributed to it, then the Trustee shall distribute such principal or income to such one or more organizations described in sections 170(c), 2055(a), and 2522(a) as the Trustee shall select in its sole discretion.

6. Additional Contributions. If any additional contributions are made to the Trust after the initial contribution, the unitrust amount for the year in which the additional contribution is made shall be [THE SAME PERCENTAGE AS IN PARAGRAPH 2] percent of the sum of (a) the net fair market value of the Trust assets as of the valuation date (excluding the assets so added and any income from, or appreciation on, such assets) and (b) that proportion of the fair market value of the assets so added that was excluded under (a) that the number of days in the period that begins with the date of contribution and ends with the earlier of the last day of the taxable year or the date of death of the survivor Recipient bears to the number of days in the period that begins on the first day of such taxable year and ends with the earlier of the last day in such taxable year or the date of death of the survivor Recipient. In the case where there is no valuation date after the time of contribution, the assets so added shall be valued as of the time of contribution.

7. Prohibited Transactions. The Trustee shall make distributions at such time and in such manner as not to subject the Trust to tax under section 4942 of the Code. Except for the payment of the unitrust amount to the Recipients, the Trustee shall not engage in any act of self-dealing, as defined in section 4941(d), and shall not make any taxable expenditures, as defined in section 4945(d). The Trustee shall not make any investments that jeopardize the charitable purpose of the Trust, within the meaning of section 4944 and the regulations thereunder, or retain any excess business holdings, within the meaning of section 4943(c).

8. Taxable Year. The taxable year of the Trust shall be the calendar year.

9. Governing Law. The operation of the Trust shall be governed by the laws of the State of _____. The Trustee, however, is prohibited from exercising any power or discretion granted under said laws that would be inconsistent with the qualification of the Trust under section 664(d)(2) of the Code and the corresponding regulations.

10. Limited Power of Amendment. The Trust is irrevocable. The Trustee, however, shall have the power, acting alone, to amend the Trust in any manner required for the sole purpose of ensuring that the Trust qualifies and continues to qualify as a charitable remainder unitrust within the meaning of section 664(d)(2) of the Code.

11. Investment of Trust Assets. Nothing in this Trust instrument shall be construed to restrict the Trustee from investing the Trust assets in a manner that could result in the annual realization of a reasonable amount of income or gain from the sale or disposition of Trust assets.

_____

[DONOR]

_____

[TRUSTEE]

By _____
[ACKNOWLEDGMENTS, WITNESSES, ETC.]

SECTION 6. SAMPLE TESTAMENTARY CHARITABLE REMAINDER UNITRUST: ONE LIFE

All the rest, residue, and remainder of my property and estate, real and personal, of whatever nature and wherever situated [ALTERNATIVELY, IF NOT A RESIDUARY BEQUEST, DESCRIBE OR IDENTIFY THE BEQUEST], I give, devise, and bequeath to my Trustee in trust. It being my intention to establish a charitable remainder unitrust within the meaning of section 6 of Rev. Proc. 90-30 and section 664(d)(2) of the Internal Revenue Code (hereinafter referred to as "the Code"), such Trust shall be known as the _____ Charitable Remainder Unitrust and I hereby designate _____ as the initial Trustee. [ALTERNATE OR SUCCESSOR TRUSTEES MAY ALSO BE DESIGNATED IF DESIRED.]

1. Payment of Unitrust Amount. In each taxable year of the Trust, the Trustee shall pay to [a living individual] (hereinafter referred to as "the Recipient") during the Recipient's life a unitrust amount equal to [at least 5] percent of the net fair market value of the assets of the Trust valued as of the first day of each taxable year of the Trust (the "valuation date"). The unitrust amount shall be paid in equal quarterly amounts from income and, to the extent that income is not sufficient, from principal. Any income of the Trust for a taxable year in excess of the unitrust amount shall be added to principal. If for any year the net fair market value of the Trust assets is incorrectly determined, then within a reasonable period after the value is finally determined for federal tax purposes, the Trustee shall pay to the Recipient (in the case of an undervaluation) or receive from the Recipient (in the case of an overvaluation) an amount equal to the difference between the unitrust amount properly payable and the unitrust amount actually paid.

2. Deferral Provision. The obligation to pay the unitrust amount shall commence with the date of my death, but payment of the unitrust amount may be deferred from such date until the end of the taxable year of the Trust in which occurs the complete funding of the Trust. Within a reasonable time after the end of the taxable year in which the complete funding of the Trust occurs, the Trustee must pay to the Recipient (in the case of an underpayment) or receive from the Recipient (in the case of an overpayment) the difference between: (1) any unitrust amounts actually paid, plus interest, compounded annually, computed for any period at the rate of interest that the federal income tax regulations under section 664 of the Code prescribe for the Trust for such computation for such period; and (2) the unitrust amounts payable, plus interest, compounded annually, computed for any period at the rate of interest that the federal income tax regulations under section 664 prescribe for the Trust for such computation for such period.

3. Proration of the Unitrust Amount. In determining the unitrust amount, the Trustee shall prorate the same on a daily basis for a short taxable year and for the taxable year ending with the Recipient's death.

4. Distribution to Charity. Upon the death of the Recipient, the Trustee shall distribute all of the then principal and income of the Trust (other than any amount due the Recipient or the Recipient's estate under the provisions above) to _____ (hereinafter referred to as "the Charitable Organization"). If the Charitable Organization is not an organization described in sections 170(c) and 2055(a) of the Code at the time when any principal or income of the Trust is to be distributed to it, then the Trustee shall distribute such principal or income to such one or more organizations described in sections 170(c) and 2055(a) as the Trustee shall select in its sole discretion.

5. Additional Contributions. No additional contributions shall be made to the Trust after the initial contribution. The initial contribution, however, shall consist of all property passing to the Trust by reason of my death.

6. Prohibited Transactions. The trustee shall make distributions at such time and in such manner as not to subject the Trust to tax under section 4942 of the Code. Except for the payment of the unitrust amount to the Recipient, the Trustee shall not engage in any act of self-dealing, as defined in section 4941(d), and shall not make any taxable expenditures, as defined in section 4945(d). The Trustee shall not make any investments that jeopardize the charitable purpose of the Trust, within the meaning of section 4944 and the regulations thereunder, or retain any excess business holdings, within the meaning of section 4943(c).

7. Taxable Year. The taxable year of the Trust shall be the calendar year.

8. Governing Law. The operation of the Trust shall be governed by the laws of the State of _____. The Trustee, however, is prohibited from exercising any power or discretion granted under said laws that would be inconsistent with the qualification of the Trust under section 664(d)(2) of the Code and the corresponding regulations.

9. Limited Power of Amendment. The Trustee shall have the power, acting alone, to amend the Trust in any manner required for the sole purpose of ensuring that the Trust qualifies and continues to qualify as a charitable remainder unitrust within the meaning of section 664(d)(2) of the Code.

10. Investment of Trust Assets. Nothing herein shall be construed to restrict the Trustee from investing the Trust assets in a manner that could result in the annual realization of a reasonable amount of income or gain from the sale or disposition of Trust assets.

_____
[DONOR]

_____
[TRUSTEE]

By _____
[ACKNOWLEDGMENTS, WITNESSES, ETC.]

IRS FORM: REV. PROC. 90-30

SECTION 7. SAMPLE TESTAMENTARY CHARITABLE REMAINDER UNITRUST: TWO LIVES, CONSECUTIVE INTERESTS

All the rest, residue, and remainder of my property and estate, real and personal, of whatever nature and wherever situated [ALTERNATIVELY, IF NOT A RESIDUARY BEQUEST, DESCRIBE OR IDENTIFY THE BEQUEST], I give, devise, and bequeath to my Trustee in trust. It being my intention to establish a charitable remainder unitrust within the meaning of section 7 of Rev. Proc. 90-30 and section 664(d)(2) of the Internal Revenue Code (hereinafter referred to as "the Code"), such Trust shall be known as the _____ Charitable Remainder Unitrust and I hereby designate _____ as the initial Trustee. [ALTERNATE OR SUCCESSOR TRUSTEES MAY ALSO BE DESIGNATED IF DESIRED.]

1. Payment of Unitrust Amount. In each taxable year of the Trust, the Trustee shall pay to [a living individual] during his or her lifetime, and after his or her death to [a living individual] (hereinafter referred to as "the Recipients"), for such time as he or she survives, a unitrust amount equal to [at least 5] percent of the net fair market value of the assets of the Trust valued as of the first day of each taxable year of the Trust (the "valuation date"). The unitrust amount shall be paid in equal quarterly amounts from income and, to the extent that income is not sufficient, from principal. Any income of the Trust for a taxable year in excess of the unitrust amount shall be added to principal. If for any year the net fair market value of the Trust assets is incorrectly determined, then within a reasonable period after the value is finally determined for federal tax purposes, the Trustee shall pay to the Recipients (in the case of an undervaluation) or receive from the Recipients (in the case of an overvaluation) an amount equal to the difference between the unitrust amount properly payable and the unitrust amount actually paid.

2. Deferral Provision. The obligation to pay the unitrust amount shall commence with the date of my death, but payment of the unitrust amount may be deferred from such date until the end of the taxable year of the Trust in which occurs the complete funding of the Trust. Within a reasonable time after the end of the taxable year in which the complete funding of the Trust occurs, the Trustee must pay to the Recipients (in the case of an underpayment) or receive from the Recipients (in the case of an overpayment) the difference between: (1) any unitrust amounts actually paid, plus interest, compounded annually, computed for any period at the rate of interest that the federal income tax regulations under section 664 of the Code prescribe for the Trust for such computation for such period, and (2) the unitrust amounts payable, plus interest, compounded annually, computed for any period at the rate of interest that the federal income tax regulations under section 664 prescribe for the Trust for such computation for such period.

3. Proration of the Unitrust Amount. In determining the unitrust amount, the Trustee shall prorate the same on a daily basis for a short taxable year and for the taxable year ending with the survivor Recipient's death.

4. Distribution to Charity. Upon the death of the survivor Recipient, the Trustee shall distribute all of the then principal and income of the Trust (other than any amount due either of the Recipients or their estates under the provisions above) to _____ (hereinafter referred to as "the Charitable Organization"). If the Charitable Organization is not an organization described in sections 170(c) and 2055(a) of the Code at the time when any principal or income of the Trust is to be distributed to it, then the Trustee shall distribute such principal or income to such one or more organizations described in sections 170(c) and 2055(a) as the Trustee shall select in its sole discretion.

5. Additional Contributions. No additional contributions shall be made to the Trust after the initial contribution. The initial contribution, however, shall consist of all property passing to the Trust by reason of my death.

6. Prohibited Transactions. The trustee shall make distributions at such time and in such manner as not to subject the Trust to tax under section 4942 of the Code. Except for the payment of the unitrust amount to

the Recipient, the Trustee shall not engage in any act of self-dealing, as defined in section 4945(d), and shall not make any taxable expenditures, as defined in section 4945(d). The Trustee shall not make any investments that jeopardize the charitable purpose of the Trust, within the meaning of section 4944 and the regulations thereunder, or retain any excess business holdings, within the meaning of section 4943(c).

7. Taxable Year. The taxable year of the Trust shall be the calendar year.

8. Governing Law. The operation of the Trust shall be governed by the laws of the State of _____. The Trustee, however, is prohibited from exercising any power or discretion granted under said laws that would be inconsistent with the qualification of the Trust under section 664(d)(2) of the Code and the corresponding regulations.

9. Limited Power of Amendment. The Trustee shall have the power, acting alone, to amend the Trust in any manner required for the sole purpose of ensuring that the Trust qualifies and continues to qualify as a charitable remainder unitrust within the meaning of section 664(d)(2) of the Code.

10. Investment of Trust Assets. Nothing herein shall be construed to restrict the Trustee from investing the Trust assets in a manner that could result in the annual realization of a reasonable amount of income or gain from the sale or disposition of Trust assets.

_____

[DONOR]

_____

[TRUSTEE]

By _____
[ACKNOWLEDGMENTS, WITNESSES, ETC.]

SECTION 8. SAMPLE TESTAMENTARY CHARITABLE REMAINDER UNITRUST: TWO LIVES, CONCURRENT AND CONSECUTIVE INTERESTS

All the rest, residue, and remainder of my property and estate, real or personal, of whatever nature and wherever situated [ALTERNATIVELY, IF NOT A RESIDUARY BEQUEST, DESCRIBE OR IDENTIFY THE BEQUEST], I give, devise, and bequeath to my Trustee in trust. It being my intention to establish a charitable remainder unitrust within the meaning of section 8 of Rev. Proc. 90-30 and section 664(d)(2) of the Internal Revenue Code (hereinafter referred to as "the Code"), such Trust shall be known as the _____ Charitable Remainder Unitrust and I hereby designate _____ as the initial Trustee. [ALTERNATE OR SUCCESSOR TRUSTEES MAY ALSO BE DESIGNATED IF DESIRED.]

1. Payment of Unitrust Amount. In each taxable year of the trust, the Trustee shall pay to [a living individual] and [a living individual] (hereinafter referred to as "the Recipients"), in equal shares during their lifetimes, a unitrust amount equal to [at least 5] percent of the net fair market value of the assets of the Trust valued as of the first day of each taxable year of the Trust (the "valuation date"). Upon the death of the first of the Recipients to die, the survivor Recipient shall be entitled to receive the entire unitrust amount. The unitrust amount shall be paid in equal quarterly amounts from income and, to the extent that income is not sufficient, from principal. Any income of the Trust for a taxable year in excess of the unitrust amount shall be added to principal. If for any year the net fair market value of the Trust assets is incorrectly determined, then within a reasonable period after the value is finally determined for federal tax purposes, the Trustee shall pay to the Recipients (in the case of an undervaluation) or receive from the Recipients (in the case of an overvaluation) an amount equal to the difference between the unitrust amount properly payable and the unitrust amount actually paid.

2. Deferral Provision. The obligation to pay the unitrust amount shall commence with the date of my death, but payment of the unitrust amount may be deferred from such date until the end of the taxable year of the Trust in which occurs the complete funding of the Trust. Within a reasonable time after the end of the taxable year in which the complete funding of the Trust occurs, the Trustee must pay to the Recipients (in the case of an underpayment) or receive from the Recipients (in the case of an overpayment) the difference between: (1) any unitrust amounts actually paid, plus interest, compounded annually, computed for any period at the rate of interest that the federal income tax regulations under section 664 of the Code prescribe for the Trust for such computation for such period; and (2) the unitrust amounts payable, plus interest, compounded annually, computed for any period at the rate of interest that the federal income tax regulations under section 664 prescribe for the Trust for such computation for such period.

3. Proration of the Unitrust Amount. In determining the unitrust amount, the Trustee shall prorate the same on a daily basis for a short taxable year and for the taxable year ending with the survivor Recipient's death.

4. Distribution to Charity. Upon the death of the survivor Recipient, the Trustee shall distribute all of the then principal and income of the Trust (other than any amount due either of the Recipients or their estates under the provisions above) to _____ (hereinafter referred to as "the Charitable Organization"). If the Charitable Organization is not an organization described in sections 170(c) and 2055(a) of the Code at the time when any principal or income of the Trust is to be distributed to it, then the Trustee shall distribute such principal or income to such one or more organizations described in sections 170(c) and 2055(a) as the Trustee shall select in its sole discretion.

5. Additional Contributions. No additional contributions shall be made to the Trust after the initial contribution. The initial contribution, however, shall consist of all property passing to the Trust by reason of my death.

6. Prohibited Transactions. The trustee shall make distributions at such time and in such manner as not to subject the Trust to tax under section 4942 of the Code. Except for the payment of the unitrust amount to the Recipient, the Trustee shall not engage in any act of self-dealing, as defined in section 4941(d), and shall not make any taxable expenditures, as defined in section 4945(d). The Trustee shall not make any investments that jeopardize the charitable purpose of the Trust, within the meaning of section 4944 and the regulations thereunder, or retain any excess business holdings, within the meaning of section 4943(c).

7. Taxable Year. The taxable year of the Trust shall be the calendar year.

8. Governing Law. The operation of the Trust shall be governed by the laws of the State of _____. The Trustee, however, is prohibited from exercising any power or discretion granted under said laws that would be inconsistent with the qualification of the Trust under section 664(d)(2) of the Code and the corresponding regulations.

9. Limited Power of Amendment. The Trustee shall have the power, acting alone, to amend the Trust in any manner required for the sole purpose of ensuring that the Trust qualifies and continues to qualify as a charitable remainder unitrust within the meaning of section 664(d)(2) of the Code.

10. Investment of Trust Assets. Nothing herein shall be construed to restrict the Trustee from investing the Trust assets in a manner that could result in the annual realization of a reasonable amount of income or gain from the sale or disposition of Trust assets.

_____

[DONOR]

_____

[TRUSTEE]

By _____
[ACKNOWLEDGMENTS, WITNESSES, ETC.]

IRS FORM: REV. PROC. 90-31

SECTION 4. SAMPLE INTER VIVOS CHARITABLE REMAINDER UNITRUST: ONE LIFE

On this _____ day of _____, I, _____ (hereinafter referred to as "the Donor"), desiring to establish a charitable remainder unitrust within the meaning of section 4 of Rev. Proc. 90-31 and section 664(d)(2) and (3) of the Internal Revenue Code (hereinafter referred to as "the Code") hereby create the _____ Charitable Remainder Unitrust and designate _____ as the initial Trustee. [ALTERNATE OR SUCCESSOR TRUSTEES MAY ALSO BE DESIGNATED IF DESIRED.]

1. Funding of Trust. The Donor transfers to the Trustee the property described in Schedule A, and the Trustee accepts such property and agrees to hold, manage, and distribute such property of the Trust under the terms set forth in this Trust instrument.

2. Payment of Unitrust Amount. In each taxable year of the Trust, the Trustee shall pay to [name of a living individual] (hereinafter referred to as "the Recipient") during the Recipient's life a unitrust amount equal to the lesser of: (a) the Trust income for the taxable year, as defined in section 643(b) of the Code and the regulations thereunder, and (b) [at least 5] percent of the net fair market value of the assets of the Trust valued as of the first day of each taxable year of the Trust (the "valuation date"). The unitrust amount for any year shall also include any amount of Trust income for such year that is in excess of the amount required to be distributed under (b) (above) to the extent that the aggregate of the amounts paid in prior years was less than the aggregate of the amounts computed as [SAME PERCENTAGE AS IN (B) ABOVE] percent of the net fair market value of the Trust assets on the valuation dates.

   The unitrust amount shall be paid in quarterly installments. Any income of the Trust for taxable year in excess of the unitrust amount shall be added to principal. If for any year the net fair market value of the Trust assets is incorrectly determined, then within a reasonable period after the value is finally determined for federal tax purposes, the Trustee shall pay to the Recipient (in the case of an undervaluation) or receive from the Recipient (in the case of an overvaluation) an amount equal to the difference between the unitrust amount properly payable and the unitrust amount actually paid.

3. Proration of the Unitrust Amount. In determining the unitrust amount, the Trustee shall prorate the same on a daily basis for a short taxable year and for the taxable year ending with the Recipient's death.

4. Distribution to Charity. Upon the death of the Recipient, the Trustee shall distribute all of the then principal and income of the Trust (other than any amount due the Recipient or the Recipient's estate under the provisions above) to _____ (hereinafter referred to as "the Charitable Organization"). If the Charitable Organization is not an organization described in sections 170(c), 2055(a), and 2522(a) of the Code at the time when any principal or income of the Trust is to be distributed to it, then the Trustee shall distribute such principal or income to such one or more organizations described in sections 170(c), 2055(a), and 2522(a) as the Trustee shall select in its sole discretion.

5. Additional Contributions. If any additional contributions are made to the Trust after the initial contribution, the unitrust amount for the year in which the additional contribution is made shall be equal to the lesser of (a) the Trust income for the taxable year, as defined in section 643(b) of the Code and the regulations thereunder, and (b) [THE SAME PERCENTAGE AS IN PARAGRAPH 2] percent of the sum of (1) the net fair market value of the Trust assets as of the valuation date (excluding the assets so added and any income from, or appreciation on, such assets) and (2) that proportion of the fair market value of the assets so added that was excluded under (1) that the number of days in the period that begins with the date of contribution and ends with the earlier of the last day of the taxable year or the day of the Recipient's death bears to the number of days in the period that begins on the first day of such taxable year and ends with the earlier of the last day in such taxable year or the day of the Recipient's death. In the case where there is no valuation date after the time of contribution, the assets so added shall be valued as of the time of contribution. The unitrust amount for any such year shall also include any amount of Trust income for such year that is in excess of the amount required to be distributed under (b) above to the extent that the aggregate of the amounts paid in prior years was less than the aggregate of the amounts computed as [SAME PERCENTAGE AS IN (B) ABOVE] percent of the net fair market value of the Trust assets on the valuation dates.

6. Prohibited Transactions. The Trustee shall make distributions at such time and in such manner as not to subject the Trust to tax under section 4942 of the Code. Except for the payment of the unitrust amount to the Recipient, the Trustee shall not engage in any act of self-dealing, as defined in section 4941(d), and shall not make any taxable expenditures, as defined in section 4945(d). The Trustee shall not make any investments that jeopardize the charitable purpose of the Trust, within the meaning of section 4944 and the regulations thereunder, or retain any excess business holdings, within the meaning of section 4943(c).

7. Taxable Year. The taxable year of the Trust shall be the calendar year.

8. Governing Law. The operation of the Trust shall be governed by the laws of the State of _____. The Trustee, however, is prohibited from exercising any power or discretion granted under said laws that would be inconsistent with the qualification of the Trust under section 664(d)(2) and (3) of the Code and the corresponding regulations.

9. Limited Power of Amendment. The Trust is irrevocable. The Trustee, however, shall have the power, acting alone, to amend the Trust in any manner required for the sole purpose of ensuring that the Trust qualifies and continues to qualify as a charitable remainder unitrust within the meaning of section 664(d)(2) and (3) of the Code.

10. Investment of Trust Assets. Nothing in this Trust instrument shall be construed to restrict the Trustee from investing the Trust assets in a manner that could result in the annual realization of a reasonable amount of income or gain from the sale or disposition of Trust assets.

IN WITNESS WHEREOF _____ and [TRUSTEE] by its duly authorized officer have signed this agreement the day and year first above written.

_____

[DONOR]

_____

[TRUSTEE]

By _____
[ACKNOWLEDGMENTS, WITNESSES, ETC.]

IRS FORM: REV. PROC. 90-31

SECTION 5. SAMPLE INTER VIVOS CHARITABLE REMAINDER UNITRUST: TWO LIVES, CONSECUTIVE INTERESTS

On this _____ day of _____, I, _____ (hereinafter referred to as "the Donor"), desiring to establish a charitable remainder unitrust within the meaning of section 5 of Rev. Proc. 90-31 and section 664(d)(2) and (3) of the Internal Revenue Code (hereinafter referred to as "the Code") hereby create the _____ Charitable Remainder Unitrust and designate _____ as the initial Trustee. [ALTERNATE OR SUCCESSOR TRUSTEES MAY ALSO BE DESIGNATED IF DESIRED.]

1. Funding of Trust. The Donor transfers to the Trustee the property described in Schedule A, and the Trustee accepts such property and agrees to hold, manage, and distribute such property of the Trust under the terms set forth in this Trust instrument.

2. Payment of Unitrust Amount. In each taxable year of the Trust, the Trustee shall pay to [a living individual] during his or her lifetime, and after his or her death, to [a living individual] (hereinafter referred to as "the Recipients"), for such time as he or she survives, a unitrust amount equal to the lesser of: (a) the Trust income for the taxable year, as defined in section 643(b) of the Code and the regulations thereunder, and (b) [at least 5] percent of the net fair market value of the assets of the Trust valued as of the first day of each taxable year of the Trust (the "valuation date"). The unitrust amount for any year shall also include any amount of Trust income for such year that is in excess of the amount required to be distributed under (b) (above) to the extent that the aggregate of the amounts paid in prior years was less than the aggregate of the amounts computed as [SAME PERCENTAGE AS IN (B) ABOVE] percent of the net fair market value of the Trust assets on the valuation dates.

   The unitrust amount shall be paid in quarterly installments. Any income of the Trust for a taxable year in excess of the unitrust amount shall be added to principal. If for any year the net fair market value of the Trust assets is incorrectly determined, then within a reasonable period after the value is finally determined for federal tax purposes, the Trustee shall pay to the Recipients (in the case of an undervaluation) or receive from the Recipients (in the case of an overvaluation) an amount equal to the difference between the unitrust amount properly payable and the unitrust amount actually paid.

3. Payment of Federal Estate Taxes and State Death Taxes. The lifetime unitrust interest of the second Recipient will take effect upon the death of the first Recipient only if the second Recipient furnishes the funds for payment of any federal estate taxes or state death taxes for which the Trustee may be liable upon the death of the first Recipient. [THIS PROVISION IS MANDATORY ONLY IF ALL OR A PORTION OF THE TRUST MAY BE SUBJECT TO SUCH TAXES ON THE DEATH OF THE FIRST RECIPIENT.]

4. Proration of the Unitrust Amount. In determining the unitrust amount, the Trustee shall prorate the same on a daily basis for a short taxable year and for the taxable year ending with the survivor Recipient's death.

5. Distribution to Charity. Upon the death of the survivor Recipient, the Trustee shall distribute all of the then principal and income of the Trust (other than any amount due either of the Recipients or their estates under the provisions above) to _____ (hereinafter referred to as "the Charitable Organization"). If the Charitable Organization is not an organization described in sections 170(c), 2055(a), and 2522(a) of the Code at the time when any principal or income of the Trust is to be distributed to it, then the Trustee shall distribute such principal or income to such one or more organizations described in sections 170(c), 2055(a), and 2522(a) as the Trustee shall select in its sole discretion.

6. Additional Contributions. If any additional contributions are made to the Trust after the initial contribution, the unitrust amount for the year in which the additional contribution is made shall be equal to the lesser of (a) the Trust income for the taxable year, as defined in section 643(b) of the Code and the regulations thereunder,

and (b) [THE SAME PERCENTAGE AS IN PARAGRAPH 2] percent of the sum of (1) the net fair market value of the Trust assets as of the valuation date (excluding the assets so added and any income from, or appreciation on, such assets) and (2) that proportion of the fair market value of the assets so added that was excluded under (1) that the number of days in the period that begins with the date of contribution and ends with the earlier of the last day of the taxable year or the date of death of the survivor Recipient bears to the number of days in the period that begins on the first day of such taxable year and ends with the earlier of the last day in such taxable year or the date of death of the survivor Recipient. In the case where there is no valuation date after the time of contribution, the assets so added shall be valued as of the time of contribution. The unitrust amount for any such year shall also include any amount of Trust income for such year that is in excess of the amount required to be distributed under (b) above to the extent that the aggregate of the amounts paid in prior years was less than the aggregate of the amounts computed as [SAME PERCENTAGE AS IN (B) ABOVE] percent of the net fair market value of the Trust assets on the valuation dates.

7. Prohibited Transactions. The Trustee shall make distributions at such time and in such manner as not to subject the Trust to tax under section 4942 of the Code. Except for the payment of the unitrust amount to the Recipients, the Trustee shall not engage in any act of self-dealing, as defined in section 4941(d), and shall not make any taxable expenditures, as defined in section 4945(d). The Trustee shall not make any investments that jeopardize the charitable purpose of the Trust, within the meaning of section 4944 and the regulations thereunder, or retain any excess business holdings, within the meaning of section 4943(c).

8. Taxable Year. The taxable year of the Trust shall be the calendar year.

9. Governing Law. The operation of the Trust shall be governed by the laws of the State of _____. The Trustee, however, is prohibited from exercising any power or discretion granted under said laws that would be inconsistent with the qualification of the Trust under section 664(d)(2) and (3) of the Code and the corresponding regulations.

10. Limited Power of Amendment. The Trust is irrevocable. The Trustee, however, shall have the power, acting alone, to amend the Trust in any manner required for the sole purpose of ensuring that the Trust qualifies and continues to qualify as a charitable remainder unitrust within the meaning of section 664(d)(2) and (3) of the Code.

11. Investment of Trust Assets. Nothing in this Trust instrument shall be construed to restrict the Trustee from investing the Trust assets in a manner that could result in the annual realization of a reasonable amount of income or gain from the sale or disposition of Trust assets.

IN WITNESS WHEREOF _____ and [TRUSTEE] by its duly authorized officer have signed this agreement the day and year first above written.

_____
[DONOR]

_____
[TRUSTEE]

By _____
[ACKNOWLEDGMENTS, WITNESSES, ETC.]

SECTION 6. SAMPLE INTER VIVOS CHARITABLE REMAINDER UNITRUST: TWO LIVES, CONCURRENT AND CONSECUTIVE INTERESTS

On this _____ day of _____, I, _____ (hereinafter referred to as "the Donor"), desiring to establish a charitable remainder unitrust, within the meaning of section 6 of Rev. Proc. 90-31 and section 664(d)(2) and (3) of the Internal Revenue Code (hereinafter referred to as "the Code") hereby create the _____ Charitable Remainder Unitrust and designate _____ as the initial Trustee. [ALTERNATE OR SUCCESSOR TRUSTEES MAY ALSO BE DESIGNATED IF DESIRED.]

1. Funding of Trust. The Donor transfers to the Trustee property described in Schedule A, and the Trustee accepts such property and agrees to hold, manage, and distribute such property of the Trust under the terms set forth in this Trust instrument.

2. Payment of Unitrust Amount. In each taxable year of the Trust, the Trustee shall pay to [a living individual] and [a living individual] (hereinafter referred to as "the Recipients") in equal shares during their lifetimes, a unitrust amount equal to the lesser of: (a) the Trust income for the taxable year, as defined in section 643(b) of the Code and the regulations thereunder, and (b) [at least 5] percent of the net fair market value of the assets of the Trust valued as of the first day of each taxable year of the Trust (the "valuation date"). The unitrust amount for any year shall also include any amount of Trust income for such year that is in excess of the amount required to be distributed under (b) (above) to the extent that the aggregate of the amounts paid in prior years was less than the aggregate of the amounts computed as [SAME PERCENTAGE AS IN (B) ABOVE] percent of the net fair market value of the Trust assets on the valuation dates. Upon the death of the first of the Recipients to die, the survivor Recipient shall be entitled to receive the entire unitrust amount. The unitrust amount shall be paid in quarterly installments. Any income of the Trust for a taxable year in excess of the unitrust amount shall be added to principal. If for any year the net fair market value of the Trust assets is incorrectly determined, then within a reasonable period after the value is finally determined for federal tax purposes, the Trustee shall pay to the Recipients (in the case of an undervaluation) or receive from the Recipients (in the case of an overvaluation) an amount equal to the difference between the unitrust amount properly payable and the unitrust amount actually paid.

3. Payment of Federal Estate Taxes and State Death Taxes. The lifetime unitrust interest of the survivor Recipient will continue in effect upon the death of the first Recipient to die only if the survivor Recipient furnishes the funds for payment of any federal estate taxes or state death taxes for which the Trustee may be liable upon the death of the first Recipient to die. [THIS PROVISION IS MANDATORY ONLY IF ALL OR A PORTION OF THE TRUST MAY BE SUBJECT TO SUCH TAXES ON THE DEATH OF THE FIRST RECIPIENT TO DIE.]

4. Proration of the Unitrust Amount. In determining the unitrust amount, the Trustee shall prorate the same on a daily basis for a short taxable year and for the taxable year ending with the survivor's death.

5. Distribution to Charity. Upon the death of the survivor Recipient, the Trustee shall distribute all of the then principal and income of the Trust (other than any amount due either of the Recipients or their estates under the provisions above) to _____ (hereinafter referred to as "the Charitable Organization"). If the Charitable Organization is not an organization described in sections 170(c), 2055(a), and 2522(a) of the Code at the time when any principal or income of the Trust is to be distributed to it, then the Trustee shall distribute such principal or income to such one or more organizations described in sections 170(c), 2055(a), and 2522(a) as the Trustee shall select in its sole discretion.

6. Additional Contributions. If any additional contributions are made to the Trust after the initial contribution, the unitrust amount for the year in which the additional contribution is made shall be equal to the lesser of (a) the Trust income for the taxable year, as defined in section 643(b) of the Code and the regulations thereunder,

and (b) [THE SAME PERCENTAGE AS IN PARAGRAPH 2] percent of the sum of (1) the net fair market value of the Trust assets as of the valuation date (excluding the assets so added and any income from, or appreciation on, such assets) and (2) that proportion of the fair market value of the assets so added that was excluded under (1) that the number of days in the period that begins with the date of contribution and ends with the earlier of the last day of the taxable year or the date of death of the survivor Recipient bears to the number of days in the period that begins on the first day of such taxable year and ends with the earlier of the last day in such taxable year or the date of death of the survivor Recipient. In the case where there is no valuation date after the time of contribution, the assets so added shall be valued as of the time of contribution. The unitrust amount for any such year shall also include any amount of Trust income for such year that is in excess of the amount required to be distributed under (b) (above) to the extent that the aggregate of the amounts paid in prior years was less than the aggregate of the amounts computed as [SAME PERCENTAGE AS IN (B) ABOVE] percent of the net fair market value of the Trust assets on the valuation dates.

7. Prohibited Transactions. The Trustee shall make distributions at such time and in such manner as not to subject the Trust to tax under section 4942 of the Code. Except for the payment of the unitrust amount to the Recipients, the Trustee shall not engage in any act of self-dealing, as defined in section 4941(d), and shall not make any taxable expenditures, as defined in section 4945(d). The Trustee shall not make any investments that jeopardize the charitable purpose of the Trust, within the meaning of section 4944 and the regulations thereunder, or retain any excess business holdings, within the meaning of section 4943(c).

8. Taxable Year. The taxable year of the Trust shall be the calendar year.

9. Governing Law. The operation of the Trust shall be governed by the laws of the State of _____. The Trustee, however, is prohibited from exercising any power or discretion granted under said laws that would be inconsistent with the qualification of the Trust under section 664(d)(2) and (3) of the Code and the corresponding regulations.

10. Limited Power of Amendment. The Trust is irrevocable. The Trustee, however, shall have the power, acting alone, to amend the Trust in any manner required for the sole purpose of ensuring that the Trust qualifies and continues to qualify as a charitable remainder unitrust within the meaning of section 664(d)(2) and (3) of the Code.

11. Investment of Trust Assets. Nothing in this Trust instrument shall be construed to restrict the Trustee from investing the Trust assets in a manner that could result in the annual realization of a reasonable amount of income or gain from the sale or disposition of Trust assets.

IN WITNESS WHEREOF _____ and [TRUSTEE] by its duly authorized officer have signed this agreement the day and year first above written.

_____
[DONOR]

_____
[TRUSTEE]

By _____
[ACKNOWLEDGMENTS, WITNESSES, ETC.]

SECTION 7. SAMPLE TESTAMENTARY CHARITABLE REMAINDER UNITRUST: ONE LIFE

All the rest, residue, and remainder of my property and estate, real and personal, of whatever nature and wherever situated [ALTERNATIVELY, IF NOT A RESIDUARY BEQUEST, DESCRIBE OR IDENTIFY THE BEQUEST], I give, devise, and bequeath to my Trustee in trust. It being my intention to establish a charitable remainder unitrust within the meaning of section 7 of Rev. Proc. 90-31 and section 664(d)(2) and (3) of the Internal Revenue Code (hereinafter referred to as "the Code"), such Trust shall be known as the _____ Charitable Remainder Unitrust and I hereby designate _____ as the initial Trustee. [ALTERNATE OR SUCCESSOR TRUSTEES MAY ALSO BE DESIGNATED IF DESIRED.]

1. Payment of Unitrust Amount. In each taxable year of the Trust, the Trustee shall pay to [a living individual] (hereinafter referred to as "the Recipient") during the Recipient's life a unitrust amount equal to the lesser of: (a) the Trust income for the taxable year as defined in section 643(b) of the Code and the regulations thereunder, and (b) [at least 5] percent of the net fair market value of the assets of the Trust valued as of the first day of each taxable year of the Trust (the "valuation date"). The unitrust amount for any year shall also include any amount of Trust income for such year that is in excess of the amount required to be distributed under (b) (above) to the extent that the aggregate of the amounts paid in prior years was less than the aggregate of the amounts computed as [SAME PERCENTAGE AS IN (B) ABOVE] percent of the net fair market value of the Trust assets on the valuation dates.

   The unitrust amount shall be paid in quarterly installments. Any income of the Trust for a taxable year in excess of the unitrust amount shall be added to principal. If for any year the net fair market value of the Trust assets is incorrectly determined, then within a reasonable period after the value is finally determined for federal tax purposes, the Trustee shall pay to the Recipient (in the case of an undervaluation) or receive from the Recipient (in the case of an overvaluation) an amount equal to the difference between the unitrust amount properly payable and the unitrust amount actually paid.

2. Deferral Provision. The obligation to pay the unitrust amount shall commence with the date of my death, but payment of the unitrust amount may be deferred from such date until the end of the taxable year of the Trust in which occurs the complete funding of the Trust. Within a reasonable time after the end of the taxable year in which the complete funding of the Trust occurs, the Trustee must pay to the Recipient (in the case of an underpayment) or receive from the Recipient (in the case of an overpayment) the difference between: (1) any unitrust amounts actually paid, plus interest compounded annually, computed for any period at the rate of interest that the federal income tax regulations under section 664 of the Code prescribe for the Trust for such computation for such period; and (2) the unitrust amounts payable, plus interest compounded annually, computed for any period at the rate of interest that the federal income tax regulations under section 664 prescribe for the Trust for such computation for such period.

3. Proration of the Unitrust Amount. In determining the unitrust amount, the Trustee shall prorate the same on a daily basis for a short taxable year and for the taxable year ending with the Recipient's death.

4. Distribution to Charity. Upon the death of the Recipient, the Trustee shall distribute all of the then principal and income of the Trust (other than any amount due the Recipient or the Recipient's estate under the provisions above) to _____ (hereinafter referred to as "the Charitable Organization"). If the Charitable Organization is not an organization described in sections 170(c) and 2055(a) of the Code at the time when any principal or income of the Trust is to be distributed to it, then the Trustee shall distribute such principal or income to such one or more organizations described in sections 170(c) and 2055 (a) as the Trustee shall select in its sole discretion.

5. Additional Contributions. No additional contributions shall be made to the Trust after the initial contribution. The initial contribution, however, shall be deemed to consist of all property passing to the Trust by reason of my death.

6. Prohibited Transactions. The Trustee shall make distributions at such time and in such manner as not to subject the Trust to tax under section 4942 of the Code. Except for the payment of the unitrust amount to the Recipient, the Trustee shall not engage in any act of self-dealing, as defined in section 4941(d), and shall not make any taxable expenditures, as defined in section 4945(d). The Trustee shall not make any investments that jeopardize the charitable purpose of the Trust, within the meaning of section 4944 and the regulations thereunder, or retain any excess business holdings, within the meaning of section 4943(c).

7. Taxable year. The taxable year of the Trust shall be the calendar year.

8. Governing Law. The operation of the Trust shall be governed by the laws of the State of _____. The Trustee, however, is prohibited from exercising any power or discretion granted under said laws that would be inconsistent with the qualification of the Trust under section 664(d)(2) and (3) of the Code and the corresponding regulations.

9. Limited Power of Amendment. The Trustee shall have the power, acting alone, to amend the Trust in any manner required for the sole purpose of ensuring that the Trust qualifies and continues to qualify as a charitable remainder unitrust within the meaning of section 664(d)(2) and (3) of the Code.

10. Investment of Trust Assets. Nothing herein shall be construed to restrict the Trustee from investing the Trust assets in a manner that could result in the annual realization of a reasonable amount of income or gain from the sale or disposition of Trust assets.

IN WITNESS WHEREOF _____ and [TRUSTEE] by its duly authorized officer have signed this agreement the day and year first above written.

_____

[DONOR]

_____

[TRUSTEE]

By _____
[ACKNOWLEDGMENTS, WITNESSES, ETC.]

SECTION 8. SAMPLE TESTAMENTARY CHARITABLE REMAINDER UNITRUST: TWO LIVES, CONSECUTIVE INTERESTS

All the rest, residue, and remainder of my property and estate, real and personal, of whatever nature and wherever situated [ALTERNATIVELY, IF NOT A RESIDUARY BEQUEST, DESCRIBE OR IDENTIFY, THE BEQUEST], I give, devise, and bequeath to my Trustee in trust. It being my intention to establish a charitable remainder unitrust within the meaning of section 8 of Rev. Proc. 90-31 and section 664(d)(2) and (3) of the Internal Revenue Code (hereinafter referred to as "the Code"), such Trust shall be known as the _____ Charitable Remainder Unitrust and I hereby designate _____ as the initial Trustee. [ALTERNATE OR SUCCESSOR TRUSTEES MAY ALSO BE DESIGNATED IF DESIRED.]

1. Payment of Unitrust Amount. In each taxable year of the Trust, the Trustee shall pay to [a living individual] during his or her lifetime, and after his or her death, to [a living individual] (hereinafter referred to as "the Recipients"), for such time as he or she survives, a unitrust amount equal to the lesser of: (a) the Trust income for the taxable year, as defined in section 643(b) of the Code and the regulations thereunder, and (b) [at least 5] percent of the net fair market value of the assets of the Trust valued as of the first day of each taxable year of the Trust (the "valuation date"). The unitrust amount for any year shall also include any amount of Trust income for such year that is in excess of the amount required to be distributed under (b) (above) to the extent that the aggregate of the amounts paid in prior years was less than the aggregate of the amounts computed as [SAME PERCENTAGE AS IN (B) ABOVE] percent of the net fair market value of the Trust assets on the valuation dates.

   The unitrust amount shall be paid in quarterly installments. Any income of the Trust for a taxable year in excess of the unitrust amount shall be added to principal. If for any year the net fair market value of the Trust assets is incorrectly determined, then within a reasonable period after the value is finally determined for federal tax purposes, the Trustee shall pay to the Recipients (in the case of an undervaluation) or receive from the Recipients (in the case of an overvaluation) an amount equal to the difference between the unitrust amount properly payable and the unitrust amount actually paid.

2. Deferral Provision. The obligation to pay the unitrust amount shall commence with the date of my death, but payment of the unitrust amount may be deferred from such date until the end of the taxable year of the Trust in which occurs the complete funding of the Trust. Within a reasonable time after the end of the taxable year in which the complete funding of the Trust occurs, the Trustee must pay to the Recipients (in the case of an underpayment) or receive from the Recipients (in the case of an overpayment) the difference between: (1) any unitrust amounts actually paid, plus interest compounded annually, computed for any period at the rate of interest that the federal income tax regulations under section 664 of the Code prescribe for the trust for such computation for such period; and (2) the unitrust amounts payable, plus interest compounded annually, computed for any period at the rate of interest that the federal income tax regulations under section 664 of Code prescribe for the Trust for such computation for such period.

3. Proration of the Unitrust Amount. In determining the unitrust amount, the Trustee shall prorate the same on a daily basis for a short taxable year and for the taxable year ending with the survivor Recipient's death.

4. Distribution to Charity. Upon the death of the survivor Recipient, the Trustee shall distribute all of the then principal and income of the Trust (other than any amount due either of the Recipients or their estates under the provisions above) to _____ (hereinafter referred to as "the Charitable Organization"). If the Charitable Organization is not an organization described in sections 170(c) and 2055(a) of the Code at the time when any principal or income of the Trust is to be distributed to it, then the Trustee shall distribute such principal or income to such one or more organizations described in sections 170(c) and 2055(a) as the Trustee shall select in its sole discretion.

5. Additional Contributions. No additional contributions shall be made to the Trust after the initial contribution. The initial contribution, however, shall be deemed to consist of all property passing to the Trust by reason of my death.

6. Prohibited Transactions. The Trustee shall make distributions at such time and in such manner as not to subject the Trust to tax under section 4942 of the Code. Except for the payment of the unitrust amount to the Recipients, the Trustee shall not engage in any act of self-dealing, as defined in section 4941(d), and shall not make any taxable expenditures, as defined in section 4944(d). The Trustee shall not make any investments that jeopardize the charitable purpose of the Trust, within the meaning of section 4944 and the regulations thereunder, or retain any excess business holdings, within the meaning of section 4943(c).

7. Taxable Year. The taxable year of the Trust shall be the calendar year.

8. Governing Law. The operation of the Trust shall be governed by the laws of the State of _____. The Trustee, however, is prohibited from exercising any power or discretion granted under said laws that would be inconsistent with the qualification of the Trust under section 664(d)(4) and (3) of the Code and the corresponding regulations.

9. Limited Power of Amendment. The Trustee shall have the power, acting alone, to amend the Trust in any manner required for the sole purpose of ensuring that the Trust qualifies and continues to qualify as a charitable remainder unitrust within the meaning of section 664(d)(2) and (3) of the Code.

10. Investment of Trust Assets. Nothing herein shall be construed to restrict the Trustee from investing the Trust assets in a manner that could result in the annual realization of a reasonable amount of income or gain from the sale or disposition of Trust assets.

IN WITNESS WHEREOF _____ and [TRUSTEE] by its duly authorized officer have signed this agreement the day and year first above written.

_____

[DONOR]

_____

[TRUSTEE]

By _____
[ACKNOWLEDGMENTS, WITNESSES, ETC.]

SECTION 9. SAMPLE TESTAMENTARY CHARITABLE REMAINDER UNITRUST: TWO LIVES, CONCURRENT AND CONSECUTIVE INTERESTS

All the rest, residue, and remainder of my property and estate, real and personal, of whatever nature and wherever situated [ALTERNATIVELY, IF NOT A RESIDUARY BEQUEST, DESCRIBE OR IDENTIFY THE BEQUEST], I give, devise, and bequeath to my Trustee in trust. It being my intention to establish a charitable remainder unitrust within the meaning of section 9 of Rev. Proc. 90-31 and section 664(d)(2) and (3) of the Internal Revenue Code (hereinafter referred to as "the Code"), such Trust shall be known as the _____ Charitable Remainder Unitrust and I hereby designate _____ as the initial Trustee. [ALTERNATE OR SUCCESSOR TRUSTEES MAY ALSO BE DESIGNATED IF DESIRED.]

1. Payment of Unitrust Amount. In each taxable year of the Trust, the Trustee shall pay to [a living individual] and [a living individual] (hereinafter referred to as "the Recipients"), in equal shares during their lifetimes, a unitrust amount equal to the lesser of: (a) the Trust income for the taxable year, as defined in section 643(b) of the Code and the regulations thereunder, and (b) [at least 5] percent of the net fair market value of the assets of the Trust valued as of the first day of each taxable year of the Trust (the "valuation date"). The unitrust amount for any year shall also include any amount of Trust income for such year that is in excess of the amount required to be distributed under (b) (above) to the extent that the aggregate of the amounts paid in prior years was less than the aggregate of the amounts computed as [SAME PERCENTAGE AS IN (B) ABOVE] percent of the net fair market value of the trust assets on the valuation dates.

   Upon the death of the first of the Recipients to die, the survivor Recipient shall be entitled to receive the entire unitrust amount. The unitrust amount shall be paid in quarterly installments. Any income of the Trust for a taxable year in excess of the unitrust amount and which is not paid pursuant to the second preceding sentence shall be added to principal. If for any year the net fair market value of the Trust assets is incorrectly determined, then within a reasonable period after the value is finally determined for federal tax purposes, the Trustee shall pay to the Recipients (in the case of an undervaluation) or receive from the Recipients (in the case of an overvaluation) an amount equal to the difference between the unitrust amount properly payable and the unitrust amount actually paid.

2. Deferral Provision. The obligation to pay the unitrust amount shall commence with the date of my death, but payment of the unitrust amount may be deferred from such date until the end of the taxable year of the Trust in which occurs the complete funding of the Trust. Within a reasonable time after the end of the taxable year in which the complete funding of the Trust occurs, the Trustee must pay to the Recipients (in the case of an underpayment) or receive from the Recipients (in the case of an overpayment) the difference between: (1) any unitrust amounts actually paid, plus interest compounded annually, computed for any period at the rate of interest that the federal income tax regulations under section 664 of the Code prescribe for the Trust for such computation for such period; and (2) the unitrust amounts payable, plus interest compounded annually, computed for any period at the rate of interest that the federal income tax regulations under section 664 of the Code prescribe for the Trust for such computation for such period.

3. Proration of the Unitrust Amount. In determining the unitrust amount, the Trustee shall prorate the same on a daily basis for a short taxable year and for the taxable year ending with the survivor Recipient's death.

4. Distribution to Charity. Upon the death of the survivor Recipient, the Trustee shall distribute all of the then principal and income of the Trust (other than any amount due either of the Recipients or their estates under the provisions above) to _____ (hereinafter referred to as "the Charitable Organization"). If the Charitable Organization is not an organization described in sections 170(c) and 2055(a) of the Code at the time when any principal or income of the Trust is to be distributed to it, then the Trustee shall distribute such principal or income to such one or more organizations described in sections 170(c) and 2055(a) as the Trustee shall select in its sole discretion.

5. Additional Contributions. No additional contributions shall be made to the Trust after the initial contribution. The initial contribution, however, shall be deemed to consist of all property passing to the Trust by reason of my death.

6. Prohibited Transactions. The Trustee shall make distributions at such time and in such manner as not to subject the Trust to tax under section 4942 of the Code. Except for the payment of the unitrust amount to the Recipients, the Trustee shall not engage in any act of self-dealing, as defined in section 4941(d), and shall not make any taxable expenditures, as defined in section 4945(d). The Trustee shall not make any investments that jeopardize the charitable purpose of the Trust, within the meaning of section 4944 and the regulations thereunder, or retain any excess business holdings, within the meaning of section 4943(c).

7. Taxable Year. The taxable year of the Trust shall be the calendar year.

8. Governing Law. The operation of the Trust shall be governed by the laws of the State of _____. The Trustee, however, is prohibited from exercising any power or discretion granted under said laws that would be inconsistent with the qualification of the Trust under section 664(d)(2) and (3) of the Code and the corresponding regulations.

9. Limited Power of Amendment. The Trustee shall have the power, acting alone, to amend the Trust in any manner required for the sole purpose of ensuring that the Trust qualifies and continues to qualify as a charitable remainder unitrust within the meaning of section 664(d)(2) and (3) of the Code.

10. Investments of Trust Assets. Nothing herein shall be construed to restrict the Trustee from investing the Trust assets in a manner that could result in the annual realization of a reasonable amount of income or gain from the sale or disposition of Trust assets.

IN WITNESS WHEREOF _____ and [TRUSTEE] by its duly authorized officer have signed this agreement the day and year first above written.

_____

[DONOR]

_____

[TRUSTEE]

By _____
[ACKNOWLEDGMENTS, WITNESSES, ETC.]

REV. PROC. 88-53(8)-APPLICATION

The Service will recognize a trust as meeting all of the requirements of a qualified pooled income fund under section 642(c)(5) of the Code if the public charity responsible for the creation and maintenance of the trust makes reference in the trust instrument of the fund to this revenue procedure and adopts substantially similar documents, provided the trust operates in a manner consistent with the terms of the trust instrument, and provided it is a valid trust under applicable local law. A trust that contains substantive provisions in addition to those provided by this revenue procedure (other than provisions necessary to establish a valid trust under applicable local law) or that omits any of these provisions will not necessarily be disqualified, but neither will it be assured of qualification under the provisions of this revenue procedure.

IRS FORM: REV. PROC. 88-53

SECTION 4. SAMPLE DECLARATION OF TRUST

On this _____ day of _____, 19_____, the Board of Trustees of the [Public Charity] (hereinafter referred to as "[Public Charity]") desiring to establish a pooled income fund within the meaning of Rev. Proc. 88-53 and section 642(c)(5) of the Internal Revenue Code (hereinafter referred to as "the Code"), hereby creates the [Public Charity] Pooled Income Fund (hereinafter referred to as "the Fund") and designates _____ as the initial trustee to hold, manage, and distribute such property hereinafter transferred to and accepted by it as part of the Fund under the following terms and conditions.

1. Gift of Remainder Interest. Each donor transferring property to the Fund shall contribute an irrevocable remainder interest in such property to [Public Charity].

2. Retention of Life Income Interest. Each donor transferring property to the Fund shall retain for himself or herself an income interest in the property transferred, or create an income interest in such property for the life of one or more named beneficiaries, provided that each income beneficiary must be a living person at the time of the transfer of property to the Fund by the donor. If more than one beneficiary of the income interest is named, such beneficiaries may enjoy their shares concurrently and/or consecutively. [Public Charity] may also be designated as one of the beneficiaries of the income interest. The donor need not retain or create a life interest in all of the income from the property transferred to the Fund and any income not payable to an income beneficiary shall be contributed to, and within the taxable year of the Fund in which it is received paid to, [Public Charity].

3. Commingling of Property. The property transferred to the Fund by each donor shall be commingled with, and invested or reinvested with, other property transferred to the Fund by other donors satisfying the requirements of this instrument and of section 642(c)(5) of the Code or corresponding provision of any subsequent federal tax law. The Fund shall not include property transferred under arrangements other than those specified in this instrument and satisfying the said provisions of the Code.

   All or any portion of the assets of the Fund may, however, be invested or reinvested jointly with other properties not a part of the Fund that are held by, or for the use of, [Public Charity]. When joint investment or reinvestment occurs, detailed accounting records shall be maintained by the Trustee specifically identifying the portion of the jointly invested property owned by the Fund and the income earned by, and attributable to, such portion.

4. Prohibition Against Exempt Securities. The property transferred to the Fund by any donor shall not include any securities whose income is exempt from taxation under subtitle A of the Code or the corresponding provisions of any subsequent federal tax law. The Trustee of the Fund shall not accept or invest in such securities as part of the assets of the Fund.

5. Maintenance by [Public Charity]. [Public Charity] shall always maintain the Fund or exercise control, directly or indirectly, over the Fund. [Public Charity] shall always have the power to remove any Trustee or Trustees and to designate a new Trustee or Trustees.

6. Prohibition Against Donor or Beneficiary Serving as Trustee. The Fund shall not have as a Trustee a donor to the Fund or a beneficiary (other than [Public Charity]) of an income interest in any property transferred to the Fund. No donor or beneficiary (other than [Public Charity]) shall have, directly or indirectly, general responsibilities with respect to the Fund that are ordinarily exercised by a Trustee.

7. Income of Beneficiary to Be Based on Rate of Return of Fund. The taxable year of the Fund shall be the calendar year. The Trustee shall pay income to each beneficiary entitled thereto in any taxable year of the Fund in the amount determined by the rate of return earned by the Fund for the year with respect to the

beneficiary's income interest. Payments must be made at least once in the year in which the income is earned. Until the Trustee determines that payments shall be made more or less frequently or at other times, the Trustee shall make income payments to the beneficiary or beneficiaries entitled to them in four quarterly payments on or about March 31, June 30, September 30, and December 31 of each year. An adjusting payment, if necessary, will be made during the taxable year or within the first 65 days following its close to bring the total payment to the actual income to which the beneficiary or beneficiaries are entitled for that year.

On each transfer of property by a donor to the Fund, there shall be assigned to the beneficiary or beneficiaries of the income interest retained or created in the property the number of units of participation equal to the number obtained by dividing the fair market value of the property transferred by the fair market value of a unit in the Fund immediately before the transfer. The fair market value of a unit in the Fund immediately before the transfer shall be determined by dividing the fair market value of all property in the Fund at the time by the number of units then in the Fund. The initial fair market value of a unit in the Fund shall be the fair market value of the property transferred to the Fund divided by the number of units assigned to the beneficiaries of the income interest in that property. All units in the Fund shall always have equal value.

If a transfer of property to the Fund by a donor occurs on other than a determination date, the number of units of participation assigned to the beneficiary or beneficiaries of the income interest in the property shall be determined by using the average fair market value of the property in the Fund immediately before the transfer, which shall be deemed to be the average of the fair market values of the property in the Fund on the determination dates immediately preceding and succeeding the date of transfer. For the purpose of determining the average fair market value, the property transferred by the donor and any other property transferred to the Fund between the preceding and succeeding dates, or on such succeeding date, shall be excluded. The fair market value of a unit in the Fund immediately before the transfer shall be determined by dividing the average fair market value of the property in the Fund at that time by the number of units then in the Fund. Units of participation assigned with respect to property transferred on other than a determination date shall be deemed to be assigned as of date of the transfer.

A determination date means each day within a taxable year of the Fund on which a valuation is made of the property in the Fund. The property of the Fund shall be valued on January 1, April 1, July 1, and October 1 of each year; provided, however, that where such date falls on a Saturday, Sunday, or legal holiday (as defined in section 7503 of the Code and the regulations thereunder), the valuation shall be made on the next succeeding day which is not a Saturday, Sunday, or legal holiday.

The amount of income allocated to each unit of participation in the Fund shall be determined by dividing the income of the Fund for the taxable year by the outstanding number of units in the Fund at the end of the year, except that income shall be allocated to units outstanding during only part of the year by taking into consideration the period of time the units are outstanding during the year.

For purposes of this instrument, the term "income" has the same meaning as it does under section 643(b) of the Code or corresponding provision of any subsequent federal tax law and the regulations thereunder.

The income interest of any beneficiary of the Fund shall terminate with the last regular payment of income that was made before the death of the beneficiary. The Trustee of the Fund shall not be required to prorate any income payment to the date of the beneficiary's death.

8. Termination of Life Income Interest. Upon the termination of the income interest of the designated beneficiary (or, in the case of successive income interests, the survivor of the designated beneficiaries) entitled to receive income pursuant to the terms of a transfer to the Fund, the Trustee shall sever from the Fund an amount equal to the value of the remainder interest in the property upon which the income interest is based. The value of the remainder interest for severance purposes shall be its value as of the date on which the last regular payment was made before the death of the beneficiary. The amount so severed from the Fund shall be paid to [Public Charity]. If at the time of severance of the remainder interest [Public Charity] has ceased to exist or is not a

public charity (an organization described in clauses (i) through (vi) of section 170(b)(1)(A) of the Code), the amount severed shall be paid to an organization selected by the Trustee that is a public charity.

9. Prohibited Activities. The income of the Fund for each taxable year shall be distributed at such time and in such manner as not to subject the Fund to tax under section 4942 of the Code. Except for making the required payments to the life income beneficiaries, the Trustee shall not engage in any act of self-dealing as defined in section 4941(d) and shall not make any taxable expenditures as defined in section 4945(d). The Trustee shall not make any investments that jeopardize the charitable purpose of the Fund within the meaning of section 4944 or retain any excess business holdings within the meaning of section 4943.

10. Depreciable or Depletable Assets. The Trustee shall not accept or invest in any depreciable or depletable assets.

11. Incorporation by Reference. The provisions of this document may be, and are intended to be, incorporated by reference in any will, trust, or other instrument by means of which property is transferred to the Fund. Any property transferred to the Fund whereby an income interest is retained or created for the life of one or more named beneficiaries, where this document is not incorporated by reference, shall become a part of the Fund and shall be held and managed under the terms and conditions of this document, unless the instrument of transfer is inconsistent with such terms and conditions, in which case the Trustee shall not accept the property.

12. Governing Law. The operation of the Fund shall be governed by the laws of the State of _____. However, the Trustee is prohibited from exercising any power or discretion granted under said laws that would be inconsistent with the qualification of the Fund under section 642(c)(5) of the Code and the corresponding regulations.

13. Power of Amendment. The Fund is irrevocable. However, [Public Charity] shall have the power, acting alone, to amend this document and the associated instruments of transfer in any manner required for the sole purpose of ensuring that the Fund qualifies and continues to qualify as a pooled income fund within the meaning of section 642(c)(5).

IN WITNESS WHEREOF _____ and [TRUSTEE] by its duly authorized officer have signed this agreement the day and year first above written.

_____

[PUBLIC CHARITY]

_____

[TRUSTEE]

By _____
[ACKNOWLEDGMENTS, WITNESSES, ETC.]

IRS FORM: REV. PROC. 88-53

SECTION 5. SAMPLE INSTRUMENT OF TRANSFER: ONE LIFE

On this _____ day of _____, 19_____, I hereby transfer to the _____ [Public Charity] Pooled Income Fund, under the terms and conditions set forth in its Declaration of Trust, the following property: _____.

The income interest attributable to the property transferred shall be paid as follows:

    A. To me during my lifetime.

    B. To _____ during his or her life. However, I reserve the right to revoke, solely by will, this income interest.

Upon the termination of the income interest, the Trustee of the Fund will sever from the Fund an amount equal to the value of the remainder interest in the transferred property and transfer it to [Public Charity]:

    A. For its general uses and purposes.

    B. For the following charitable purpose(s): _____. However, if it is not possible for [Public Charity] in its sole discretion to use the severed amount for the specified purpose(s), then it may be used for the general purposes of [Public Charity]. This instrument and the transfer of property made pursuant thereto shall be effective after acceptance by both Donor and the Trustee.

IN WITNESS WHEREOF _____ and [TRUSTEE] by its duly authorized officer have signed this agreement the day and year first above written.

_____
[DONOR]

_____
[TRUSTEE]

By _____
[ACKNOWLEDGMENTS, WITNESSES, ETC.]

IRS FORM: REV. PROC. 88-53

SECTION 6. SAMPLE INSTRUMENT OF TRANSFER: TWO LIVES, CONSECUTIVE INTERESTS

On this _____ day of _____, 19_____, I hereby transfer to the [Public Charity] Pooled Income Fund, under the terms and conditions set forth in its Declaration of Trust, the following property: _____.

The income interest attributable to the property transferred shall be paid as follows:

A. To me during my lifetime, and after my death to _____ during his or her lifetime. However, I reserve the right to revoke, solely by will, his or her income interest.

B. To _____ during his or her lifetime, and after his or her death to _____ during his or her lifetime. However, I reserve the right to revoke, solely by will, the income interest of either or both beneficiaries.

Upon the termination of the income interest, the Trustee of the Fund will sever from the Fund an amount equal to the value of the remainder interest in the transferred property and transfer it to [Public Charity]:

A. For its general uses and purposes.

B. For the following charitable purpose(s): _____. However, if it is not possible for [Public Charity] in its sole discretion to use the severed amount for the specified purpose(s), then it may be used for the general purposes of [Public Charity]. This instrument and the transfer of property made pursuant thereto shall be effective after acceptance by both Donor and the Trustee.

IN WITNESS WHEREOF _____ and [TRUSTEE] by its duly authorized officer have signed this agreement the day and year first above written.

_____

[DONOR]

_____

[TRUSTEE]

By _____
[ACKNOWLEDGMENTS

IRS FORM: REV. PROC. 88-53

SECTION 7. SAMPLE INSTRUMENT OF TRANSFER: TWO LIVES, CONCURRENT AND CONSECUTIVE INTERESTS

On this _____ day of _____, 19_____, I hereby transfer to the [Public Charity] Pooled Income Fund, under the terms and conditions set forth in its Declaration of Trust, the following property: _____.

The income interest attributable to the property transferred shall be paid as follows:

A. _____% to me during my lifetime, and _____% to _____ during his or her lifetime. After the death of the first income beneficiary to die, the survivor shall be entitled to the entire income. However, I reserve the right to revoke, solely by will, _____'s income interest.

B. _____% to _____ during his or her lifetime and _____% to _____ during his or her lifetime. Upon the death of the first income beneficiary to die, the survivor shall be entitled to receive the entire income. However, I reserve the right to revoke, solely by will, the income interest of either or both beneficiaries.

Upon the termination of the income interest, the Trustee of the Fund will sever from the Fund an amount equal to the value of the remainder interest in the transferred property and transfer it to [Public Charity]:

A. For its general uses and purposes.

B. For the following charitable purpose(s): _____. However, if it is not possible for [Public Charity] in its sole discretion to use the severed amount for the specified purpose(s), then it may be used for the general purposes of [Public Charity].

This instrument and the transfer of property made pursuant thereto shall be effective after acceptance by both the Donor and the Trustee.

IN WITNESS WHEREOF _____ and [TRUSTEE] by its duly authorized officer have signed this agreement the day and year first above written.

_____
[DONOR]

_____
[TRUSTEE]

By _____
[ACKNOWLEDGMENTS, WITNESSES, ETC.]

SAMPLE RETAINED LIFE ESTATE AGREEMENTS

Worthy Charity

THIS AGREEMENT entered into this _____ day of _____, 19_____ by and between Worthy Charity and [DONOR] of [STREET, CITY, STATE], (the "Grantor").

WITNESSETH THAT:

WHEREAS, the Grantor has this day executed a deed giving to Worthy Charity a remainder interest in [HIS/HER] personal residence located at [STREET, CITY, STATE] (the "Property"), NOW, THEREFORE, the parties hereto agree as follows:

1. The Grantor shall, during [HIS/HER] lifetime, have the sole right to occupy and utilize the premises as [HIS/HER] residence and to lease the premises to any other person for use as a personal residence.

2. Worthy Charity shall join in any lease of the premises to another in order to permit the lease term to continue beyond the death of the Grantor, provided that such term shall not continue for more than one year beyond the date of death of the Grantor and provided further that Worthy Charity shall be entitled to the rent from the property from the date of death of the Grantor.

3. The Grantor shall have the sole responsibility for maintaining the property, paying real estate taxes, insuring the property against loss and liability, and shall not, without the consent of Worthy Charity, suffer any lien or mortgage to be placed on the property other than liens or mortgages which may now exist, and shall not, without the consent of Worthy Charity, permit the amount of any lien or mortgage now existing to increase.

4. In the event of any damage to the property, the Grantor, at [HIS/HER] sole expense, shall cause such damage to be repaired unless the Grantor and Worthy Charity shall agree that is impractical to do so, in which case, any insurance proceeds resulting from such damage shall be divided between Worthy Charity and the Grantor in accordance with the value of their respective interests as of the date such damage occurred. For purposes of determining the value of Worthy Charity's interest in the event of such loss, the value shall be determined in the same manner as is used to value a gift of a remainder interest in a personal residence or a farm as is provided in U.S. Treasury Regulation (Section) 1.170A-12 or any corresponding U.S. Treasury Regulations then in effect, using the rate of interest determined under IRC (Section) 7520 in effect for the month in which the loss occurred.

5. The Grantor agrees to hold Worthy Charity harmless against any and all liability arising from the property during the lifetime of the Grantor.

6. The Grantor may at any time or times at [HIS/HER] sole expense make improvements to the property, provided that such improvements shall not result in a reduction of the value of the property.

IN WITNESS WHEREOF, the parties hereto have set their hands and seals the day and year first above written.

For Worthy Charity:

By: _____
    [NAME] [TITLE]

_____
[NAME], Grantor

Sample Quitclaim Deed with Retained Life Estate

Worthy Charity

I, [DONOR], of [CITY, COUNTY, STATE] (the "Grantor"), for One Dollar ($1.00) consideration paid, grant to Worthy Charity, a [STATE] charitable corporation with an address of [ADDRESS], with QUITCLAIM COVENANTS, a certain parcel of land with the buildings thereon, situated at [ADDRESS], more particularly bounded and described as follows:

[DESCRIPTION OF PROPERTY FROM DEED TO GRANTOR]

There is expressly excluded from this conveyance, and the Grantor does hereby reserve for [HIMSELF/HERSELF], the full use, control, income, and possession of all of the premises for the remainder of [HIS/HER] life. The Grantor shall not have the power to sell, mortgage, exchange, or dispose of the premises. The interest reserved in this paragraph is hereinafter referred to as the "Life Estate." The Life Estate may be terminated only by the death of the Grantor or by an instrument of release, executed by the Grantor or Grantor's legal representative in a form suitable for recording and delivered to Worthy Charity.

The Grantor hereby agrees that during the Life Estate, [HE/SHE] will do the following at [HIS/HER] own cost and expense:

1. Keep the buildings on the premises insured against loss or damage by fire (with extended coverage) in an amount sufficient to avoid being deemed a coinsurer and naming Worthy Charity as additional insured;

2. Pay all real estate taxes assessed on the premises, and if the expiration of the Life Estate is on a date other than at the commencement or expiration of any fiscal year, the taxes in such year shall be apportioned between the Grantor and Worthy Charity;

3. Keep the premises in substantially such repair, order, and condition as the same are in on the date hereof, reasonable use and wear excepted.

Consideration for this deed being nominal, no [STATE] Deed Excise Stamps are affixed hereto, none being required by law.

WITNESS my hand and seal this _____ day of _____, 19_____.

_____

[DONOR]

[STATE or COMMONWEALTH]

County of [COUNTY], S.S.

On this _____ day of _____, 19_____, personally appeared before me, _____, and satisfactorily proved to me to be the signer of the above instrument by the oath of [NAME OF WITNESS], a competent and credible witness for that purpose, by me duly sworn, and [HE/SHE], the said [GRANTOR] acknowledged that [HE/SHE] executed the same.

_____

Notary Public
My Commission Expires: [DATE]

SAMPLE GIFT ANNUITY AGREEMENTS

NOTE:
BEFORE PROCEEDING, CHECK THE MOST CURRENT INFORMATION REGARDING THE LANGUAGE AND OTHER CHARITABLE GIFT ANNUITY REQUIREMENTS OF THE STATE IN WHICH THE CHARITY IS LOCATED *AND* THE STATE IN WHICH THE DONOR IS LOCATED.

Worthy Charity

One-Beneficiary Charitable Gift Annuity

Worthy Charity, a charitable corporation located in [CITY, STATE], agrees to pay to [DONOR] of [CITY, STATE], (hereinafter called the "Donor"), for [HIS/HER] life an annuity in the annual sum of [AMOUNT IN WORDS] ([DOLLAR AMOUNT]) from date hereof, in equal quarterly installments on the last day of March, June, September, and December. The first installment shall be payable on [DATE]. This annuity shall be nonassignable, except in the case of a voluntary transfer of part or all of such annuity to Worthy Charity.

The obligation of Worthy Charity to make annuity payments shall terminate with the payment preceding the death of the Donor.

Worthy Charity certifies that the Donor, as an evidence of the Donor's desire to support the work of Worthy Charity and to make a charitable gift, has this day contributed to Worthy Charity the property listed in Schedule A attached hereto, receipt of which is acknowledged for its general charitable purposes.

IN WITNESS WHEREOF, Worthy Charity has executed this instrument this _____ day of _____, 19_____.

For Worthy Charity:

By: _____

Worthy Charity

Two-Beneficiary Charitable Gift Annuity

NOTE:
BEFORE PROCEEDING, CHECK THE MOST CURRENT INFORMATION REGARDING THE LANGUAGE AND OTHER CHARITABLE GIFT ANNUITY REQUIREMENTS OF THE STATE IN WHICH THE CHARITY IS LOCATED *AND* THE STATE IN WHICH THE DONOR IS LOCATED.

Worthy Charity, a charitable corporation located in [CITY, STATE], agrees to pay to [DONOR], of [CITY, STATE] (hereinafter called the "Donor"), for the Donor's life and thereafter to the Donor's spouse, [SPOUSE'S NAME], for (HIS/HER) life if (HE/SHE) survives the Donor, an annuity in the annual sum of [AMOUNT IN WORDS] ([DOLLAR AMOUNT]) from the date hereof, in equal quarterly installments of [DOLLAR AMOUNT] on the last day of March, June, September, and December; provided, however, that the Donor may by the Donor's last will revoke the annuity to be paid to the Donor's said spouse. The first installment shall be payable on [DATE]. This annuity shall be nonassignable, except in the case of a voluntary transfer of part or all of such annuity to Worthy Charity.

The obligation of Worthy Charity to make annuity payments shall terminate with the payment preceding the death of the survivor of the Donor and the Donor's said spouse, unless the Donor revokes the annuity payable to the Donor's said spouse, in which case Worthy Charity's obligation shall terminate with the payment preceding the death of the Donor.

Worthy Charity certifies that the Donor, as an evidence of the Donor's desire to support the work of Worthy Charity and to make a charitable gift, has this day contributed to Worthy Charity the property listed in Schedule A attached hereto, receipt of which is acknowledged for its general charitable purposes.

IN WITNESS WHEREOF, Worthy Charity has executed this instrument this _____ day of _____, 19_____.

For Worthy Charity:

By: _____

Worthy Charity

Deferred Gift Annuity for One Beneficiary

NOTE:
BEFORE PROCEEDING, CHECK THE MOST CURRENT INFORMATION REGARDING THE LANGUAGE AND OTHER CHARITABLE GIFT ANNUITY REQUIREMENTS OF THE STATE IN WHICH THE CHARITY IS LOCATED *AND* THE STATE IN WHICH THE DONOR IS LOCATED.

Worthy Charity, a nonprofit organization incorporated in the state of [STATE] and having its principal place of business at [ADDRESS] hereby agrees to pay to [DONOR] of [DONOR'S ADDRESS], during his/her lifetime, an annuity in the annual amount of [ANNUAL PAYMENT AMOUNT] beginning [DATE PAYMENT BEGINS]. The annuity shall be payable in quarterly installments on the last day of each quarter. The first payment shall be a pro rata amount. The payments under this Agreement shall cease with the last payment preceding the death of [DONOR] . The annuity payable hereunder shall not be assignable.

Worthy Charity hereby certifies that [DONOR], as evidence of his/her desire to support the work of Worthy Charity and to make a charitable gift, has given to Worthy Charity this day the property listed in the attached Schedule A, receipt of which is hereby acknowledged.

This Agreement shall be administered and construed in accordance with the laws of [STATE]. IN WITNESS WHEREOF, Worthy Charity, by its duly authorized officer, has executed this instrument this _____ day of _____, 19_____.

For Worthy Charity:

By: _____

Worthy Charity

Deferred Gift Annuity for Two Beneficiaries

NOTE:

BEFORE PROCEEDING, CHECK THE MOST CURRENT INFORMATION REGARDING THE LANGUAGE AND OTHER CHARITABLE GIFT ANNUITY REQUIREMENTS OF THE STATE IN WHICH THE CHARITY IS LOCATED *AND* THE STATE IN WHICH THE DONOR IS LOCATED.

Worthy Charity, a nonprofit organization incorporated in the state of [STATE] and having its principal place of business at [ADDRESS] hereby agrees to pay to [DONORS] of [DONORS' ADDRESS] during their lifetimes, an annuity in the annual amount of [ANNUAL PAYMENT AMOUNT] beginning [DATE PAYMENT BEGINS]. The annuity shall be payable in quarterly installments on the last day of each quarter. The first payment shall be a pro rata amount. The payments under this Agreement shall cease with the last payment preceding the death of the second donor. The annuity payable hereunder shall not be assignable.

Worthy Charity hereby certifies that [DONORS], as evidence of their desire to support the work of Worthy Charity and to make a charitable gift, have given to Worthy Charity this day the property listed in the attached Schedule A, receipt of which is hereby acknowledged.

This Agreement shall be administered and construed in accordance with the laws of [STATE]. IN WITNESS WHEREOF, Worthy Charity, by its duly authorized officer, has executed this instrument this _____ day of _____, 19_____.

For Worthy Charity:

By: _____

Appendix D

IRS Forms for Gifts of Tangible Personal Property

Form **8282**

(Rev. September 1998)

Department of the Treasury
Internal Revenue Service

Donee Information Return

(Sale, Exchange, or Other Disposition of Donated Property)

▶ See instructions on back.

OMB No. 1545-0908

Give a Copy to Donor

Please Print or Type

Name of charitable organization (donee)	Employer identification number
Address (number, street, and room or suite no.)	
City or town, state, and ZIP code	

Part I Information on ORIGINAL DONOR and DONEE Receiving the Property

1a Name(s) of the original donor of the property	1b Identifying number

Note: *Complete lines 2a–2d only if you gave this property to another charitable organization (successor donee).*

2a Name of charitable organization	2b Employer identification number
2c Address (number, street, and room or suite no.)	
2d City or town, state, and ZIP code	

Note: *If you are the original donee, skip Part II and go to Part III now.*

Part II Information on PREVIOUS DONEES–Complete this part only if you were not the first donee to receive the property.

If you were the second donee, leave lines 4a–4d blank. If you were a third or later donee, complete lines 3a–4d. On lines 4a–4d, give information on the preceding donee (the one who gave you the property).

3a Name of original donee	3b Employer identification number
3c Address (number, street, and room or suite no.)	
3d City or town, state, and ZIP code	
4a Name of preceding donee	4b Employer identification number
4c Address (number, street, and room or suite no.)	
4d City or town, state, and ZIP code	

Part III Information on DONATED PROPERTY– If you are the original donee, leave column (c) blank.

(a) Description of donated property sold, exchanged, or otherwise disposed of (if you need more space, attach a separate statement)	(b) Date you received the item(s)	(c) Date the first donee received the item(s)	(d) Date item(s) sold, exchanged, or otherwise disposed of	(e) Amount received upon disposition	

For Paperwork Reduction Act Notice, see back of form.

Cat. No. 62307Y

Form **8282** (Rev. 9-98)

General Instructions

Section references are to the Internal Revenue Code.

Purpose of Form

Donee organizations use Form 8282 to report information to the IRS about dispositions of certain charitable deduction property made within 2 years after the donor contributed the property.

Definitions

Note: *For Form 8282 and these instructions, the term "donee" includes all donees, unless specific reference is made to "original" or "successor" donees.*

Original donee. The first donee to or for which the donor gave the property. The original donee is required to sign an Appraisal Summary presented by the donor for charitable deduction property.

Successor donee. Any donee of property other than the original donee.

Appraisal summary. Section B of **Form 8283,** Noncash Charitable Contributions.

Charitable deduction property. Property (other than money or certain publicly traded securities) for which the original donee signed, or was presented with for signature, the Appraisal Summary (Form 8283, Section B).

Generally, only items or groups of similar items for which the donor claimed a deduction of more than $5,000 are included on the Appraisal Summary. There is an exception if a donor gives similar items to more than one donee organization and the total deducted for these similar items exceeds $5,000. For example, if a donor deducts $2,000 for books given to a donee organization and $4,000 for books to another donee organization, the donor must present a separate Appraisal Summary to each organization. For more information, see the Instructions for Form 8283.

Who Must File

Original and successor donee organizations must file Form 8282 if they sell, exchange, consume, or otherwise dispose of (with or without consideration) charitable deduction property within 2 years after the date the original donee received the property. See **Charitable deduction property** earlier.

Exceptions. There are two situations where Form 8282 does not have to be filed.

1. Items valued at $500 or less. You do not have to file Form 8282 if, at the time the original donee signed the Appraisal Summary, the donor had signed a statement on Form 8283 that the appraised value of the specific item was not more than $500. If Form 8283 contains more than one similar item, this exception applies only to those items that are clearly identified as having a value of $500 or less. However, for purposes of the donor's

determination of whether the appraised value of the item exceeds $500, all shares of nonpublicly traded stock, or items that form a set, are considered one item. For example, a collection of books written by the same author, components of a stereo system, or six place settings of a pattern of silverware are considered one item.

2. Items consumed or distributed for charitable purpose. You do not have to file Form 8282 if an item is consumed or distributed, without consideration, in fulfilling your purpose or function as a tax-exempt organization. For example, no reporting is required for medical supplies consumed or distributed by a tax-exempt relief organization in aiding disaster victims.

When To File

If you dispose of charitable deduction property within 2 years of the date the original donee received it and you do not meet exception **1** or **2** above, you must file Form 8282 within 125 days after the date of disposition.

Exception. If you did not file because you had no reason to believe the substantiation requirements applied to the donor, but you later become aware that they did apply, file Form 8282 within 60 days after the date you become aware you are liable. For example, this exception would apply where an Appraisal Summary is furnished to a successor donee after the date that donee disposes of the charitable deduction property.

Missing Information

If Form 8282 is filed by the due date, you must enter your organization's name, address, and EIN and complete at least Part III, column (a). You do not have to complete the remaining items if the information is not available. For example, you may not have the information necessary to complete all entries if the donor's Appraisal Summary is not available to you.

Where To File

Send Form 8282 to the Internal Revenue Service, Ogden, UT 84201-0027.

Penalty

You may be subject to a penalty if you fail to file this form by the due date, fail to include all of the information required to be shown on this form, or fail to include correct information on this form (see **Missing Information** above). The penalty is generally $50. For more details, see section 6721.

Other Requirements

Information you must give a successor donee. If the property is transferred to another charitable organization within the 2-year period discussed earlier, you must give your successor donee all of the following information.

1. The name, address, and EIN of your organization.

2. A copy of the Appraisal Summary (the Form 8283 that you received from the donor or a preceding donee).

3. A copy of this Form 8282, within 15 days after you file it.

You must furnish items **1** and **2** above within 15 days after the latest of the date:

● You transferred the property,

● The original donee signed the Appraisal Summary, or

● You received a copy of the Appraisal Summary from the preceding donee if you are also a successor donee.

Information the successor donee must give you. The successor donee organization to whom you transferred this property is required to give you their organization's name, address, and EIN within 15 days after the later of:

● The date you transferred the property, or

● The date they received a copy of the Appraisal Summary.

Information you must give the donor. You must give a copy of your Form 8282 to the original donor of the property.

Recordkeeping. You must keep a copy of the Appraisal Summary in your records.

Paperwork Reduction Act Notice. We ask for the information on this form to carry out the Internal Revenue laws of the United States. You are required to give us the information. We need it to ensure that you are complying with these laws and to allow us to figure and collect the right amount of tax.

You are not required to provide the information requested on a form that is subject to the Paperwork Reduction Act unless the form displays a valid OMB control number. Books or records relating to a form or its instructions must be retained as long as their contents may become material in the administration of any Internal Revenue law. Generally, tax returns and return information are confidential, as required by section 6103.

The time needed to complete this form will vary depending on individual circumstances. The estimated average time is:

Recordkeeping	3 hr., 7 min.
Learning about the law or the form	35 min.
Preparing and sending the form to the IRS	41 min.

If you have comments concerning the accuracy of these time estimates or suggestions for making this form simpler, we would be happy to hear from you. You can write to the Tax Forms Committee, Western Area Distribution Center, Rancho Cordova, CA 95743-0001. **DO NOT** send the form to this address. Instead, see **Where To File** on this page.

Form **8283**
(Rev. October 1998)

Department of the Treasury
Internal Revenue Service

Noncash Charitable Contributions

▶ Attach to your tax return if you claimed a total deduction
of over $500 for all contributed property.

▶ See separate instructions.

Name(s) shown on your income tax return

Identifying number

Note: *Figure the amount of your contribution deduction before completing this form. See your tax return instructions.*

Section A– List in this section **only** items (or groups of similar items) for which you claimed a deduction of $5,000 or less. Also, list certain publicly traded securities even if the deduction is over $5,000 (see instructions).

| Part I | Information on Donated Property– If you need more space, attach a statement. |

1

	(a) Name and address of the donee organization	**(b)** Description of donated property
A		
B		
C		
D		
E		

Note: *If the amount you claimed as a deduction for an item is $500 or less, you do not have to complete columns (d), (e), and (f).*

	(c) Date of the contribution	**(d)** Date acquired by donor (mo., yr.)	**(e)** How acquired by donor	**(f)** Donor's cost or adjusted basis	**(g)** Fair market value	**(h)** Method used to determine the fair market value
A						
B						
C						
D						
E						

| Part II | Other Information– Complete line 2 if you gave less than an entire interest in property listed in Part I. Complete line 3 if conditions were attached to a contribution listed in Part I. |

2 If, during the year, you contributed less than the entire interest in the property, complete lines a–e.

a Enter the letter from Part I that identifies the property ▶ _____. If Part II applies to more than one property, attach a separate statement.

b Total amount claimed as a deduction for the property listed in Part I: **(1)** For this tax year ▶ _____ .
                                                     (2) For any prior tax years ▶ _____ .

c Name and address of each organization to which any such contribution was made in a prior year (complete only if different from the donee organization above):

Name of charitable organization (donee)

Address (number, street, and room or suite no.)

City or town, state, and ZIP code

d For tangible property, enter the place where the property is located or kept ▶ _____

e Name of any person, other than the donee organization, having actual possession of the property ▶ _____

3 If conditions were attached to any contribution listed in Part I, answer questions a–c and attach the required statement (see instructions).

		Yes	No
a	Is there a restriction, either temporary or permanent, on the donee's right to use or dispose of the donated property?		
b	Did you give to anyone (other than the donee organization or another organization participating with the donee organization in cooperative fundraising) the right to the income from the donated property or to the possession of the property, including the right to vote donated securities, to acquire the property by purchase or otherwise, or to designate the person having such income, possession, or right to acquire?		
c	Is there a restriction limiting the donated property for a particular use?		

For Paperwork Reduction Act Notice, see page 4 of separate instructions.   Cat. No. 62299J   Form **8283** (Rev. 10-98)

Form 8283 (Rev. 10-98)

Name(s) shown on your income tax return	Identifying number

Section B–Appraisal Summary– List in this section only items (or groups of similar items) for which you claimed a deduction of more than $5,000 per item or group. **Exception.** Report contributions of certain publicly traded securities only in Section A.

If you donated art, you may have to attach the complete appraisal. See the **Note** in Part I below.

Part I	**Information on Donated Property–** To be completed by the taxpayer and/or appraiser.

4   Check type of property:

☐ Art* (contribution of $20,000 or more)   ☐ Real Estate   ☐ Gems/Jewelry   ☐ Stamp Collections
☐ Art* (contribution of less than $20,000)   ☐ Coin Collections   ☐ Books   ☐ Other

*Art includes paintings, sculptures, watercolors, prints, drawings, ceramics, antique furniture, decorative arts, textiles, carpets, silver, rare manuscripts, historical memorabilia, and other similar objects.

Note: *If your total art contribution deduction was $20,000 or more, you must attach a complete copy of the signed appraisal. See instructions.*

5	**(a)** Description of donated property (if you need more space, attach a separate statement)	**(b)** If tangible property was donated, give a brief summary of the overall physical condition at the time of the gift	**(c)** Appraised fair market value
A			
B			
C			
D			

	(d) Date acquired by donor (mo., yr.)	**(e)** How acquired by donor	**(f)** Donor's cost or adjusted basis	**(g)** For bargain sales, enter amount received	**(h)** Amount claimed as a deduction	**(i)** Average trading price of securities
					See instructions	
A						
B						
C						
D						

Part II	**Taxpayer (Donor) Statement–** List each item included in Part I above that the appraisal identifies as having a value of $500 or less. See instructions.

I declare that the following item(s) included in Part I above has to the best of my knowledge and belief an appraised value of not more than $500 (per item). Enter identifying letter from Part I and describe the specific item. See instructions. ▶ _____

Signature of taxpayer (donor) ▶ _____   Date ▶ _____

Part III	**Declaration of Appraiser**

I declare that I am not the donor, the donee, a party to the transaction in which the donor acquired the property, employed by, or related to any of the foregoing persons, or married to any person who is related to any of the foregoing persons. And, if regularly used by the donor, donee, or party to the transaction, I performed the majority of my appraisals during my tax year for other persons.

Also, I declare that I hold myself out to the public as an appraiser or perform appraisals on a regular basis; and that because of my qualifications as described in the appraisal, I am qualified to make appraisals of the type of property being valued. I certify that the appraisal fees were not based on a percentage of the appraised property value. Furthermore, I understand that a false or fraudulent overstatement of the property value as described in the qualified appraisal or this appraisal summary may subject me to the penalty under section 6701(a) (aiding and abetting the understatement of tax liability). I affirm that I have not been barred from presenting evidence or testimony by the Director of Practice.

Sign Here

Signature ▶	Title ▶	Date of appraisal ▶
Business address (including room or suite no.)		Identifying number
City or town, state, and ZIP code		

Part IV	**Donee Acknowledgment–** To be completed by the charitable organization.

This charitable organization acknowledges that it is a qualified organization under section 170(c) and that it received the donated property as described in Section B, Part I, above on ▶ _____
(Date)

Furthermore, this organization affirms that in the event it sells, exchanges, or otherwise disposes of the property described in Section B, Part I (or any portion thereof) within 2 years after the date of receipt, it will file **Form 8282**, Donee Information Return, with the IRS and give the donor a copy of that form. This acknowledgment does not represent agreement with the claimed fair market value.

Does the organization intend to use the property for an unrelated use? . . . . ▶ ☐ Yes   ☐ No

Name of charitable organization (donee)	Employer identification number
Address (number, street, and room or suite no.)	City or town, state, and ZIP code
Authorized signature	Title	Date

✪

Instructions for Form 8283

(Revised October 1998)

Department of the Treasury
Internal Revenue Service

Noncash Charitable Contributions

Section references are to the Internal Revenue Code unless otherwise noted.

General Instructions

Purpose of Form

Use Form 8283 to report information about noncash charitable contributions.

Do not use Form 8283 to report out-of-pocket expenses for volunteer work or amounts you gave by check or credit card. Treat these items as cash contributions. Also, **do not** use Form 8283 to figure your charitable contribution deduction. For details on how to figure the amount of the deduction, see your tax return instructions.

Additional Information

You may want to see **Pub. 526,** Charitable Contributions (for individuals), and **Pub. 561,** Determining the Value of Donated Property. If you contributed depreciable property, see **Pub. 544,** Sales and Other Dispositions of Assets.

Who Must File

You must file Form 8283 if the amount of your deduction for all noncash gifts is more than $500. For this purpose, "amount of your deduction" means your deduction **before** applying any income limits that could result in a carryover. The carryover rules are explained in Pub. 526. Make any required reductions to fair market value (FMV) before you determine if you must file Form 8283. See **Fair Market Value (FMV)** on page 2.

Form 8283 is filed by individuals, partnerships, and corporations.

Note: *C corporations, other than personal service corporations and closely held corporations, must file Form 8283 only if the amount claimed as a deduction is over $5,000.*

Partnerships and S corporations. A partnership or S corporation that claims a deduction for noncash gifts over $500 must file Form 8283 with Form 1065, 1065-B, or 1120S. If the total deduction of any item or group of similar items exceeds $5,000, the partnership or S corporation must complete Section B of Form 8283 even if the amount allocated to each partner or shareholder does not exceed $5,000.

The partnership or S corporation must give a completed copy of Form 8283 to each partner or shareholder receiving an allocation of the contribution deduction shown in Section B of the partnership's or S corporation's Form 8283.

Partners and shareholders. The partnership or S corporation will provide information about your share of the contribution on your Schedule K-1 (Form 1065 or 1120S).

In some cases, the partnership or S corporation must give you a copy of its Form 8283. If you received a copy of Form 8283 from the partnership or S corporation, attach a copy to your tax return. Deduct the amount shown on your Schedule K-1, not the amount shown on the Form 8283.

If the partnership or S corporation is not required to give you a copy of its Form 8283, combine the amount of noncash contributions shown on your Schedule K-1 with your other noncash contributions to see if you must file Form 8283. If you need to file Form 8283, you do not have to complete all the information requested in Section A for your share of the partnership's or S corporation's contributions. Complete only column (g) of line 1 with your share of the contribution and enter "From Schedule K-1 (Form 1065 or 1120S)" across columns (c)–(f).

When To File

File Form 8283 with your tax return for the year you contribute the property and first claim a deduction.

Which Sections To Complete

If you must file Form 8283, you may need to complete Section A, Section B, or both, depending on the type of property donated and the amount claimed as a deduction.

Section A. Include in Section A only items (or groups of similar items as defined on this page) for which you claimed a deduction of $5,000 or less per item (or group of similar items). Also, include the following publicly traded securities even if the deduction is more than $5,000.

- Securities listed on an exchange in which quotations are published daily,
- Securities regularly traded in national or regional over-the-counter markets for which published quotations are available, or
- Securities that are shares of a mutual fund for which quotations are published on a daily basis in a newspaper of general circulation throughout the United States.

Section B. Include in Section B only items (or groups of similar items) for which you claimed a deduction of more than $5,000 (omit publicly traded securities reportable in Section A). With certain exceptions, items reported in Section B will require information based on a written appraisal by a qualified appraiser.

Similar Items of Property

Similar items of property are items of the same generic category or type, such as stamp collections, coin collections, lithographs, paintings, books, nonpublicly traded stock, land, or buildings.

Example. You claimed a deduction of $400 for clothing, $7,000 for publicly traded securities (quotations published daily), and $6,000 for a collection of 15 books ($400 each). Report the clothing and securities in Section A and the books (a group of similar items) in Section B.

Special Rule for Certain C Corporations

A special rule applies for deductions taken by certain C corporations under section 170(e)(3) or (4) for contributions of inventory or scientific equipment.

Cat. No. 62730R

To determine if you must file Form 8283 or which section to complete, use the difference between the amount you claimed as a deduction and the amount you would have claimed as cost of goods sold (COGS) had you sold the property instead. This rule is **only** for purposes of Form 8283. It does not change the amount or method of figuring your contribution deduction.

If you do not have to file Form 8283 because of this rule, you must attach a statement to your tax return (similar to the one in the example below). Also, attach a statement if you must complete Section A, instead of Section B, because of this rule.

Example. You donated clothing from your inventory for the care of the needy. The clothing cost you $5,000 and your claimed charitable deduction is $8,000. Complete Section A instead of Section B because the difference between the amount you claimed as a charitable deduction and the amount that would have been your COGS deduction is $3,000 ($8,000 − $5,000). Attach a statement to Form 8283 similar to the following:

Form 8283—Inventory

Contribution deduction	$8,000
COGS (if sold, not donated)	− 5,000
For Form 8283 filing purposes	=$3,000

Fair Market Value (FMV)

Although the **amount** of your deduction determines if you have to file Form 8283, you also need to have information about the **value** of your contribution to complete the form.

FMV is the price a willing, knowledgeable buyer would pay a willing, knowledgeable seller when neither has to buy or sell.

You may not always be able to deduct the FMV of your contribution. Depending on the type of property donated, you may have to reduce the FMV to get to the deductible amount, as explained next.

Reductions to FMV. The amount of the reduction (if any) depends on whether the property is ordinary income property or capital gain property. Attach a statement to your tax return showing how you figured the reduction.

Ordinary income property is property that would result in ordinary income or short-term capital gain if it were sold at its FMV on the date it was contributed. Examples of ordinary income property are inventory, works of art created by the donor, and capital assets held for 1 year or less. The deduction for a gift of ordinary income property is limited to the FMV minus the amount that would be ordinary income or short-term capital gain if the property were sold.

Capital gain property is property that would result in long-term capital gain if it were sold at its FMV on the date it was contributed. It includes certain real property and depreciable property used in your trade or business, and generally held for more than 1 year. You usually may deduct gifts of capital gain property at their FMV. However, you must reduce the FMV by the amount of any appreciation if any of the following apply.

- The capital gain property is contributed to certain private nonoperating foundations. This rule does not apply to qualified appreciated stock.
- You choose the 50% limit instead of the special 30% limit.

- The contributed property is tangible personal property that is put to an **unrelated use** (as defined in Pub. 526) by the charity.

Qualified conservation contribution. If your donation qualifies as a "qualified conservation contribution" under section 170(h), attach a statement showing the FMV of the underlying property before and after the gift and the conservation purpose furthered by the gift. See Pub. 561 for more details.

Specific Instructions

Identifying number. Individuals must enter their social security number or individual taxpayer identification number. All other filers should enter their employer identification number.

Section A

Part I, Information on Donated Property

Line 1

Column (b). Describe the property in sufficient detail. The greater the value, the more detail you need. For example, a car should be described in more detail than pots and pans.

For securities, include the following:
- Name of the issuer,
- Kind of security,
- Whether a share of a mutual fund, and
- Whether regularly traded on a stock exchange or in an over-the-counter market.

Note: *If the amount you claimed as a deduction for the item is $500 or less, you do not have to complete columns (d), (e), and (f).*

Column (d). Enter the approximate date you acquired the property. If it was created, produced, or manufactured by or for you, enter the date it was substantially completed.

Column (e). State how you acquired the property (i.e., by purchase, gift, inheritance, or exchange).

Column (f). **Do not** complete this column for publicly traded securities or property held 12 months or more. Keep records on cost or other basis.

Note: *If you have reasonable cause for not providing the information in columns (d) and (f), attach an explanation.*

Column (g). Enter the FMV of the property on the date you donated it. If you were required to reduce the FMV of your deduction or you gave a qualified conservation contribution, you must attach a statement. See **Fair Market Value (FMV)** on this page for the type of statement to attach.

Column (h). Enter the method(s) you used to determine the FMV. The FMV of used household goods and clothing is usually much lower than when new. A good measure of value might be the price that buyers of these used items actually pay in consignment or thrift shops.

Examples of entries to make include "Appraisal," "Thrift shop value" (for clothing or household goods), "Catalog" (for stamp or coin collections), or "Comparable sales" (for real estate and other kinds of assets). See Pub. 561.

Part II, Other Information

If Part II applies to more than one property, attach a separate statement. Give the required information for each property separately. Identify which property listed in Part I the information relates to.

Lines 2a Through 2e

Complete lines 2a–2e only if you contributed less than the entire interest in the donated property during the tax year. On line 2b, enter the amount claimed as a deduction for this tax year and in any prior tax years for gifts of a partial interest in the same property.

Lines 3a Through 3c

Complete lines 3a–3c only if you attached restrictions to the right to the income, use, or disposition of the donated property. An example of a "restricted use" is furniture that you gave only to be used in the reading room of an organization's library. Attach a statement explaining **(1)** the terms of any agreement or understanding regarding the restriction, and **(2)** whether the property is designated for a particular use.

Section B

Part I, Information on Donated Property

You must have a written appraisal from a qualified appraiser that supports the information in Part I. However, see the **Exceptions** below.

Use Part I to summarize your appraisal(s). Generally, you do not need to attach the appraisals but you should keep them for your records. But see **Art valued at $20,000 or more** below.

Exceptions. You do not need a written appraisal if the property is:

- Nonpublicly traded stock of $10,000 or less,
- Certain securities considered to have market quotations readily available (see Regulations section 1.170A-13(c)(7)(xi)(B)),
- A donation by a C corporation (other than a closely held corporation or personal service corporation), or
- Inventory and other property donated by a closely held corporation or a personal service corporation that are "qualified contributions" for the care of the ill, the needy, or infants, within the meaning of section 170(e)(3)(A).

Although a written appraisal is not required for the types of property listed above, you must provide certain information in Part I of Section B (see Regulations section 1.170A-13(c)(4)(iv)) and have the donee organization complete Part IV.

Art valued at $20,000 or more. If your total deduction for art is $20,000 or more, you must attach a complete copy of the signed appraisal. For individual objects valued at $20,000 or more, a photograph must be provided upon request. The photograph must be of sufficient quality and size (preferably an 8 x 10 inch color photograph or a color transparency no smaller than 4 x 5 inches) to fully show the object.

Appraisal Requirements

The appraisal must be made not earlier than 60 days before the date you contribute the property. You must receive the appraisal before the due date (including extensions) of the return on which you first claim a deduction for the property. For a deduction first claimed on an amended return, the appraisal must be received before the date the amended return was filed.

A separate qualified appraisal and a separate Form 8283 are required for each item of property except for an item that is part of a group of similar items. Only one appraisal is required for a group of similar items contributed in the same tax year, if it includes all the required information for each item. The appraiser may group similar items with a collective value appraised at $100 or less.

If you gave similar items to more than one donee for which you claimed a total deduction of more than $5,000, you must attach a separate form for each donee.

Example. You claimed a deduction of $2,000 for books given to College A, $2,500 for books given to College B, and $900 for books given to a public library. You must attach a separate Form 8283 for each donee.

See Regulations section 1.170A-13(c)(3)(i)–(ii) for the definition of a "qualified appraisal" and information to be included in the appraisal.

Line 5

Note: *You **must** complete at least column (a) of line 5 (and column (b) if applicable) before submitting Form 8283 to the donee. You may then complete the remaining columns.*

Column (a). Provide enough detail so a person unfamiliar with the property could identify it in the appraisal.

Column (c). Include the FMV from the appraisal. If you were not required to get an appraisal, include the FMV you determine to be correct.

Columns (d)–(f). If you have reasonable cause for not providing the information in columns (d), (e), or (f), attach an explanation so your deduction will not automatically be disallowed.

Column (g). A bargain sale is a transfer of property that is in part a sale or exchange and in part a contribution. Enter the amount received for bargain sales.

Column (h). Complete column (h) only if you were not required to get an appraisal, as explained earlier.

Column (i). Complete column (i) only if you donated securities for which market quotations are considered to be readily available because the issue satisfies the five requirements described in Regulations section 1.170A-13(c)(7)(xi)(B).

Part II, Taxpayer (Donor) Statement

Complete Part II for each item included in Part I that has an appraised value of $500 or less. Because you do not have to show the value of these items in Part I of the donee's copy of Form 8283, clearly identify them for the donee in Part II. Then, the donee does not have to file **Form 8282**, Donee Information Return, for items valued at $500 or less. See the **Note** on page 4 for more details about filing Form 8282.

The amount of information you give in Part II depends on the description of the donated property you enter in Part I. If you show a single item as "Property A" in Part I and that item is appraised at $500 or less, then the entry "Property A" in Part II is enough. However, if "Property A" consists of several items and the total appraised value is over $500, list in Part II any item(s) you gave that is valued at $500 or less.

All shares of nonpublicly traded stock or items in a set are considered one item. For example, a book collection by the same author, components of a stereo system, or six place settings of a pattern of silverware are one item for the $500 test.

Example. You donated books valued at $6,000. The appraisal states that one of the items, a collection of books by author "X," is worth $400. On the Form 8283 that you are required to give the donee, you decide not to show the appraised value of all of the books. But you also do not want the donee to have to file Form 8282 if the collection of books is sold. If your description of Property A on line 5 includes all the books, then specify in Part II the "collection of books by X included in Property A." But if your Property A description is "collection of books by X," the only required entry in Part II is "Property A."

In the above example, you may have chosen instead to give a completed copy of Form 8283 to the donee. The donee would then be aware of the value. If you include all the books as Property A on line 5, and enter $6,000 in column (c), you may still want to describe the specific collection in Part II so the donee can sell it without filing Form 8282.

Part III, Declaration of Appraiser

If you had to get an appraisal, the appraiser **must** complete Part III to be considered qualified. See Regulations section 1.170A-13(c)(5) for a definition of a qualified appraiser.

Persons who cannot be qualified appraisers are listed in the Declaration of Appraiser. Usually, a party to the transaction will not qualify to sign the declaration. But a person who sold, exchanged, or gave the property to you may sign the declaration if the property was donated within 2 months of the date you acquired it and the property's appraised value did not exceed its acquisition price.

An appraiser may not be considered qualified if you had knowledge of facts that would cause a reasonable person to expect the appraiser to falsely overstate the value of the property. An example of this is an agreement between you and the appraiser about the property value when you know that the appraised amount exceeds the actual FMV.

Usually, appraisal fees cannot be based on a percentage of the appraised value unless the fees were paid to certain not-for-profit associations. See Regulations section 1.170A-13(c)(6)(ii).

Part IV, Donee Acknowledgment

The donee organization that received the property described in Part I of Section B must complete Part IV. Before submitting page 2 of Form 8283 to the donee for acknowledgment, complete at least your name, identifying number, and description of the donated property (line 5, column (a)). If tangible property is donated, also describe its physical condition (line 5, column (b)) at the time of the gift. Complete Part II, if applicable, before submitting the form to the donee. See the instructions for Part II.

The person acknowledging the gift must be an official authorized to sign the tax returns of the organization, or a person specifically designated to sign Form 8283. After completing Part IV, the organization must return Form 8283 to you, the donor. You must give a copy of Section B of this form to the donee organization. You may then complete any remaining information required in Part I. Also, Part III may be completed at this time by the qualified appraiser.

In some cases, it may be impossible to get the donee's signature on the Appraisal Summary. The deduction will not be disallowed for that reason if you attach a detailed explanation why it was impossible.

Note: *If the donee (or a successor donee) organization disposes of the property within 2 years after the date the original donee received it, the organization must file **Form 8282**, Donee Information Return, with the IRS and send a copy to the donor. An exception applies to items having a value of $500 or less if the donor identified the items and signed the statement in Part II (Section B) of Form 8283. See the instructions for Part II.*

Failure To File Form 8283, Section B

If you fail to attach Form 8283 to your return for donated property that is required to be reported in Section B, your deduction will be disallowed unless your failure was due to a good-faith omission. If the IRS asks you to submit the form, you have 90 days to send a completed Section B of Form 8283 before your deduction is disallowed.

Paperwork Reduction Act Notice. We ask for the information on this form to carry out the Internal Revenue laws of the United States. You are required to give us the information. We need it to ensure that you are complying with these laws and to allow us to figure and collect the right amount of tax.

You are not required to provide the information requested on a form that is subject to the Paperwork Reduction Act unless the form displays a valid OMB control number. Books or records relating to a form or its instructions must be retained as long as their contents may become material in the administration of any Internal Revenue law. Generally, tax returns and return information are confidential, as required by section 6103.

The time needed to complete and file this form will vary depending on individual circumstances. The estimated average time is: **Recordkeeping,** 20 min.; **Learning about the law or the form,** 29 min.; **Preparing the form,** 37 min.; **Copying, assembling, and sending the form to the IRS,** 35 min.

If you have comments concerning the accuracy of these time estimates or suggestions for making this form simpler, we would be happy to hear from you. See the instructions for the tax return with which this form is filed.

Page 4

Form **990**

Return of Organization Exempt From Income Tax

Under section 501(c) of the Internal Revenue Code (except black lung benefit trust or private foundation), section 527, or section 4947(a)(1) nonexempt charitable trust

Department of the Treasury
Internal Revenue Service

▶ The organization may have to use a copy of this return to satisfy state reporting requirements.

OMB No. 1545-0047

2000

Open to Public Inspection

A For the 2000 calendar year, or tax year period beginning _____, 2000, and ending _____, 20 _____

B Check if applicable:	Please use IRS label or print or type. See Specific Instructions.	**C** Name of organization	**D** Employer identification number
☐ Change of address			
☐ Change of name		Number and street (or P.O. box if mail is not delivered to street address) Room/suite	**E** Telephone number ( )
☐ Initial return			
☐ Final return		City or town, state or country, and ZIP code	**F** Check ▶ ☐ if application pending
☐ Amended return			

G Organization type (check only one) ▶ ☐ 501(c) ( ) ◀ (insert no.) ☐ 527 or ☐ 4947(a)(1)

● **Section 501(c)(3) organizations and 4947(a)(1) nonexempt charitable trusts must attach a completed Schedule A (Form 990 or 900-EZ).**

J Accounting method: ☐ Cash ☐ Accrual ☐ Other (specify) ▶

K Check here ▶ ☐ if the organization's gross receipts are normally not more than $25,000. The organization need not file a return with the IRS; but if the organization received a Form 990 Package in the mail, it should file a return without financial data. **Some states require a complete return.**

Note: H *and* **I** *are not applicable to section 527 orgs.*

H(a) Is this a group return for affiliates? ☐ Yes ☐ No
H(b) If "Yes," enter number of affiliates ▶ _____
H(c) Are all affiliates included? ☐ Yes ☐ No
(If "No," attach a list. See inst.)
H(d) Is this a separate return filed by an organization covered by a group ruling? ☐ Yes ☐ No
I Enter 4-digit group exemption no. (GEN) ▶
L Check this box if the organization is **not** required to attach Schedule B (Form 990 or 990-EZ) ▶ ☐

Part I Revenue, Expenses, and Changes in Net Assets or Fund Balances (See Specific Instructions on page 16.)

1	Contributions, gifts, grants, and similar amounts received:			
a	Direct public support	1a		
b	Indirect public support	1b		
c	Government contributions (grants)	1c		
d	**Total** (add lines 1a through 1c) (cash $ _____ noncash $ _____)		1d	
2	Program service revenue including government fees and contracts (from Part VII, line 93)		2	
3	Membership dues and assessments		3	
4	Interest on savings and temporary cash investments		4	
5	Dividends and interest from securities		5	
6a	Gross rents	6a		
b	Less: rental expenses	6b		
c	Net rental income or (loss) (subtract line 6b from line 6a)		6c	
7	Other investment income (describe ▶)		7	
8a	Gross amount from sales of assets other than inventory	**(A) Securities** 8a	**(B) Other**	
b	Less: cost or other basis and sales expenses	8b		
c	Gain or (loss) (attach schedule)	8c		
d	Net gain or (loss) (combine line 8c, columns (A) and (B))		8d	
9	Special events and activities (attach schedule)			
a	Gross revenue (not including $ _____ of contributions reported on line 1a)	9a		
b	Less: direct expenses other than fundraising expenses	9b		
c	Net income or (loss) from special events (subtract line 9b from line 9a)		9c	
10a	Gross sales of inventory, less returns and allowances	10a		
b	Less: cost of goods sold	10b		
c	Gross profit or (loss) from sales of inventory (attach schedule) (subtract line 10b from line 10a)		10c	
11	Other revenue (from Part VII, line 103)		11	
12	**Total revenue** (add lines 1d, 2, 3, 4, 5, 6c, 7, 8d, 9c, 10c, and 11)		12	
13	Program services (from line 44, column (B))		13	
14	Management and general (from line 44, column (C))		14	
15	Fundraising (from line 44, column (D))		15	
16	Payments to affiliates (attach schedule)		16	
17	**Total expenses** (add lines 16 and 44, column (A))		17	
18	Excess or (deficit) for the year (subtract line 17 from line 12)		18	
19	Net assets or fund balances at beginning of year (from line 73, column (A))		19	
20	Other changes in net assets or fund balances (attach explanation)		20	
21	Net assets or fund balances at end of year (combine lines 18, 19, and 20)		21	

For Paperwork Reduction Act Notice, see page 1 of the separate instructions.   Cat. No. 11282Y   Form **990** (2000)

Part II	Statement of Functional Expenses		(A) Total	(B) Program services	(C) Management and general	(D) Fundraising

All organizations must complete column (A). Columns (B), (C), and (D) are required for section 501(c)(3) and (4) organizations and section 4947(a)(1) nonexempt charitable trusts but optional for others. (See Specific Instructions on page 20.)

Do not include amounts reported on line 6b, 8b, 9b, 10b, or 16 of Part I.

			(A) Total	(B) Program services	(C) Management and general	(D) Fundraising
22	Grants and allocations (attach schedule) (cash $_____ noncash $_____)	22			/////	/////
23	Specific assistance to individuals (attach schedule)	23			/////	/////
24	Benefits paid to or for members (attach schedule)	24			/////	/////
25	Compensation of officers, directors, etc.	25				
26	Other salaries and wages	26				
27	Pension plan contributions	27				
28	Other employee benefits	28				
29	Payroll taxes	29				
30	Professional fundraising fees	30				
31	Accounting fees	31				
32	Legal fees	32				
33	Supplies	33				
34	Telephone	34				
35	Postage and shipping	35				
36	Occupancy	36				
37	Equipment rental and maintenance	37				
38	Printing and publications	38				
39	Travel	39				
40	Conferences, conventions, and meetings	40				
41	Interest	41				
42	Depreciation, depletion, etc. (attach schedule)	42				
43	Other expenses (itemize): a	43a				
b		43b				
c		43c				
d		43d				
e		43e				
44	Total functional expenses (add lines 22 through 43). *Organizations completing columns (B)-(D), carry these totals to lines 13–15*	44				

Reporting of Joint Costs. Did you report in column (B) (Program services) any joint costs from a combined educational campaign and fundraising solicitation? ▶ ☐ Yes ☐ No
If "Yes," enter **(i)** the aggregate amount of these joint costs $_____; **(ii)** the amount allocated to Program services $_____;
(iii) the amount allocated to Management and general $_____; and **(iv)** the amount allocated to Fundraising $_____

Part III	Statement of Program Service Accomplishments (See Specific Instructions on page 23.)

What is the organization's primary exempt purpose? ▶------------

All organizations must describe their exempt purpose achievements in a clear and concise manner. State the number of clients served, publications issued, etc. Discuss achievements that are not measurable. (Section 501(c)(3) and (4) organizations and 4947(a)(1) nonexempt charitable trusts must also enter the amount of grants and allocations to others.)

Program Service Expenses (Required for 501(c)(3) and (4) orgs., and 4947(a)(1) trusts; but optional for others.)

a _____ (Grants and allocations $)

b _____ (Grants and allocations $)

c _____ (Grants and allocations $)

d _____ (Grants and allocations $)

e Other program services (attach schedule) (Grants and allocations $)

f **Total of Program Service Expenses** (should equal line 44, column (B), Program services) ▶

Form **990** (2000)

| **Part IV** | **Balance Sheets** (See Specific Instructions on page 23.) | | | | |

Note:	*Where required, attached schedules and amounts within the description column should be for end-of-year amounts only.*		**(A)** Beginning of year		**(B)** End of year
Assets	**45** Cash—non-interest-bearing			**45**	
	46 Savings and temporary cash investments			**46**	
	47a Accounts receivable	**47a**		**47c**	
	b Less: allowance for doubtful accounts . .	**47b**			
	48a Pledges receivable	**48a**			
	b Less: allowance for doubtful accounts . .	**48b**		**48c**	
	49 Grants receivable			**49**	
	50 Receivables from officers, directors, trustees, and key employees (attach schedule)			**50**	
	51a Other notes and loans receivable (attach schedule).	**51a**			
	b Less: allowance for doubtful accounts . .	**51b**		**51c**	
	52 Inventories for sale or use			**52**	
	53 Prepaid expenses and deferred charges			**53**	
	54 Investments—securities (attach schedule). . . ▶ ☐ Cost ☐ FMV			**54**	
	55a Investments—land, buildings, and equipment: basis	**55a**			
	b Less: accumulated depreciation (attach schedule).	**55b**		**55c**	
	56 Investments—other (attach schedule) . .			**56**	
	57a Land, buildings, and equipment: basis .	**57a**			
	b Less: accumulated depreciation (attach schedule).	**57b**		**57c**	
	58 Other assets (describe ▶ _____)			**58**	
	59 **Total assets** (add lines 45 through 58) (must equal line 74)			**59**	
Liabilities	**60** Accounts payable and accrued expenses			**60**	
	61 Grants payable			**61**	
	62 Deferred revenue			**62**	
	63 Loans from officers, directors, trustees, and key employees (attach schedule).			**63**	
	64a Tax-exempt bond liabilities (attach schedule)			**64a**	
	b Mortgages and other notes payable (attach schedule)			**64b**	
	65 Other liabilities (describe ▶ _____)			**65**	
	66 **Total liabilities** (add lines 60 through 65)			**66**	
Net Assets or Fund Balances	Organizations that follow SFAS 117, check here ▶ ☐ and complete lines 67 through 69 and lines 73 and 74.				
	67 Unrestricted.			**67**	
	68 Temporarily restricted			**68**	
	69 Permanently restricted			**69**	
	Organizations that do not follow SFAS 117, check here ▶ ☐ and complete lines 70 through 74.				
	70 Capital stock, trust principal, or current funds			**70**	
	71 Paid-in or capital surplus, or land, building, and equipment fund . .			**71**	
	72 Retained earnings, endowment, accumulated income, or other funds			**72**	
	73 **Total net assets or fund balances** (add lines 67 through 69 OR lines 70 through 72; column (A) must equal line 19 and column (B) must equal line 21)			**73**	
	74 **Total liabilities and net assets / fund balances** (add lines 66 and 73)			**74**	

Form 990 is available for public inspection and, for some people, serves as the primary or sole source of information about a particular organization. How the public perceives an organization in such cases may be determined by the information presented on its return. Therefore, please make sure the return is complete and accurate and fully describes, in Part III, the organization's programs and accomplishments.

Part IV-A	Reconciliation of Revenue per Audited Financial Statements with Revenue per Return (See Specific Instructions, page 25.)

a Total revenue, gains, and other support per audited financial statements . . ▶ **a**

b Amounts included on line **a** but not on line 12, Form 990:

　(1) Net unrealized gains on investments . . $

　(2) Donated services and use of facilities . $

　(3) Recoveries of prior year grants . . . $

　(4) Other (specify):

　------------------------- $

　Add amounts on lines **(1)** through **(4)** ▶ **b**

c Line **a** minus line **b**. . . . . . ▶ **c**

d Amounts included on line 12, Form 990 but not on line **a**:

　(1) Investment expenses not included on line 6b, Form 990 . . . $

　(2) Other (specify):

　------------------------- $

　Add amounts on lines **(1)** and **(2)** ▶ **d**

e Total revenue per line 12, Form 990 (line **c** plus line **d**) . . . . . . ▶ **e**

Part IV-B	Reconciliation of Expenses per Audited Financial Statements with Expenses per Return

a Total expenses and losses per audited financial statements . . ▶ **a**

b Amounts included on line **a** but not on line 17, Form 990:

　(1) Donated services and use of facilities $

　(2) Prior year adjustments reported on line 20, Form 990 . . . . $

　(3) Losses reported on line 20, Form 990 . $

　(4) Other (specify):

　------------------------- $

　Add amounts on lines **(1)** through **(4)** ▶ **b**

c Line **a** minus line **b** . . . . . ▶ **c**

d Amounts included on line 17, Form 990 but not on line **a**:

　(1) Investment expenses not included on line 6b, Form 990. . . $

　(2) Other (specify):

　------------------------- $

　Add amounts on lines **(1)** and **(2)** ▶ **d**

e Total expenses per line 17, Form 990 (line **c** plus line **d**) . . . . . ▶ **e**

Part V	List of Officers, Directors, Trustees, and Key Employees (List each one even if not compensated; see Specific Instructions on page 25.)

(A) Name and address	(B) Title and average hours per week devoted to position	(C) Compensation (If not paid, enter -0-.)	(D) Contributions to employee benefit plans & deferred compensation	(E) Expense account and other allowances

75 Did any officer, director, trustee, or key employee receive aggregate compensation of more than $100,000 from your organization and all related organizations, of which more than $10,000 was provided by the related organizations? ▶ ☐ **Yes** ☐ **No**
　　If "Yes," attach schedule—see Specific Instructions on page 26.

Form **990** (2000)

Part VI	**Other Information** (See Specific Instructions on page 26.)	N/A	Yes	No
76	Did the organization engage in any activity not previously reported to the IRS? If "Yes," attach a detailed description of each activity .	76		
77	Were any changes made in the organizing or governing documents but not reported to the IRS? . . . If "Yes," attach a conformed copy of the changes.	77		
78a	Did the organization have unrelated business gross income of $1,000 or more during the year covered by this return?.	78a		
b	If "Yes," has it filed a tax return on **Form 990-T** for this year?	78b		
79	Was there a liquidation, dissolution, termination, or substantial contraction during the year? If "Yes," attach a statement	79		
80a	Is the organization related (other than by association with a statewide or nationwide organization) through common membership, governing bodies, trustees, officers, etc., to any other exempt or nonexempt organization? . . .	80a		
b	If "Yes," enter the name of the organization ▶ ------------------------------------ ------------------------------------ and check whether it is ☐ exempt **OR** ☐ nonexempt.			
81a	Enter the amount of political expenditures, direct or indirect, as described in the instructions for line 81. . . . . |81a|			
b	Did the organization file **Form 1120-POL** for this year?.	81b		
82a	Did the organization receive donated services or the use of materials, equipment, or facilities at no charge or at substantially less than fair rental value?	82a		
b	If "Yes," you may indicate the value of these items here. Do not include this amount as revenue in Part I or as an expense in Part II. (See instructions for reporting in Part III). . . . . |82b|			
83a	Did the organization comply with the public inspection requirements for returns and exemption applications?	83a		
b	Did the organization comply with the disclosure requirements relating to quid pro quo contributions? . .	83b		
84a	Did the organization solicit any contributions or gifts that were not tax deductible?	84a		
b	If "Yes," did the organization include with every solicitation an express statement that such contributions or gifts were not tax deductible?	84b		
85	*501(c)(4), (5), or (6) organizations.* **a** Were substantially all dues nondeductible by members?	85a		
b	Did the organization make only in-house lobbying expenditures of $2,000 or less?	85b		
	If "Yes" was answered to either 85a or 85b, **do not** complete 85c through 85h below unless the organization received a waiver for proxy tax owed for the prior year.			
c	Dues, assessments, and similar amounts from members . . . . |85c|			
d	Section 162(e) lobbying and political expenditures . . . . |85d|			
e	Aggregate nondeductible amount of section 6033(e)(1)(A) dues notices . . |85e|			
f	Taxable amount of lobbying and political expenditures (line 85d less 85e) . |85f|			
g	Does the organization elect to pay the section 6033(e) tax on the amount in 85f?.	85g		
h	If section 6033(e)(1)(A) dues notices were sent, does the organization agree to add the amount in 85f to its reasonable estimate of dues allocable to nondeductible lobbying and political expenditures for the following tax year?. . .	85h		
86	*501(c)(7) orgs.* Enter: **a** Initiation fees and capital contributions included on line 12 . |86a|			
b	Gross receipts, included on line 12, for public use of club facilities. . . . . |86b|			
87	*501(c)(12) orgs.* Enter: **a** Gross income from members or shareholders. . . . |87a|			
b	Gross income from other sources. (Do not net amounts due or paid to other sources against amounts due or received from them.) . . . . |87b|			
88	At any time during the year, did the organization own a 50% or greater interest in a taxable corporation or partnership, or an entity disregarded as separate from the organization under Regulations sections 301.7701-2 and 301.7701-3? If "Yes," complete Part IX	88		
89a	*501(c)(3) organizations.* Enter: Amount of tax imposed on the organization during the year under: section 4911 ▶---------------- ; section 4912 ▶---------------- ; section 4955 ▶----------------			
b	*501(c)(3) and 501(c)(4) orgs.* Did the organization engage in any section 4958 excess benefit transaction during the year or did it become aware of an excess benefit transaction from a prior year? If "Yes," attach a statement explaining each transaction.	89b		
c	Enter: Amount of tax imposed on the organization managers or disqualified persons during the year under sections 4912, 4955, and 4958. . . . . ▶ ----------------			
d	Enter: Amount of tax on line 89c, above, reimbursed by the organization. . . . . ▶ ----------------			
90a	List the states with which a copy of this return is filed ▶ ----------------------------------			
b	Number of employees employed in the pay period that includes March 12, 2000 (See inst.) . |90b|			
91	The books are in care of ▶ ---------------------- Telephone no. ▶ (------) Located at ▶ ---------------------------- ZIP code ▶ ----------			
92	*Section 4947(a)(1) nonexempt charitable trusts filing Form 990 in lieu of* **Form 1041**—Check here . . . . . . ▶ ☐ and enter the amount of tax-exempt interest received or accrued during the tax year . . ▶ |92|			

Form **990** (2000)

Part VII	Analysis of Income-Producing Activities (See Specific Instructions on page 30.)				

Enter gross amounts unless otherwise indicated.	Unrelated business income		Excluded by section 512, 513, or 514		**(E)** Related or exempt function income
	(A) Business code	**(B)** Amount	**(C)** Exclusion code	**(D)** Amount	
93 Program service revenue:					
a _____					
b _____					
c _____					
d _____					
e _____					
f Medicare/Medicaid payments					
g Fees and contracts from government agencies					
94 Membership dues and assessments . . .					
95 Interest on savings and temporary cash investments					
96 Dividends and interest from securities . . .					
97 Net rental income or (loss) from real estate:					
a debt-financed property					
b not debt-financed property					
98 Net rental income or (loss) from personal property					
99 Other investment income					
100 Gain or (loss) from sales of assets other than inventory					
101 Net income or (loss) from special events . .					
102 Gross profit or (loss) from sales of inventory .					
103 Other revenue: **a** _____					
b _____					
c _____					
d _____					
e _____					
104 Subtotal (add columns (B), (D), and (E)) . .					

105 **Total** (add line 104, columns (B), (D), and (E)). . . . . ▶ _____

Note: *Line 105 plus line 1d, Part I, should equal the amount on line 12, Part I.*

Part VIII	Relationship of Activities to the Accomplishment of Exempt Purposes (See Specific Instructions on page 31.)

Line No. ▼	Explain how each activity for which income is reported in column (E) of Part VII contributed importantly to the accomplishment of the organization's exempt purposes (other than by providing funds for such purposes).

Part IX	Information Regarding Taxable Subsidiaries and Disregarded Entities (See Specific Instructions on page 31.)				
(A) Name, address, and EIN of corporation, partnership, or disregarded entity	**(B)** Percentage of ownership interest	**(C)** Nature of activities	**(D)** Total income	**(E)** End-of-year assets
	%			
	%			
	%			
	%			

Part X	Information Regarding Transfers Associated with Personal Benefit Contracts (See Specific Instructions on page 31.)

(a) Did the organization, during the year, receive any funds, directly or indirectly, to pay premiums on a personal benefit contract? . . . . ☐ Yes ☐ No

(b) Did the organization, during the year, pay premiums, directly or indirectly, on a personal benefit contract? ☐ Yes ☐ No

Note: *If "Yes" to **(b)**, file Form 8870 **and** Form 4720 (see instructions).*

Please Sign Here	Under penalties of perjury, I declare that I have examined this return, including accompanying schedules and statements, and to the best of my knowledge and belief, it is true, correct, and complete. Declaration of preparer (other than officer) is based on all information of which preparer has any knowledge. (**Important:** See General Instruction W, on page 14.)		
	▶ _____ Signature of officer	_____ Date	▶ _____ Type or print name and title.

Paid Preparer's Use Only	Preparer's signature ▶		Date	Check if self-employed ▶ ☐	Preparer's SSN or PTIN
	Firm's name (or yours if self-employed) and address, and ZIP code ▶			EIN ▶	
				Phone no. ▶ ( )	

✺

Form **990** (2000)

Index

About the Authors

RICHARD D. BARRETT is president of Barrett Planned Giving, Inc., a consulting firm that provides marketing, coaching, and telephone donor consulting services to a wide range of not-for-profit organizations. Previously Mr. Barrett directed Georgetown University's Office of Gift Planning, and he combines the experience of establishing that university's successful planned giving program with three decades of banking in which he established marketing, international, and private banking functions and managed internal operations and branch systems, as well as serving as trustee for numerous not-for-profit organizations. He is a frequent conference speaker on planned giving topics.

MOLLY E. WARE, CFRE, Principal of Ware Development Consulting, specializes in donor-centered, integrated fundraising, board development, and coaching services to the not-for-profit community. She has worked for local and national organizations as Vice President for Development at the Washington Home and Hospice, a major and planned gifts officer with Epilepsy Foundation of America, and as a development officer working with corporations at the Library of Congress. Her professional experience in the for-profit sector includes estate planning work with clients as a stock broker and as a bank trust officer. She is an active board member and volunteer in the community, and a frequent presenter on major and planned gift topics.